About Typography 38————————————————
————————————————————————————————

For the past sixty-three years,————————
the Type Directors Club has encouraged———
the graphic arts community to achieve————
excellence in typography through its——————
annual competitions.———————————————

————————————————————————————————

Typography 38 is the TDC's newest annual—
volume devoted exclusively to typography;
the book presents the finest work in this
field from 2016.————————————————————

————————————————————————————————

Selected from more than 2,000————————————
international submissions, the 215————————
winning designs are models of excellence—
— and innovation in contemporary——————————
typography and type design. This year's——
selection encompasses a wide range of————
categories, including books, magazines,——
corporate identities, logotypes,————————
packaging, video and webgraphics, posters,
and type design.————————————————————

————————————————————————————————

THE TYPOGRAPHIC LANDSCAPE

by Doug Clouse, TDC President

Once a year, the Type Directors Club invites 11 judges to help choose the best typography and type design in the world. Everything about the two TDC competitions grows out of an international community that cares about type, a world of self- proclaimed type nerds and snobs. Passionate designers send us their work, expert practitioners judge it, and the Type Directors Club coordinates the process and celebrates and promotes the final selection.

This community determines the selection standards, which emerge organically from its combined experience and ambition. The desire to do the best design stimulates sensitivity and insight that accumulates into expertise about design quality.

Here you see what our judges chose, an unexplored landscape of new design. From this close vantage point, lacking the perspective of time, the vista is not completely clear. Graphic design and typography now are stylistically diverse, unfettered by restrictive ideologies, governed by standards of quality that transcend geographic boundaries.

Instead of being driven by salient style leaders or design schools, design is made in shifting nodes of creativity around the world.

Within this landscape of diversity, some features stand out. A familiar characteristic of contemporary design that continues to impress our judges

is the revival of nineteenth-century-style ornamented lettering. Contemporary designers have mastered this kind of work, which is especially popular for alcohol packaging.

Delicate, interlocking, angled lettering that evokes the Industrial Revolution complements the brewing and distilling industries, which emphasize slow, deliberate craftsmanship and the value of historical knowledge.

Respectful revivals of other periods appear among the winners, from Art Deco to Swiss Modernism. Would this work have garnered praise if it was new in 1928 or 1958? Again, designers have become so adept at revivals that the answer is probably "yes."

Is it wrong to be inspired by historical styles?

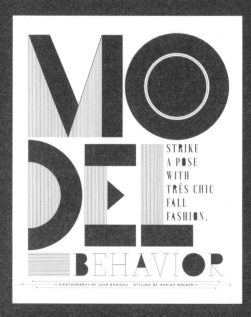

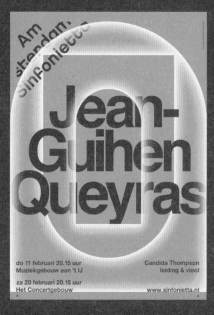

Left: Page from *Earnshaw's Magazine,* designed by Nancy Campbell and Trevett McCandliss → **page 67**
Right: Poster designed by Vincent Vrints → **page 180**

The question is so twentieth century. Historical styles are simply familiar visual languages, and questioning them is akin to questioning the diversity of the languages spoken in the United Nations.

Left: Sign painting project by Petra Dočekalová, Prague → **page 205**
Right: Lettering by Juan Ramon Pastor → **page 14**

Another notable feature among the winners is the continued popularity of lettering. Reasons for this are related to the nineteenth-century design of alcohol packaging; lettering indicates skill, value, and customization. The lettering trend originates in the now-familiar taste for hand-crafted products, whether coffee, haircuts, or typography. Its occasional casualness and lack of complexity reveals there are other reasons for its popularity, however. More schools are teaching lettering; it is a craft that distinguishes designers from their competitors and is an evolution of the microscopic control of letterforms that computers have made possible. Whatever the style being drawn, lettering reveals a designer's focused engagement with letterforms.

Lettering is related to another trend noted by our judges— type that stretches, expands, contracts, and folds. This work is essentially lettering, type tailored for a custom fit. By extending crossbars and alternating wide and narrow letters, letterforms become more expressive and also suggest the

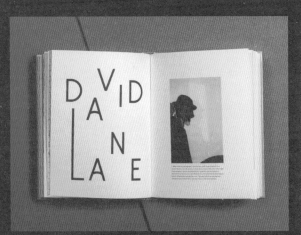

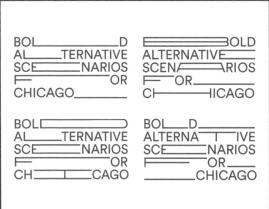

contemporary malleability of digital type.

The stylistic instability of type that is evident in historical revivals is reflected in the shape-shifting of screen type, the elasticity of pixels and vectors unrestrained by paper and ink.

And what happens to type affects language.

Our profession has struggled to describe this impermanence and novelty, sometimes using terms suggesting taint and corruption. Does a typeface stop being a typeface when it stretches or moves? Is this good or bad? Perhaps it depends on whether one is a type designer and how much one wants to control credit, copyright, and a typographic experience.

v

With their designs for the TDC competition materials and this book, Milan design team Leftloft explores the typographic "corruption" of language by non-alphabetic glyphs. Larger type families and online security features that disguise words have made uncommon glyphs familiar typographic intruders, a kind of alien species.

This message was brought to you by cigarette chemicals

<u>Left:</u> Rubber band book cover designed by Yan-Ting Chen, Taiwan → **page 30**
<u>Right:</u> Smoke type by Jose Maria Almeida Neves, New York → **page 199**

For many years, the TDC competitions have noted experimental letterforms made in novel, non-digital ways. This year is no different; among our winners are letters made from rubber bands, plastic tubes, vines and leaves, and even smoke. These ingenious constructions are useful primarily as illustrations but may some day inform the design of typefaces.

Within the competition categories of editorial design—magazine, book covers, book interiors— neat trends analyses are impossible. Any style is possible as long as it supports the text, so among the selection here we see work inspired by 1970s

Lubalin-esque lettering, 1940s movie titles, and Hindi vernacular design. Imagine a young designer facing this beautiful cacophony and trying to find a path into the design field! This work is an open call to design analysts to help articulate the combination of expertise, taste, and power that brings such work to life.

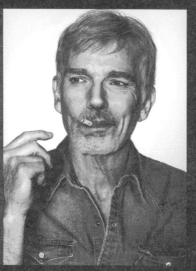

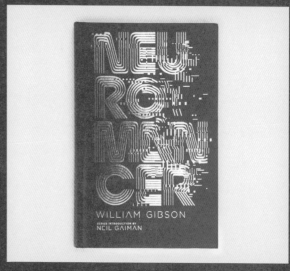

Left, top: *GQ* magazine spread by Griffin Funk and Fred Woodward → **page 87**
Right, top: Book cover designed by Alex Trochut and Paul Buckley → **page 28**
Left: *Wired UK* spread by Maris Falcigno and Shantanu Suman → **page 77**

If our typography competition metaphor is a varied landscape, the typeface competition is geological and elemental, and type is the bedrock of graphic design. Type designers continue building an immense periodic table of enticing designs.

New styles quote older ones, more or less literally.

Among our few typeface winners, we see the reverse stress of the nineteenth-century-style Salvaje, the vernacular ease of Pilot, and the humanist, Akzidenz-like sans-serif Gräbenbach. To western eyes, non-Latin designs, especially Asian ones, are more willing to experiment.

¡KING KONG!

Astounding

Gräbenbach

Time will clarify the view of the work gathered in these competitions. Meanwhile, the language we use is important; words matter. Is historical and formal variety "diversity" or is it "corruption"? One is challenging but accepting and open, while the other is negative, suggesting the need for control, sanitation, uniformity. Word choice becomes political and moral.

TYPOGRAPHY 38

THE WORLD'S BEST TYPE AND TYPOGRAPHY 2017

THE ANNUAL OF THE TYPE DIRECTORS CLUB

Advertising, Annual Reports, Book Jackets, Books, Brochure & Direct Mail, Calendars, Catalog, Editorial, Exhibits, Experimental, Identity , Logotypes, Miscellaneous, Motion experimental, Motion online titles, Motion TV shows, Packaging, Posters, Student, Websites.

230 submissions, 40 countries— 15 winning typefaces

A facsimile of the TDC's publication featuring the winning work for 1965.

→EMIGRE ZUZANA LICKO, RUDY VANDERLANS

FABLE LII. *The* Mock-bird.

— [SET IN MRS EAVES XL] —

There is a certain bird

in the West-Indies,

WHICH HAS THE *faculty* OF

MIMICKING THE NOTES

of *every* other songster,
without being able himself to add *any* original strains to the concert.

As one of these Mock-birds was displaying

HIS TALENTS *of* RIDICULE

among the branches of a venerable wood:

'Tis very well,

SAID A LITTLE WARBLER,

speaking in the name of all the rest,

we grant you that our music
is *not* without its faults:

but why will you not favour us

with a strain of

YOUR OWN?

FABLE LIII. *The* Trumpeter.

— [SET IN MRS EAVES XL NARROW] —

A Trumpeter in a certain army happened to be taken prisoner.

HE WAS ORDERED *immediately* TO EXECUTION

but pleaded **excuse** for

HIMSELF,

that it was *unjust*

a person should suffer *death*, who, far from an intention
of mischief, *did not even wear* an offensive weapon.

So much the rather,

replied one of the enemy

SHALT THOU DIE;

since without any design of *fighting thyself*,

THOU EXCITEST OTHERS TO THE

bloody business:

for he that is the *abettor* of a

BAD ACTION

IS AT LEAST EQUALLY WITH HIM THAT

commit it.

20

21

THE MAGAZINE AND FOUNDRY THAT IGNORED TYPOGRAPHIC BOUNDARIES

The Type Directors Club is pleased to award its 29th TDC medal of excellence to Zuzana Licko and Rudy VanderLans of Emigre,whose typeface designs and publishing projects have influenced the graphic design profession since 1984.

Emigre began life in 1984 as "a magazine for exiles," a reflection of its creators' own status as outsiders in the United States. Rudy VanderLans, its designer, was born in Voorburg, Netherlands in 1955. In 1981 he moved to the United States to study photography at the University of California, Berkeley. There he met Zuzana Licko who was studying graphic communications.

Licko, who was born in 1961 in Bratislava, Czechoslovakia, had emigrated to the United States in 1968. Their shared background was the seed that started *Emigre*, a cultural magazine with the "unique perspective of contemporary poets, writers, journalists, graphic designers, photographers, architects and artists who live or have lived outside their native countries."

The magazine was a vehicle for their graphic design, an opportunity to explore the possibilities of the new Macintosh computer. At the outset graphic design and typography were not its principal subject.

Emigre was essentially a zine and the use of the Macintosh was as much practical—a way to save on typesetting and other costs—as it was experimental. By *Emigre* no. 3 the magazine was produced using MacWrite and MacPaint programs. And, more importantly, it was set in low-resolution bitmapped fonts designed by Licko. The Lo-Res series of fonts was the beginning of Emigre as a digital type foundry, though initially the fonts were not for sale. But it was these first fonts that captured the attention of the graphic design world. Although they were wildly criticized for their crudeness, some designers—especially younger ones—found them both fascinating and refreshing.

Unwittingly, Emigre had become the lightning rod for debate in the late 1980s over the quality and viability of digital type and hence of digital design in general. Rather than shy away from the unexpected attention, VanderLans and Licko recognized the zeitgeist and embraced it fervently.

The occasional article on graphic design (e.g. a profile of Henk Elenga, co-founder of Hard Werken, in Emigre no. 6), gave way to issues devoted solely to the subject. Then, beginning with issue no.10 (1988), focused on the graduate design program at Cranbrook Academy of Art, Emigre became the locus of the design arguments that roiled the profession during that time of technological turmoil.

This was fully recognized with *Emigre* no. 11 (1990), the Ambition/Fear issue devoted to "Graphic Designers and the Macintosh Computer." Most importantly, Emigre became the voice for younger designers, especially design students caught in the upheaval, to challenge the corporate modernism and historicism that then dominated the profession. "The Magazine that Ignores Boundaries," the slogan that graced *Emigre* no. 4, had taken on a new meaning.

By the early 1990s *Emigre* had become important both as a forum for discussion about design in general and as a vehicle for experimentation in type design. Its first issue devoted solely to type was no. 15 which showcased Template Gothic by Barry Deck and Keedy Sans by Mr. [Jeffery] Keedy, the first non-Licko typefaces to be sold by the new Emigre Fonts.

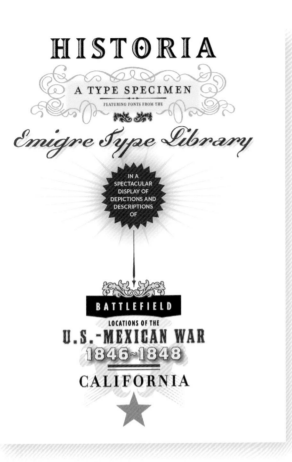

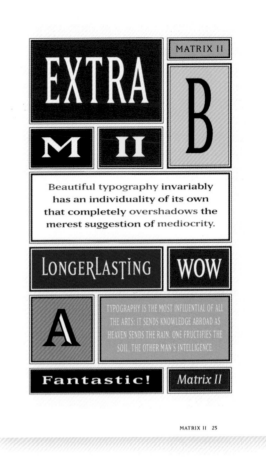

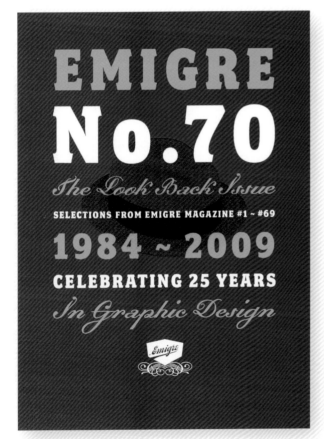

While Licko's early typefaces had been technologically driven, designed to adapt to the limitations and changes in printing resolution and computer memory, many of the first typefaces submitted to Emigre by outside designers were inspired more by iconoclasm. With names like Dead History, Not Caslon and Remedy—an antidote to Helvetica—they thumbed their nose at the type establishment. Emigre Fonts was the aesthetic and psychological alternative to its Bay Area neighbor, Adobe Systems. While Adobe was proving to skeptics that digital type could be as good—if not better—than the classical metal typefaces established typographers pined for, Emigre was thrilling less-reverent designers with typefaces truly of their time.

As digital type matured and digital design became accepted in the 1990s, *Emigre* continued to be relevant. As a magazine it shifted from being a goad to the design establishment to being its forum and its conscience. It became simultaneously both more mainstream and more academic, but never predictable. As both editor and designer VanderLans constantly surprised his readers. The anarchic page layouts of the late 1980s and early1990s gave way to a more scholarly appearance that masked subtle design experiments. VanderLans let the texts speak rather than competing with them. Similarly, Licko went historicist—but in a sly way—with the designs of Mrs. Eaves and Filosofia in 1996, two designs that have become modern classics. She followed them up with more original designs in a traditional vein such as Tarzana (1998), Fairplex (2002) and Program (2013). These fonts and others proved that Licko, like the magazine, was more than an emblem of the 1980s.

It is the longevity, marked by continual creativity, of both *Emigre* the magazine and Emigre Fonts that make VanderLans and Licko deserving of the TDC medal. *Emigre* magazine lasted for twenty-one years and 69 issues, a remarkable feat, especially when one realizes how short-lived iconic design magazines such as *Wendingen*, *The Fleuron*, *The Dolphin*, *Motif*, *Neue Grafik*, and *Dot Zero* were. It may have shrunk in size with "No Small Issue", no. 33, but it never shrank in substance.

At the same time Emigre Fonts went from being an outlet for Licko's experiments to a pioneer of digital typefounding, challenging the behemoths of the industry and inspiring countless young designers to set up their own foundries. In its dual roles, Emigre was simultaneously a vital contributor to, and a central observer of, the design scene in the final decade and a half of the 20th century.

Chronological List of Zuzana Licko's Type Designs

1985
→ Lo-Res [revised 2001]—Emigre, Emperor, Oakland
→ Modula

1986
→ Citizen
→ Matrix

1988
→ Lunatix
→ Oblong
→ Senator
→ Variex

1989
→ Elektrix
→ Triplex

1990
→ Journal
→ Tall Pack

→ Totally Gothic

1992
→ Matrix Display

1993
→ Narly

1994
→ Dogma
→ Whirligig

1995
→ Base 9 and Base 12
→ Modula Round
→ Soda Script

1996
→ Filosofia
→ Mrs. Eaves

1997
→ Hypnopaedia

1998
→ Tarzana

2000
→ Solex

2002
→ Fairplex

2005
→ Puzzler

2009
→ Mrs. Eaves XL Serif and Modern
→ Mrs. Eaves Sans and Modern
→ Mrs. Eaves XL Sans and Modern

2013
→ Program

Selected List of the Most Important Issues of Emigre magazine from the Perspective of Type and Design

→ Emigre no. 9 (1988)—4AD
Emigre no. 10 (1988)—Cranbrook Graphic Design Special Xchange Dutch Issue
→ Emigre no. 11 (1989)—Ambition Fear "Graphic Designers and the Macintosh Computer"
→ Emigre no. 14 (1990)—heritage
→ Emigre no. 15 (1990)—do you read me?
→ Emigre no. 17 (1991)—wise guys
→ Emigre no. 18 (1991)—Type-Site
→ Emigre no. 19 (1991)—Starting from Zero
→ Emigre no. 21 (1992)—New Faces
→ Emigre no. 23 (1992)—Culprits
→ Emigre no. 24 (1992)—neomania
→ Emigre no. 25 (1993)—Made in Holland
→ Emigre no. 26 (1993)—All Fired Up
→ Emigre no. 27 (1993)—David Carson
→ Emigre no. 29 (1994)—The Designers Republic
→ Emigre no. 30 (1994)—Fallout
Emigre no. 34 (1995)—The Rebirth of Design
→ Emigre no. 36 (1995)—Mouthpiece 2
→ Emigre no. 38 (1996)—The Authentic Issue
→ Emigre no. 42 (1997)—The Mercantile Issue
Emigre no. 43 (1997)—Designers Are People Too
Emigre no. 49 (1999)—The Everything Is For Sale Issue
Emigre no. 57 (2001)—Lost Formats Preservation Society
→ Emigre no. 58 (2001)—Everyone Is a Designer: Manifest for the Design Economy
→ Emigre no. 64 (2003)—Rant
Emigre no. 65 (2003)—If We're Standing on the Shoulders of Giants...
→ Emigre no. 67 (2004)—Graphic design vs. style, globalism, criticism, science, authenticity, and humanism

→JOE NEWTON AND ANGELA VOULANGAS

"The world needs more type snobs."*

Be a type snob. We believe it's a good thing—because typography can amplify meaning, clarify messages, and help us navigate the ever-increasing cacophony of modern communication. At the Type Directors Club, we're type snobs because we believe in fine typography—and knowing the difference. We want better communication for everyone, and we think type is the most powerful tool in the designer's arsenal to achieve that.

The club is authoritative and analytical, yet passionate about nurturing newcomers—an exclusive club that is inclusive to all who share our joy of typography and type design. Partake in a passion with like-minded people, and improve your knowledge and expertise, whether you are a master of your craft or a novice seeking growth and guidance.

The book in your hands, *The World's Best Typography*, contains the winners of our 63rd annual competition, painstakingly selected by an international panel of judges, from more than 1,700 entries from 52 countries. As competition co-chairs, we wish to extend our gratitude to this year's judges for generously sharing their wisdom, expertise, and time. We were edified by our weekend with these most excellent type snobs—a selection of professionals at the top of their game—and the competition couldn't have happened without them.

The book also represents a celebration of the seventieth anniversary of the Type Directors Club and its mission. The first iteration of the club, in September 1946, brought together an unprecedented cohort of type professionals from New York's design community, including such historic design icons as Louis Dorfsman, Herb Lubalin, Bradbury Thompson, and Hermann Zapf. The club is no longer a cadre of white men from North America—today, the TDC boasts a diverse membership from forty-one countries. Our mission, however, remains the same: to promote excellence in typography and type design.

This excellence can be seen in aesthetic terms certainly—excellence furthers the craft of typography and propels the whole profession forward. But great typography also embraces the task of improving communication, and this competition recognizes that the most vibrant and innovative work strives to meet that challenge on both fronts. To promote that objective beyond the confines of this book, TDC showcases the award-winning work annually in exhibits touring multiple cities in more than fifteen countries worldwide. This work, a snapshot of the best of the best, will bring inspiration and, perhaps, influence the choices we designers make.

We invite you to join us in this essential endeavor. Become a TDC member and benefit from engaging with typographic excellence and those who recognize and revere it: through this book, through the worldwide touring exhibits, and through lectures and workshops in person or online.

In type—and type snobs—we trust.

Joe Newton, Angela Voulangas
TDC63 competition co-chairs

*Our motto, ready for a T-shirt, thanks to
 branding expert Scott Lerman.

↓DESIGN
Juan Ramon Pastor, El Prat, Barcelona
↓CREATIVE DIRECTION
Kashka Pregowska-Czerw
↓URL
wetecacahuete.com
↓TWITTER
@weteone
↓STUDIO
Wete
↓CLIENT
Adobe Systems, Inc.
↓PRINCIPAL TYPE
Adobe Clean
↓DIMENSIONS
18.9 x 26 in. (48 x 56 cm)
↓CONCEPT
The intention was to create a lettering
with the words "blood", "sweat",
"tears", and "trophies" (represented
by bronze, copper, silver, and gold)
merging with it to reinforce the idea
of the creative effort to receive a prize
at Cannes Lions.

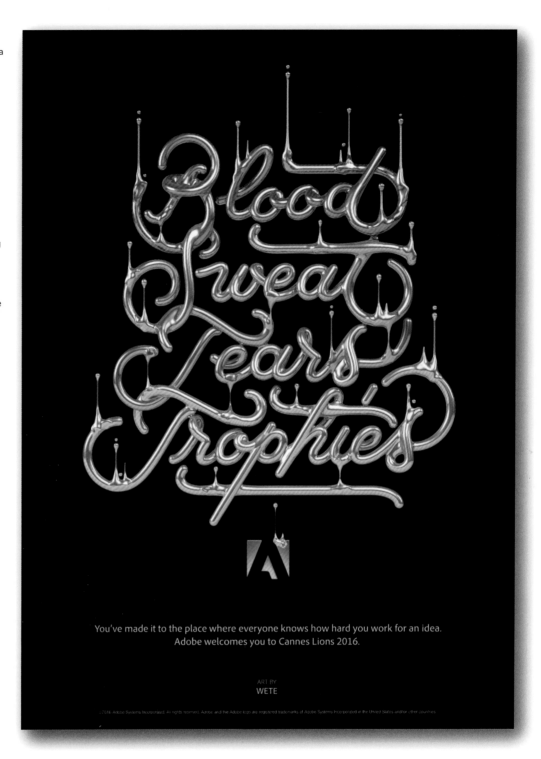

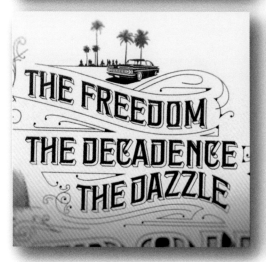

↓ART DIRECTION
Cesar Finamori, New York
↓CREATIVE DIRECTION
Cesar Finamori and Kara Goodrich
↓EXECUTIVE CREATIVE DIRECTORS
Danilo Boer and Marcos Kotlhar
↓CHIEF CREATIVE OFFICERS
David Lubars and Greg Hahn
↓LETTERING
Kevin Cantrell°
↓ILLUSTRATOR
Andre Maciel
↓PHOTOGRAPHER
Dan Smith
↓RETOUCHER
Blane Robison
↓PRODUCERS
Mary Cook, Mike Musano,
and Ilona Siller, Salt Lake City,
São Paulo, and New York
↓URL
kevincantrell.com
↓TWITTER
@kevinrcantrell
↓DESIGN FIRM
Kevin Cantrell Studio
↓AGENCY
BBDO NY
↓CLIENT
Bacardi Havana Club
↓PRINCIPAL TYPE
Bauer Bodoni and handlettering
↓DIMENSIONS
Various
↓CONCEPT
The decadence, the glamour, the
dazzle: Meet Havana Club's premium
rum. BBDO NY commissioned KCS
to produce an opulent campaign with
custom lettering and ornamentation
as regal as the product itself. KCS
created a toolbox of opulent and
versatile ornamentation components
for an ongoing campaign as well as
one-off ads so rich in detail as to be
impossible to replicate.

↓ART DIRECTION
Jamie Axford, Manchester, UK
↓URL
mccannmanchester.com
↓TWITTER
@McCannMcr
↓AGENCY
McCann Manchester
↓CLIENT
British Liver Trust
↓PRINCIPAL TYPE
Arial (body copy) and custom
(imagery)
↓DIMENSIONS
16.5 x 23.4 in. (59.4 x 42 cm)
↓CONCEPT
This is a drink-awareness campaign
that appeared in doctors' waiting
rooms around the UK.

BRITISH LIVER TRUST

Liver disease is on the increase.
A bit less booze could save your life.
britishlivertrust.org.uk

LOVE YOUR LIVER

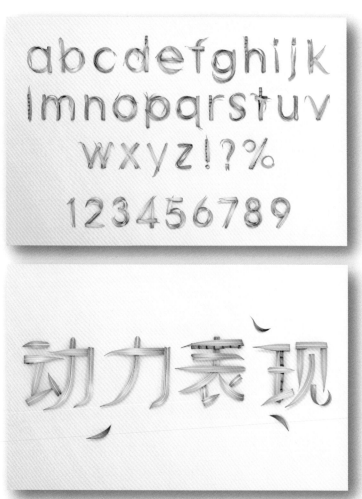

動力表現

fast

forward with plants

↓CREATIVE DIRECTION
Garrick Hamm
↓LEAD AND ART DIRECTION
Craig Kirk
↓ARTWORK
Jason Budgen and Spencer Taylor
↓ACCOUNT MANAGER
Emmanuelle Hilson
↓TYPOGRAPHERS
Craig Kirk, Jason Budgen, and Tom Waterhouse
↓3D MODELERS
Jason Budgen and Tom Waterhouse
↓LEAF TEXTURE PHOTOGRAPHER
Carol Sharp
↓COPYWRITER
Jerry Gallaher
↓URL
wmhagency.com
↓DESIGN AGENCY
Williams Murray Hamm
↓CLIENT
Susan Frame at Castrol
↓PRINCIPAL TYPE
Biosynthetic Leaf Alphabet (3D typeface)
↓CONCEPT
Plants are the future of engine protection. They can be surprisingly powerful yet protective at the same time. We brought together this natural tension, creating a world, visual language, and new typeface unique to Castrol Biosynthetic oils.

↓ART DIRECTION
Cyla Costa, Silmo Bonomi,
Rodrigo Marinheiro, and Yumi Shimada,
Curitiba, Brazil
↓CREATIVE DIRECTION
Jairo Anderson
↓LETTERING AND EXECUTION
Cyla Costa Studio°
↓AGENCY
VML Brazil
↓CLIENT
Intimus
↓PRINCIPAL TYPE
Handlettering
↓DIMENSIONS
16.5 x 23.4 in. (42 x 59.4 cm)
↓CONCEPT
VML Brazil invited me to embody the
digital version of Maria, a visual artist
who is the main character of Intimus's
ad campaign "Sou Maria mas não vou
com as outras." The campaign was
a success and had several phases,
including the recording of a film in
my studio, where I built this very
piece. The different layers and forms
represent the many personalities of
the girls who use Intimus's products.
The hand-cut lettering represents
great care and uniqueness.

↓DESIGN
Katharina Bergmann, Bianca Bunsas,
and Ulla Oberdörffer,
Berlin and Stuttgart
↓CREATIVE DIRECTION
Jochen Theurer
↓PROJECT MANAGER AND
PRODUCTION
Jeannette Kohnle
↓PRINT
raff media group GmbH
↓URL
strichpunkt-design.de
↓TWITTER
@strichpunkt
↓DESIGN AGENCY
Strichpunkt Design
↓CLIENT
Baden-Württemberg Stiftung Gmbh,
Christoph Dahl, managing director,
and Julia Kovar-Mühlhausen, head of
communications
↓PRINCIPAL TYPE
Flama, Letter Gothic, and The Serif
↓DIMENSIONS
8.5 x 11.2 in. (21.5 x 28.5 cm)
↓CONCEPT
"Human dignity is inviolable."
This basic sentence forms the
constitutional and substantive
basis of the Baden-Württemberg
Foundation's work. It is both its duty
and consistent commitment. The
report highlights, even more than
before, the attitude, motivation, and
social mission of the foundation.
The image section convinces by its
image and text collage that by means
of individual interpretations of the
nuclear issue, "dignity" provides
impetus for readers' own thinking.
The personal essay of the manager
and the lively reportage section
provide deliberate counterpoints.

↓ART DIRECTOR
Mariela Hsu, Washington, D.C.
↓CHIEF CREATIVE OFFICER
Pum Lefebure°
↓CREATIVE DIRECTOR
Pum Lefebure°
↓CEO
Jake Lefebure
↓URL
designarmy.com
↓TWITTER
@designarmy
↓DESIGN AGENCY
Design Army
↓CLIENT
Human Rights Campaign
↓PRINCIPAL TYPE
Swiss721 and SwissBT
↓DIMENSIONS
22 x 25 in. (55.8 x 63.5 cm)
↓CONCEPT
The HRC asked us to reimagine
their 2016 annual report. Typically
full-color, text-heavy brochures
with financial summaries, these are
forgettable items that rarely grab
the attention of donors. That risk
couldn't be taken in today's political
environment. As a nod to grassroots
beginnings, and a vehicle for impactful
headlines, we created an oversized
newspaper. Spreads feature clean
layouts and captivating messages,
demanding to be shared. We used a
single-color, custom typography and
spacing to present data impactfully.
We produced an inexpensive, bold
report serving as a keepsake while
driving the HRC's 1.5 million members
to fight for equal rights.

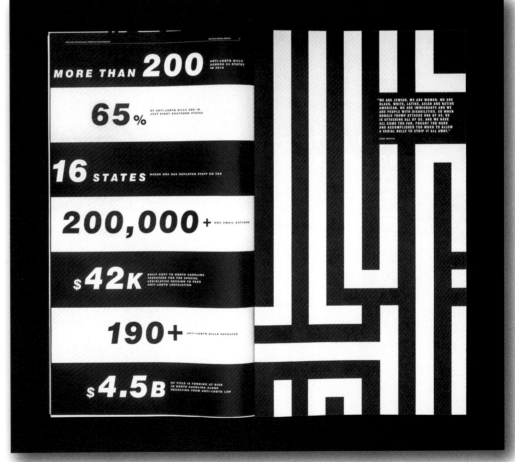

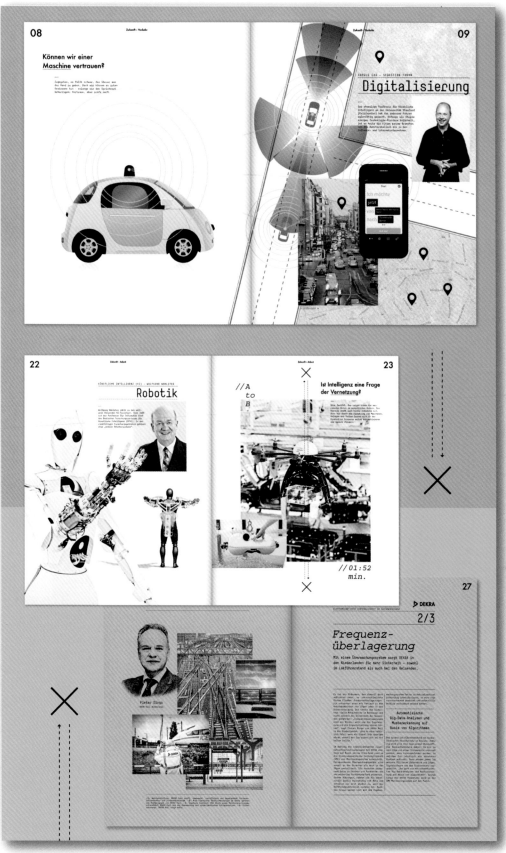

↓DESIGN
Ulla Oberdörffer, Berlin and Stuttgart
↓CREATIVE DIRECTION
Jochen Theurer
↓PROJECT MANAGER AND
PRODUCTION
Jeannette Kohnle
↓PRINT
raff media group GmbH
↓URL
strichpunkt-design.de
↓TWITTER
@strichpunkt
↓DESIGN AGENCY
Strichpunkt Design
↓CLIENT
DEKRA e.V., Stephan Heigl, director
Communications & Marketing, and Dr.
Torsten Knödler, Communications
↓PRINCIPAL TYPE
Courier Std, Futura, Futura Std,
Minion Pro, and Simple
↓DIMENSIONS
8.7 x 11.2 in. (22 x 28.5 cm)
↓CONCEPT
The Safety of Things is a magazine
from the future! Three focus areas
explore fascinating opportunities
and the potential risks of digital
transformation. The result is a
multifaceted picture of the world
of tomorrow in which DEKRA has
positioned itself as a responsible
thinker and initiator in a massive
global-growth market. This
corresponds exactly to the expert
Organization's Vision 2025: "We
will become the global partners
for a safer world." To this end, the
company focuses on safety in the
three worlds—"in traffic, at work, and
at home."

↓DESIGN AND PHOTOGRAPHY
Anne Jordan and Mitch Goldstein,
Rochester, New York
↓ART DIRECTION
Rob Ehle
↓URLS
annatype.com and mitchgoldstein.com
↓TWITTER
@annatype and @mgoldst
↓CLIENT
Stanford University Press
↓PRINCIPAL TYPE
DIN
↓DIMENSIONS
6.1 x 9.25 in. (15.5 x 23.5 cm)
↓CONCEPT
Impossible Modernism is a literary
studies book about the writings of
philosopher Walter Benjamin and
poet T. S. Eliot. The book examines
the relationship between literary and
historical form during the modernist
period and focuses on how both
writers reimagined the forms that
historical representation might take.
To communicate literature breaking
out of historical boundaries, we built
and photographed a typographic
sculpture made out of cut paper. The
final cover is a composite of many
photographs, generating a sense
of movement and creating a visual
metaphor for "Impossible Modernism."

PROF HOF'S THIRTY NEARLY IMPOSSIBLE ÉTUDES FOR GUITAR DUO

↓DESIGN
Benjamin Shaykin°,
Providence, Rhode Island
↓URL
benjaminshaykin.com
↓TWITTER
@bshaykin
↓DESIGN STUDIO
Benjamin Shaykin graphic design
↓CLIENT
Eric Hofbauer, Creative Nation Music
↓PRINCIPAL TYPE
Atlantik and Local Gothic
↓DIMENSIONS
8.5 x 11 in. (21.6x 27.9 cm)
↓CONCEPT
A book of unconventional "nearly
impossible" études for guitar duo
required an unconventional cover.
The author wanted to avoid clichés
common on books of this sort.
We decided to let the typography
represent his musicality and off-kilter
approach.

↓DESIGN
Utku Lomlu°, Istanbul
↓URL
utkulomlu.com
↓DESIGN STUDIO
Lom Creative
↓CLIENT
Can Publishing
↓PRINCIPAL TYPE
Custom
↓DIMENSIONS
4.9 x 7.6 in. (12.5 x 19.5 cm)
↓CONCEPT
The cover design of *Jean-Paul Sartre* originates from his own fundamental ideas; it is intended as a series cover design. Sartre had never shied away from facing the realities and conflicts of his era. With this in mind, a means was sought to represent both his unyielding political stance on current events and existential thought. Analytically, the name was used to create a typography-based structure; through the use of forms and lines, a sense of place, route, and direction was created. It evokes Sartre, moving determinedly through a path toward the metaphor of the door—toward himself, toward essence, toward his existentialist philosophy.

STORIES OF THE GAME

WAYNE GRETZKY

WITH KIRSTIE McLELLAN DAY

↓DESIGN
Stephen Brayda, New York
↓ART DIRECTION
Monica Cordova
↓URL
stephenbrayda.com
↓DESIGN FIRM
Penguin Art Group
↓PUBLISHER
Penguin Random House
↓PRINCIPAL TYPE
Abolition and LTC Octic Gothic
↓DIMENSIONS
6 x 9 in. (15.2 x 22.9 cm)
↓CONCEPT
To mark the NHL's ninety-ninth
anniversary, Wayne Gretzky shares
his stories along with hockey's most
memorable moments in *99: Stories of
the Game.* The goal of this design was
to convey the weight of the content
and occasion as well as the grace of
Gretzky and the game.

↓DESIGN
Ben Denzer°, New York
↓ART DIRECTION
Jason Booher°
↓PUBLISHER
Plume Books
↓URL
bendenzer.com
↓PRINCIPAL TYPE
Handwriting
↓DIMENSIONS
5.3 x 8 in. (13.5 x 20.3 cm)
↓CONCEPT
It runs out of space.

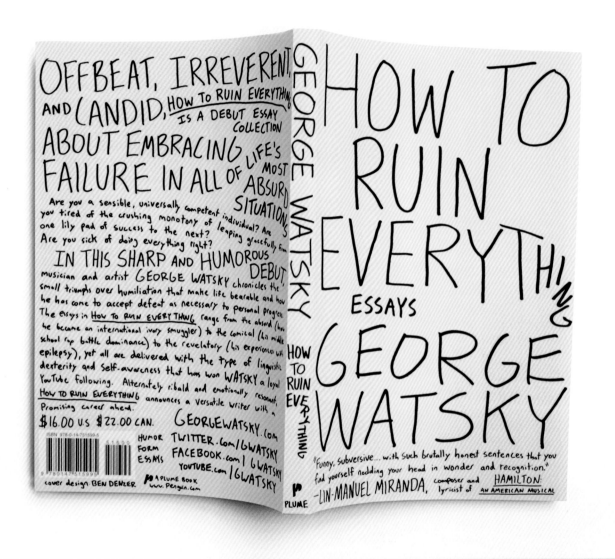

"I READ IT WITH MY HEART IN MY MOUTH....A THUNDEROUSLY GOOD STORY." —EMMA DONOGHUE, AUTHOR OF ROOM

THE
LIFE
AND
DEATH
OF SOPHIE
STARK

A NOVEL BY
ANNA NORTH

↓DESIGN
Rachel Willey, New York
↓ART DIRECTION
Jason Booher°
↓URL
rachelwilley.com
↓PUBLISHER
Plume Books
↓PRINCIPAL TYPE
Signage, warped on scanner
↓DIMENSIONS
5.5 x 8.25 in. (14 x 21 cm)
↓CONCEPT
This book is about a filmmaker and the people who weave in and out of her work and life while trying to get close to her. Using the filmstrip format and a scanner, I made distortions of the pieces of type. This warped end result was my attempt at giving a slight sense of foreboding and hinting at the deceptions and misconceptions within.

↓DESIGN
Alex Trochut, New York
↓ART DIRECTION
Paul Buckley°
↓URL
alextrochut.com
↓INSTAGRAM
@paul.buckley
↓PUBLISHER
Penguin Art Group
↓PRINCIPAL TYPE
Custom
↓DIMENSIONS
5.5 x 8.25 in. (14 x 21 cm)
↓CONCEPT
The brief consisted of a strictly
typographical solution that developed
a consistent style throughout the
whole series, from the shortest title,
Dune, to the longest, *The Left Hand
of Darkness.* This demanded that
decisions be made so as to approach
the project as a series, rather than
with a custom solution for each book.

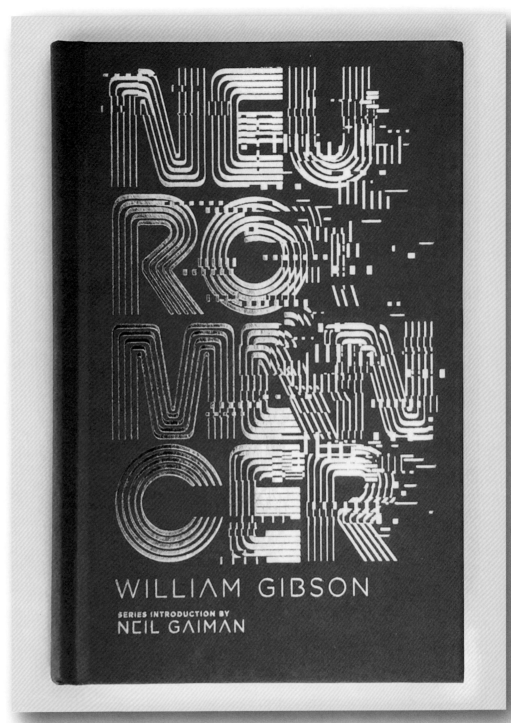

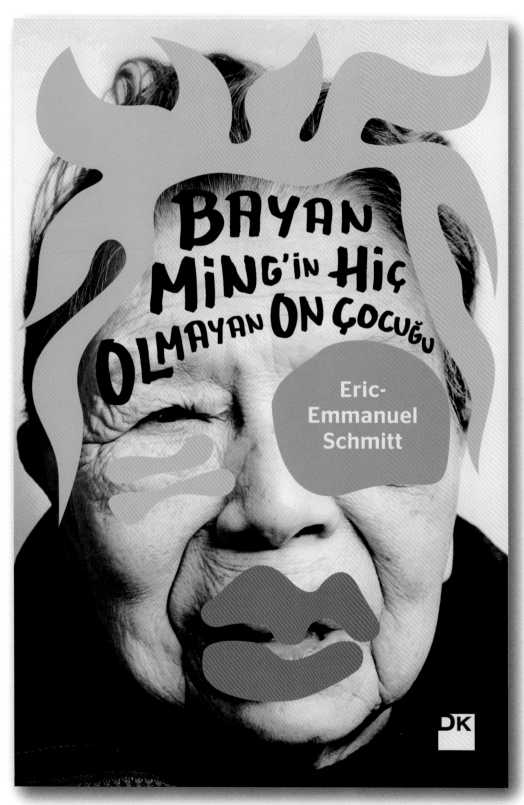

↓DESIGN
Geray Gencer, Istanbul
↓URL
geraygencer.com
↓STUDIO
Studio Geray Gencer
↓CLIENT
Dogan Egmont Publishing
↓PRINCIPAL TYPE
Stag Sans and Handlettering
↓DIMENSIONS
5.3 x 7.6 in. (13.5 x 19.5 cm)
↓CONCEPT
The design is for *Ten Children Ms. Ming Never Had* by Eric-Emmanuel Schmitt. The book is about a tragedy of a Chinese mother who can't have children and who deals with that tragedy by inventing the lives of the children her country has forbidden her to have. The colorful touches on the real photo are inspired by the way children roughly paint everything around them. It is also a scattered image referring to Ms. Ming's "lost" mind.

Annual Design Portfolio

↓DESIGN
Yan-Ting Chen, Taiwan
↓URL
yantingchen.com
↓DESIGN FIRM
Yantingchen Design
↓CLIENT
NTUST Architecture
↓PRINCIPAL TYPE
Original
↓DIMENSIONS
8.3 x 11.7 in. (2 1 x 29.7 cm)

↓COMMENT

Annual Design Portfolio is a book designed by Yan-Ting Chen for National Taiwan University of Science and Technology Department of Architecture in Taiwan. Readers can design their own "Rubber Alphabets" to represent a new idea and concept.

Yan-Ting Chen's playful book design is very engaging; we all wanted to pick it up and start arranging our own rubber alphabets! The bright and multi-toned elastics are a playful contrast to the stark-black peg and boards. The design is visually dynamic as well as tactile. It's a clever and unusual solution for a university of architecture—one assumes that the students are being taught creative exploration and design thinking and are immersed in a world of possibility and discovery. A hefty, sculptural cover with minimal printing seems all the more appropriate for a readership dedicated to the technology of building and the construction of ideas.
Janine Vangool

↓DESIGN
Geray Gencer, Istanbul
↓URL
geraygencer.com
↓STUDIO
Studio Geray Gencer
↓CLIENT
Dogan Egmont Publishing
↓PRINCIPAL TYPE
Neutraface and Skolar
↓DIMENSIONS
5.3 x 7.6 in. (13.5 x 19.5 cm)
↓CONCEPT
Deconstructive body shapes on each
cover symbolize the main characters
of the book series, who experienced
personal tragedies in their lifetimes.

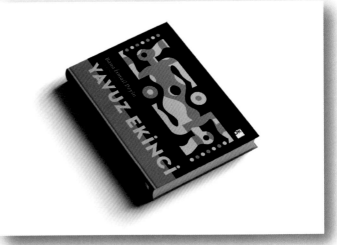

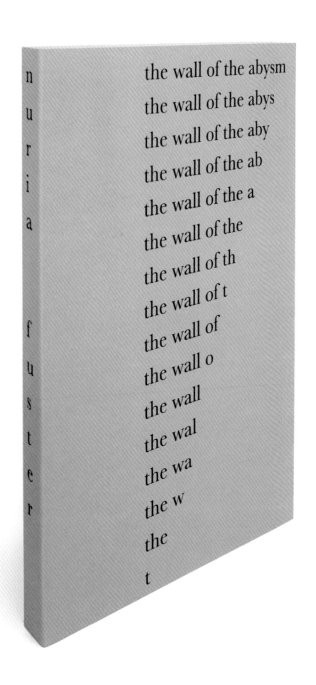

↓DESIGN
Ena Cardenal de la Nuez, Madrid
↓PREPRESS
Antonio Rubio
↓PRINTER
TF Artes Gráficas
↓CLIENT
Nuria Fuster and Fundación Botín
↓PRINCIPAL TYPE
Baskerville
↓DIMENSIONS
10.1 x 6.5 in. (25.7 x 16.4 cm)
↓CONCEPT
In the selection of works that make up
this bilingual publication, artist Fuster
proposes installations with objects
in an unconventional perspective in
what comes to be a reflection on the
current sculpture. The title, *T*, refers
to the mental approach that lies
behind her works and is represented
typographically. In the cover, the title
creates that wall playing with font and
recreates the fall and the deepness by
way of visual poetry. The title appears
in English in the front and in Spanish
in the back; the name of the artist is in
the book spine.

↓DESIGN
Adalis Martinez, New York
↓ART DIRECTION
Robin Bilardello
↓URL
adalismartinez.com
↓PUBLISHER
Harper
↓PRINCIPAL TYPE
Berthold Akzidenz Grotesk Bold
(Modified)
↓DIMENSIONS
6 x 9 in. (15.2 x 22.9 cm)

↓DESIGN
Rachel Ake, New York
↓ART DIRECTION
Joseph Perez
↓ILLUSTRATOR
Brian Levy
↓URL
rachelake.com
↓PUBLISHER
Random House Publishing Group,
Penguin Random House
↓PRINCIPAL TYPE
Helvetica
↓DIMENSIONS
5.5 x 8.5 in. (14 x 21.6 cm)
↓CONCEPT
These essays slowly reveal an
incredible web of interconnected
thoughts by the author, who still
writes all of his manuscripts on his
ancient typewriter.

↓DESIGN
Janet Hansen, New York
↓URL
janet-hansen.com
↓TWITTER
@janetehansen
↓CLIENT
Rebecca Schiff
↓PUBLISHER
Alfred A. Knopf
↓PRINCIPAL TYPE
Futura
↓DIMENSION S
5.6 x 8.25 in. (14.3 x 21 cm)
↓CONCEPT
This story collection reminds me of all the funny and odd things my friends and I were doing in our early twenties. The title story, "The Bed Moved," is hardly longer than a page, but I found myself relating it to the rest of the stories—the movement of relationships, sex, death, and drugs. Rebecca's writing is intentionally disordered, and I thought it would be really interesting to somehow express that with just the words of the title. The pink and bold letters give a nod to her strong, feminine voice, and anchoring the word "Bed" so it is the strongest word on the cover is a playful reference to the sexual nature of her stories—without having to literally visualize it.

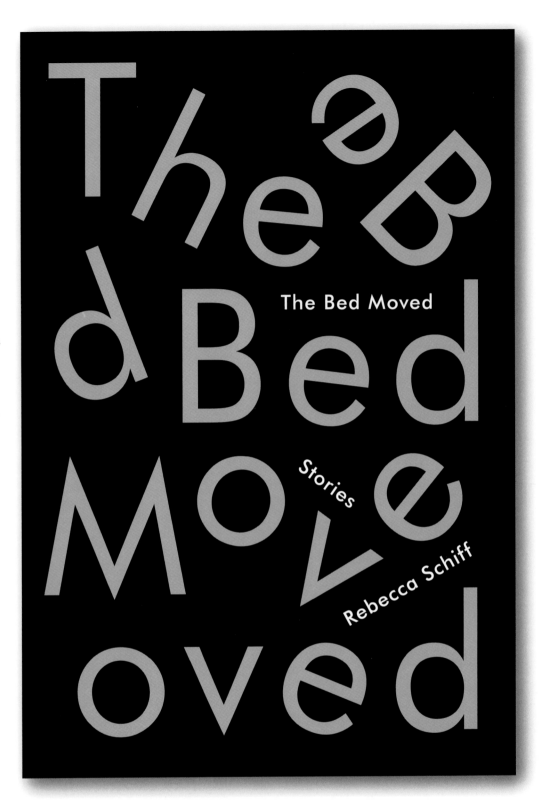

The Bed Moved

Stories

Rebecca Schiff

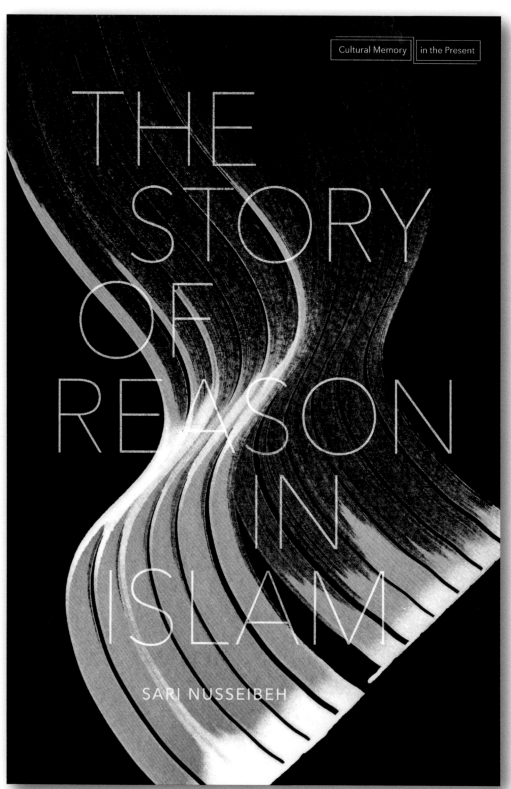

THE
STORY
OF
REASON
IN
ISLAM

Cultural Memory | in the Present

SARI NUSSEIBEH

↓DESIGN, PHOTOGRAPHY, AND ILLUSTRATIONS
Anne Jordan and Mitch Goldstein, Rochester, New York
↓ART DIRECTION
Rob Ehle
↓URLS
annatype.com
and mitchgoldstein.com
↓TWITTER
@annatype and @mgoldst
↓CLIENT
Stanford University Press
↓PRINCIPAL TYPE
Avenir
↓DIMENSIONS
6.1 x 9.25 in. (15.5 x 23.5 cm)
↓CONCEPT
This is the cover for a philosophy/ religion book about Islam and the Arabic writing system. The book describes how the rapid development of writing in the Arab world created a magnificent cultural flowering. Our design is inspired by calligraphic art and the concept of enlightenment. We created an original ink drawing, layered it with physical typography, and then photographed the construction with light shining through it. The material effect fuses the type and image together and creates a sensation of sweeping light.

↓DESIGN AND CREATIVE
DIRECTION
Benson Chong and Felix Sng,
Singapore
↓URL
swell.sg
↓DESIGN STUDIO
SWELL
↓PRINCIPAL TYPE
DTL VandenKeere and handlettering
↓DIMENSIONS
6.5 x 9.25 in. (16.5 x 23.5 cm)
↓CONCEPT

Pulp: A Short Biography of the Banished Book is a decade-long project by artist Shubigi Rao about the history of book destruction, censorship, and other forms of repression as well as the book as symbol and resistance. This publication is a manifestation of the research. Pulp is "the book as content-driven object," where design and typography extend the subject, not decorate it. The use of cinnabar is historically significant, as is employing margins as profane spaces against the "sanctified" text. The handwritten marginalia also point to the contemporary theme of marginalization in the book.

↓DESIGN, ART DIRECTION, AND ILLUSTRATION
Tim Jetis, Sydney
↓PRINTER
Theo Pettaras, Digital Press
↓URLS
cabinetofwonder.com and ameetingofwords.com
↓DESIGN STUDIO
Cabinet of Wonder
↓PRINCIPAL TYPE
Caslon
↓DIMENSIONS
11 x 13 in. (28 x 33 cm)
↓CONCEPT
A Meeting of Words is a celebration of books and the written word. It is an exploratory collaboration between art director and designer Tim Jetis and printer Theo Petarras realized in this digitally printed, clothbound book. After exploring passages from significant literature and speeches that have changed history and illuminated the heights and depths of the human spirit, I chose Caslon, inspired by Benjamin Franklin, who used it on the Declaration of Independence, imbuing a certain political elegance to the project. The challenge was to employ expressive use of typography, illustration, and print to create a book to powerfully share these works.

↓DESIGN AND CREATIVE
DIRECTION
Carolina de Bartolo,
San Anselmo, California
↓AUTHOR
Carolina de Bartolo
↓CONTRIBUTORS
Stephen Coles and Erik Spiekermann°
↓URL
explorationsintypography.com
↓TWITTER
@carodebartolo, @stewf,
and @espiekermann
↓PUBLISHER
101 Editions, LLC,
San Anselmo, California
↓PRINCIPAL TYPE
Output Sans and custom "X"
letterform designed by
Chiharu Tanaka
↓DIMENSIONS
9.25 x 12 in. (23.5 x 30.5 cm)
↓CONCEPT
This is the second edition of
the popular intermediate-level
typography textbook *Explorations in
Typography*. It has been redesigned,
revised, and expanded. Along with
more typesetting examples and more
typefaces, this new edition also has
more type combos as well as some
handy new appendices: a visual index
of page layouts and a list of free or
low-cost alternative typefaces.

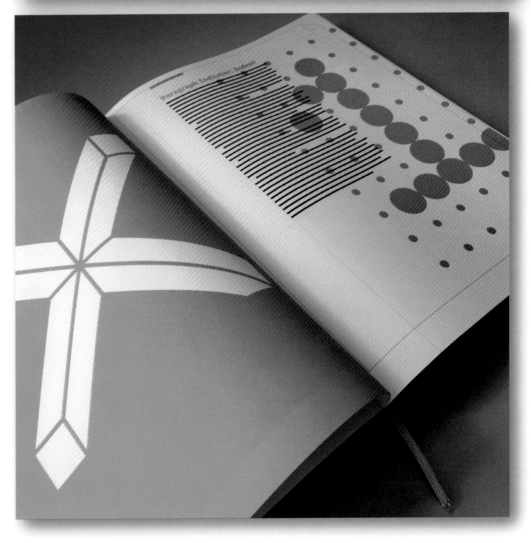

↓PRINCIPAL
Andrew Hoyne, Sydney
↓ART DIRECTOR
Nichole Trionfi
↓LETTERER
Wanissa Somsuphangsri
↓TYPESETTER
Nicholas Fels
↓URL
hoyne.com.au
↓TWITTER
@HoyneDesign
↓DESIGN FIRM
Hoyne
↓PRINCIPAL TYPE
GT Sectra Display
↓DIMENSIONS
10 x 11.8 in. (25.5 x 30 cm)
↓CONCEPT
Momentous, provoking, and beautiful,
The Place Economy is a resource
book that discusses best-practice
place making from around the world.
The book sets out to showcase all
that is possible when government,
commerce, and communities listen
to one another and collaborate in the
building of cities. *The Place Economy*
was designed as a coffee table
book, something people would want
to proudly display that would also
ignite conversation and debate. It is
both beautiful and engaging, with a
mix of photography, illustration, and
typography used to help bring each
story, interview, or case study to life.

↓DESIGN AND ART DIRECTION
Sun Xiaoxi, Beijing
↓URL
sunxiaoxi.me
↓CLIENT
Shanghai People's Publishing House,
Horizon Books
↓PRINCIPAL TYPE
DIN, DIN Alternate, FZLTCHK-GBK,
and FZLTZHUNHK-GBK
↓DIMENSIONS
9.8 x 9.4 in. (25 x 24 cm)
↓CONCEPT
Murmurs of Earth tells the story
of the Voyager Golden Record, a
record that traveled with the space
probe launched in 1977 by NASA in
an attempt to find extraterrestrial
life. This simplified Chinese edition
is the redesign of the 1978 English
version. The whole book is designed
as a "CD" package and is full of black.
The graphic of the cover implies a CD
with color varying through light, which
implies the mystery and the romance
of the universe.

↓DESIGN, CONCEPT, AND
ILLUSTRATION
Franziska Morlok
and Miriam Waszelewski, Berlin
↓PHOTOGRAPHY
Matthias Weingärtner
(matthiasweingaertner.com)
↓URLS
rimini-berlin.de and
miriamwaszelewski.com
↓CLIENT
Verlag Hermann Schmidt,
Mainz, Germany
↓PRINCIPAL TYPE
Circular and Larish
↓DIMENSIONS
7 x 9.4 in. (18 x 24 cm)
↓CONCEPT

Vom Blatt zum Blättern is a unique publication about bookbinding for graphic designers. We are celebrating the book as an object, explaining a wide range of techniques, how they work, and what their advantages are. We see binding as a crucial and underrated part of the design process. In addition to texts, the publication contains playful, bold illustrations explaining techniques of industrial bookbinding step by step. Black-and-white photographs give more detailed insight and reduce the technical appearance of the publication.

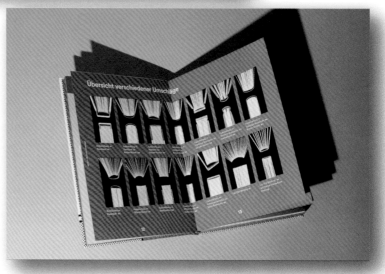

↓DESIGN
Stephanie Kaplan and Isabel Naegele
Basel, Switzerland, and
Mainz, Germany
↓ARTWORK AND ILLUSTRATIONS
Stephanie Kaplan
↓EDITORS
Petra Eisele, Annette Ludwig,
and Isabel Naegele
↓PHOTOS AND REPRODUCTIONS
Bianca Rother, Florian Schimanski,
Tobias Wenz, Carina Willenbrink,
Daniel Wolfrath, and Erdem Yildirim
↓PRINT
Gutenberg Beuys, Langenhagen,
Germany
↓BOOKBINDING
Schaumann, Darmstadt, Germany
↓URLS
www.designlabor-gutenberg.de
and www.futura-typeface.de
↓DESIGN STUDIO
Institute Designlab Gutenberg,
University of Applied Sciences Mainz
↓CLIENT
Gutenberg-Museum, Mainz, Germany,
and Institute Designlab Gutenberg,
University of Applied Sciences
↓PUBLISHER
Verlag Hermann Schmidt,
Mainz, Germany
↓PRINCIPAL TYPE
Futura and Futura Alternate
↓DIMENSIONS
6.8 x 9.4 in. (17.3 x 24 cm)
↓CONCEPT
Happy ninetieth birthday, Futura!
Introduced in Frankfurt/Mainz in
1927, the typeface quickly became
an international bestseller, spread
throughout all the world's major
metropolises and even reaching
the moon. Inspired by the Apollo 11
images, we decided to pay tribute
to silver and cite the cover of the
wonderful silver specimen of 1933.
Instead of citing the classic red-and-
black new typography look, we used
the color palette of a folder with job
works from the 1950s and combined it
with the elegant Futura light typeface
wherever possible. The dimensions of
the book derive from the dimensions
of the original type proofs. They are
reproduced in a special chapter on
lightweight paper.

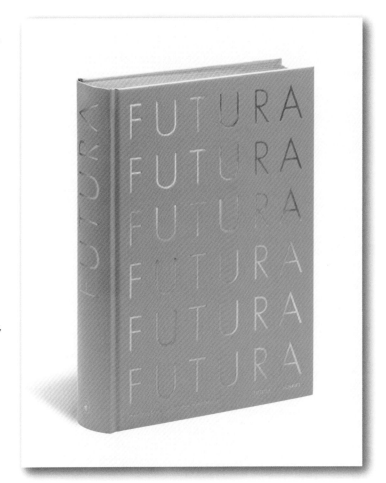

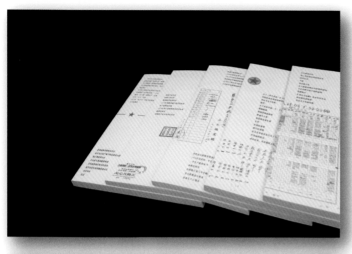

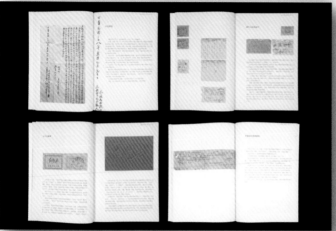

↓CREATIVE DIRECTION
Mo Guangping
Dongguan City, Guangdong Province,
China
↓URL
dongdidesign.com
↓DESIGN STUDIO
Dongdi Design Studio
↓CLIENT
Sun Yat-Sen University Press
↓PRINCIPAL TYPE
FZNew BaoSong-Z12S
↓DIMENSIONS
6.9 x 9.7 in. (17.5 x 24.5 cm)
↓CONCEPT
Breaking the conventional way of
thinking, the book is categorized
to agriculture, people's livelihood,
agricultural and sideline, agricultural
finance, and agricultural policy.
By way of categorized design, the
book caters more to the aesthetic
demands of modern people. In order
to be closer to file, a fully enclosed
book cover was designed. Readers
can open the book only after tearing
it. This involvement lets the readers
experience the process of opening
a file. Moreover, some old farming
symbols such as "Suzhou code" and
some typographies used in particular
ages were extracted from the file
collected by Liu Songtai and used on
the book cover, showing the lifestyle
of particular ages.

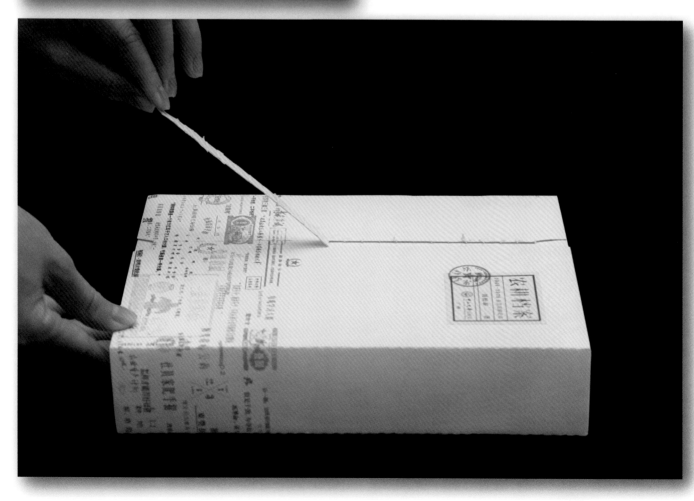

↓DESIGN
Lauren Barber, Olivia King,
and Jason Little°, Sydney
↓CREATIVE DIRECTION
Jason Little
↓ILLUSTRATOR
Ben Walker
↓URL
forthepeople.agency
↓TWITTER
@forthepeopleAU
↓DESIGN FIRM
For The People
↓CLIENT
The Biennale of Sydney
↓PRINCIPAL TYPE
BOS Embassy Display, Larish, GT
Pressura Mono, and GT Walsheim
↓DIMENSIONS
15.7 x 19.7 in. (40 x 50 cm)
↓CONCEPT
The theme of the twentieth edition
was "The future is already here—
it's just not evenly distributed." It
speaks to our expectations of a
future yet to materialize and that
today's physical and virtual reality
has already bypassed it. The *20th
Biennale of Sydney* book provides
an in-depth overview of the themes,
ideas, and concerns informing the
exhibition. The various "embassies
of thought" are presented in seven
distinctive sections containing
essays, roundtable discussions,
texts by participating artists, and a
compendium of excerpts of key texts
informing the exhibition.

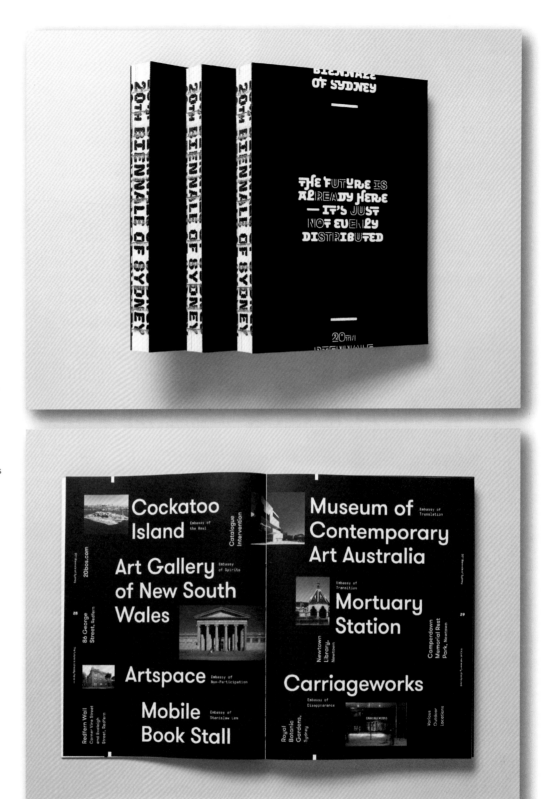

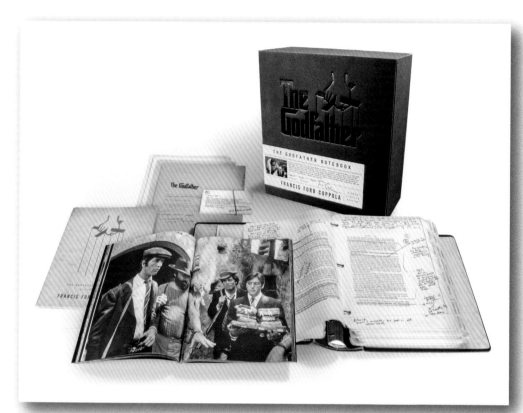

↓ART AND CREATIVE DIRECTION
Richard Ljoenes°, New York
↓COVER DESIGN
Richard Ljoenes
↓INTERIOR DESIGN
Nancy Singer
↓PRODUCTION DIRECTOR
Kurt Andrews
↓EDITOR
Lucas Wittman
↓URL
reganarts.com
↓PUBLISHER
Judith Regan, Regan Arts
↓PRINCIPAL TYPE
Alternate Gothic, Helvetica,
Neutraface 2 Text, Orator, Pica,
and Trade Gothic
↓DIMENSIONS
11.25 x 12.25 in. (28.5 x 31 cm)
↓CONCEPT
When Coppola was preparing to
shoot *The Godfather*, he took a razor
blade to Mario Puzo's 1969 book, cut
out every page, and pasted them into
a notebook. Then he scribbled in the
margins and underlined important
passages, while slashing others. For
each section he planned to film, he
included notes on synopsis, texture,
tone, and pitfalls to avoid. That
700-plus-page notebook has been
made available for the first time
in this exact reproduction, which
also includes an introduction by
Coppola himself, never-before-seen
photographs, alternate casting lists,
pre-production meeting memos, etc.
This is a rare, behind-the-scenes look
at Coppola's creative process.

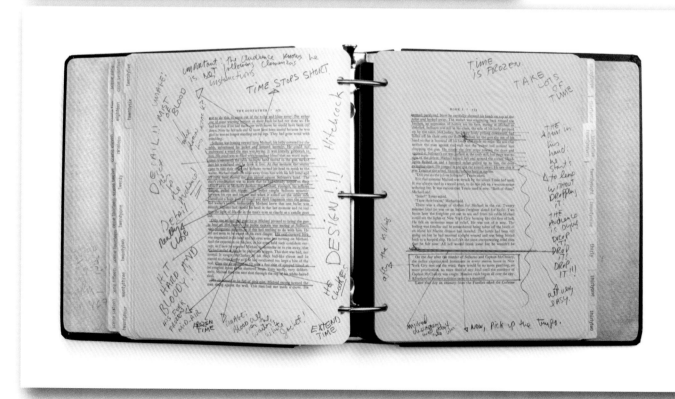

↓DESIGN
Geray Gencer, Istanbul
↓URL
geraygencer.com
↓STUDIO
Geray Gencer
↓CLIENT
Dogan Egmont Publishing
↓PRINCIPAL TYPE
Gotham Rounded and Skolar
↓DIMENSIONS
5.3 x 9.2 in. (6.7 x 23.5 cm)
↓CONCEPT
Yüz is a limited-edition book that
included my hundred book covers
select from ten years archives of
Dogan Edmont Publishing.

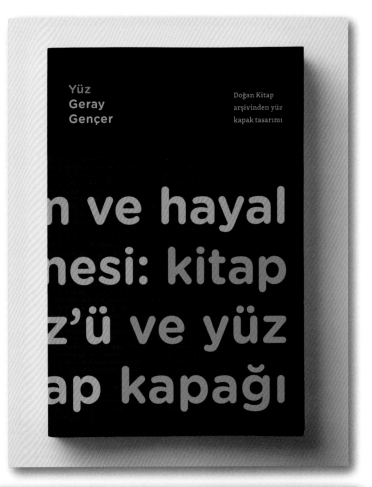

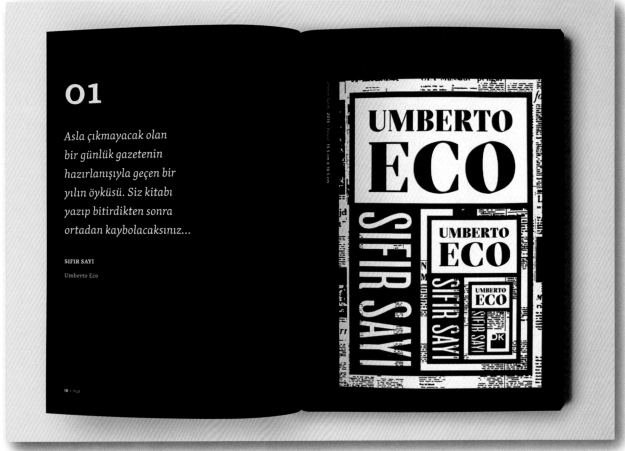

↓URL
fuenfwerken.com
↓AGENCY
Fuenfwerken, Berlin
↓PRINCIPAL TYPE
Fugue, Minion Pro, and Noe Display
↓DIMENSIONS
9.4 x 13 in. (24 x 33 cm)
↓CONCEPT

The House of Happiness tells three stories—that of the architecture of an impressive house, that of the people who created the house, and that of those who now live in it. It is a book that explores the question of how we build houses when happiness can be at home. From the outside, the book resembles a biblical work, restrained and reduced to the essentials. If you leaf through it, a veritable expressive world unfolds before your eyes: spacious, diverse, and vibrant. The special color gold predominates, seeping regularly into powerful colors, while the typography reflects both clear architectural lines and playful emotions. Moreover, various materials are used, all providing subtle haptic stimuli that support the quest for happiness.

↓DESIGN
Studio Frith, London
↓URLS
studiofrith.com, visual-editions.com,
and wetransfer.com
↓TWITTER
@VisualEditions and @WeTransfer
↓CONCEPT CREATION, CREATIVE
PRODUCTION, AND EDITOR-IN-
CHIEF
Visual Editions
↓CLIENT
WeTransfer
↓PRINCIPAL TYPE
Long Face
↓DIMENSIONS
5.9 x 7.5 in. (15 x 19 cm)
↓CONCEPT
WeTransfer wanted to celebrate
the creative values of our online
file-sending service in a tangible way.
We wanted to translate our aesthetic
into something playful that didn't
feel like a basic branded book. It had
to be about our world but not about
us. Working with Visual Editions
and Studio Frith, we produced three
hardback books focusing on doubt,
time, and magic, explored through
twenty-eight creatives' work. We
developed bespoke typography and
used a bold, bright color system
for the books and accompanying
postcards and tote bags. The books
appeal to clients, creative partners,
press, and WeTransfer users alike.

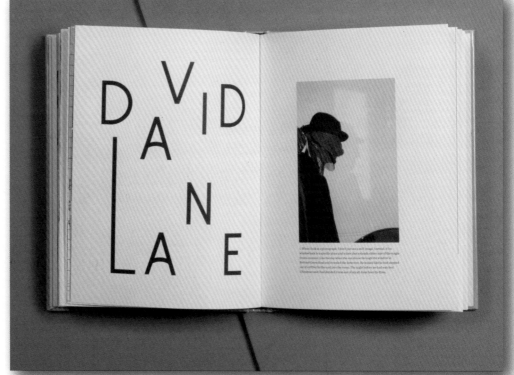

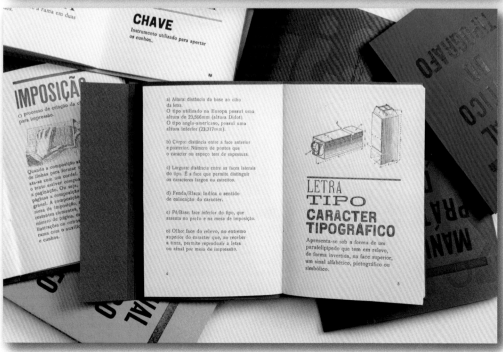

↓DESIGN
Joana Monteiro (Clube dos Tipos),
Ricardo Dantas and Rúben Dias
(Tipografia Dias),
Coimbra and Lisbon, Portugal
↓ART DIRECTION
Joana Monteiro (Clube dos Tipos)
↓PRODUCTION
Rui Damasceno and José Lage
(Tipografia Damasceno)
↓HAND TYPESETTERS
Maria Antunes, Pedro Bandeira,
Tomás Capa, Ana Coelho,
Inês Correia, Filipa Cruz,
Ricardo Dantas, Rúben Dias,
Marina Ermakova, Diana Ferreira,
Alexandre Gigas, Bruno Inácio, Carla
Martins, Xana Martins,
Joana Monteiro, Sal Nunkachov,
Sophia Pagano, Rúben Silva,
Raquel Simões, and Lisa Teles
↓URLS
clubedostipos.com
and tipografiadias.com
↓STUDIOS
Clube dos Tipos and Tipografia Dias
↓PRINCIPAL TYPE
Multiple letterpress hand-setting
typefaces
↓DIMENSIONS
6.5 x 4.5 in. (16.5 x 11.5 cm)
↓CONCEPT
The publication consists of a key-term
glossary describing the phases and
materials used for a good practice in
traditional typography workshops. As
an answer to the current letterpress
revival, this book proposes to facilitate
communication, attempting to narrow
the gap between new practitioners,
technicians, and designers. It is
essential that apprentices have a
manual in their hands. The same
hands that will fill wth lead dust and
paint should be able to let through,
without fear of getting dirty, your own
manual. Composed with eighteenth-
century hand-carved wood type and
myriad twentieth-century currently
unnamed metal typefaces.

↓DESIGN AND ART DIRECTION
Area of Practice, Kevin Brainard,
and Cybele Grandjean, New York
↓CREATIVE DIRECTION
Stefan Sagmeister and Jessica Walsh
↓ILLUSTRATION (commissioned)
Na Kim, Eugenia Loli, and Trey Wright
↓PHOTOGRAPHY (commissioned)
Stephanie Gonot, Sarah Illenberger,
Brian Kelley, and Elise Mesner
↓EDITOR
Christopher Bollen
↓IMAGE RESEARCH
Elisa Gallagher
↓RETOUCHING
Blue Soho and Jason Nuttall
Barneys New York
↓CREATIVE DIRECTOR
Dennis Freedman
↓DIRECTOR OF SPECIAL PROJECTS
Michael King
↓SENIOR PRODUCTION DIRECTOR
Christine Hackett
↓MANAGING EDITOR
George Madisson
Rizzoli, New York
↓PUBLISHER
Charles Miers
↓MANAGING EDITOR
Anthony Petrillose
EDITORIAL ASSISTANT
Gisela Aguilar
PRODUCTION MANAGER
Kaija Markoe
↓URLS
area-of-practice.com and
sagmeisterwalsh.com
↓AGENCY AND DESIGN FIRM
Area of Practice and
Sagmeister & Walsh
↓CLIENTS
Barneys New York and Rizzoli
↓PRINCIPAL TYPE
Eksell Display, GT Sectra,
and GT Walsheim
↓DIMENSIONS
10 x 13 in. (25.4 x 33 cm)

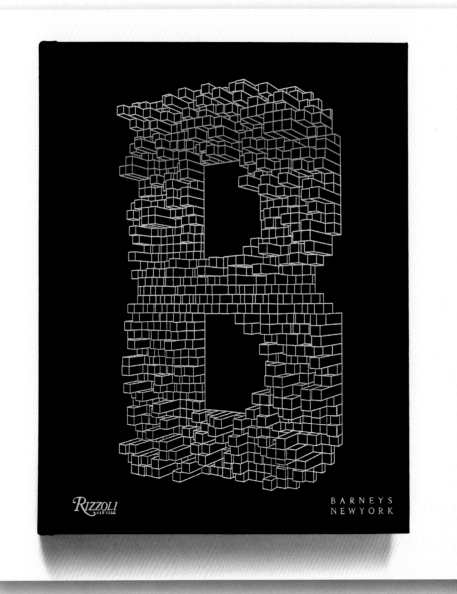

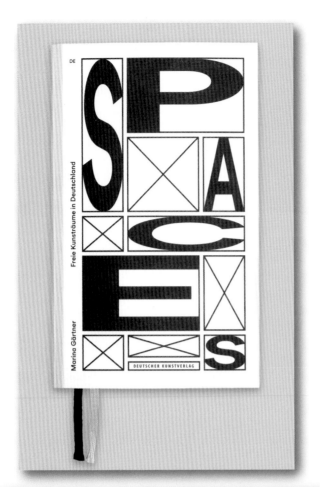

↓DESIGNER AND EDITOR
Marina Gärtner, Basel
↓URLS
marinagaertner.de
and spaces-guide.de
↓TWITTER
@SpacesGuide
↓PUBLISHER
Deutscher Kunstverlag GmbH Berlin/
Munich, Germany
↓PRINCIPAL TYPE
LL Circular
↓DIMENSIONS
4.5 x 7.3 in. (11.5 x 18.5 cm)
↓CONCEPT
Spaces is the first city guide featuring
project spaces and noncommercial
initiatives for contemporary art in
Germany. The book started as a
diploma project at Stuttgart State
Academy of Art and Design in 2014,
yearly followed by further editions.
The current, second edition features
250 project spaces in 41 cities across
the country. The design mirrors
the characteristics of its topic: All
initiatives make temporary use of
spaces within cities—their identity
comes through change within a
recurring set of parameters. The
design makes use of two colors and a
modular layout based on a rectangle
that outlines and maps the spaces,
which become specific only through
the initiatives and their program.
They perform as working tools of a
"dynamic identity" playfully put into
practice per edition.

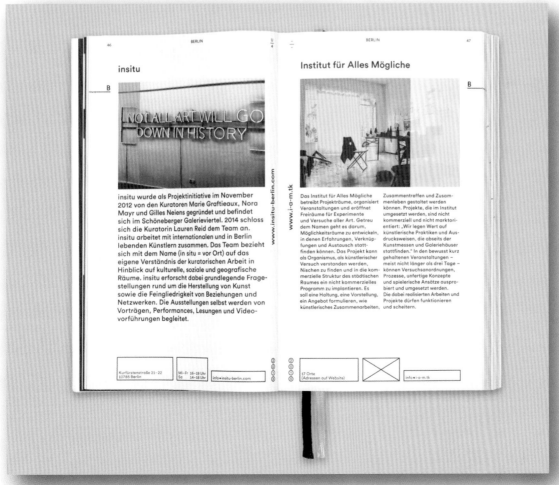

↓CREATIVE DIRECTION
Daniela Herweg, Alexandros
Michalakopoulos, Andreas Ruhe,
and Marco Schmidt, Düsseldorf
↓GRAPHIC DESIGN
Jazzer Pozalla
↓PHOTOGRAPHY
Pavel Becker, Nora Luther, and
Christian Rolfes
↓EDITORS
Kristin Braun
↓URL
morphoria.com
↓TWITTER
@morphoria_dc
↓INSTAGRAM
@morphoria_design
↓DESIGN STUDIO
The Morphoria Collective
↓CLIENT
Karl's Restaurant
↓PRINCIPAL TYPE
GT Walsheim Medium. We expanded
and modified the font with 368
ligatures for the mixture of underlined
and strike-through letters
↓DIMENSIONS
6.5 x 8.8 in. (16.5 x 22.5 cm)
↓CONCEPT
We cooked, photographed, wrote,
and designed to create a book filled
with the favorite recipes of four
of Düsseldorf´s finest chefs. Our
network created content and a visual
appearance that needed to reflect
the contemporary and high-quality
cuisine featured in the book. For us,
the characteristics of good food are
shown not only through its processing
but also by the initial quality of the
ingredients. This is why we chose
a photography style that was not
intended to be flattering but to be
honest. Every aspect had to correlate
with the typographic simplicity so as
to not outshine the initial purpose—
to cook. One hundred percent of the
revenue is going directly to four local
social organizations.

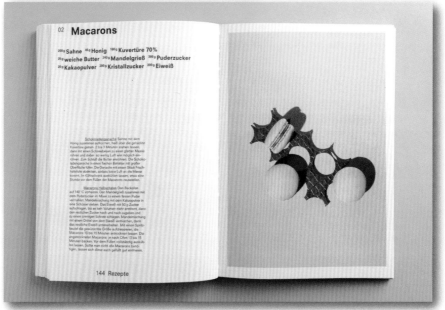

↓DESIGN
Qing Zhao, Nanjing, China
↓DESIGN FIRM
Nanjing Han Qing Tang Design Co., LTD.
↓CLIENT
Nanjing Publishing Group
↓PRINCIPAL TYPE
VT Portable Remington, Times,
and HYZiDianSongJ
↓DIMENSIONS
7.3 x 10.2 in. (18.5 x 26 cm)
↓CONCEPT
I reached back to the 32-bit world of
manuscripts for the content of the
design. The left of the book is the
original manuscript and the right is
the manuscript in English and Chinese
annotation. So, in the beginning of
the directory, the reader can compare
both versions.

↓DESIGN
Qing Zhao, Nanjing, China
↓DESIGN FIRM
Nanjing Han Qing Tang Design Co., LTD.
↓CLIENT
Jiangsu Phoenix literature and art publishing
↓PRINCIPAL TYPE
FZFangSong-Z02S, Futura Std Book, FZLanTingHei-L-GBK, FZLanTingHei-R-GBK, Letter Gothic Std Medium, FZShuSong-Z01S, and Trajan Pro Regular
↓DIMENSIONS
4.1 x 5.7 in. (10.5 x 145 cm)
↓CONCEPT
This book can be a Valentine's Day gift. It has 365 pages with different compositions. When the book is opened fully, you can read it horizontally. The page number position rotates continuously, referencing the twelve hours on the clock. The opposite pays tribute to the traditional Chinese vertical reading; at the same time, it has been divided into day and night.

↓DESIGN
Vanessa Alexandra Zúñiga Tinizaray,
Loja, Ecuador
↓URL
amuki.com.ec
↓TWITTER
@amuki
↓STUDIO
Amuki Studio
↓PRINCIPAL TYPE
Amaru Creador, Modular 46, Oráculo,
Sara/Maíz, Taypi, and twelve
additional experimental typefaces
↓DIMENSIONS
9.8 x 9.8 in. (25 x 25 cm)
↓CONCEPT
The Visual Chronicles, Abya Yala's
book, is a collection of experiments
based on the signs from the ancient
cultures of Ecuador. The 216 pages
showcase 17 experimental typefaces,
425 Andean patterns, over 40
illustrations, and 115 visual signs.

↓CREATIVE DIRECTION
Lloyd Osborne and Shabnam Shiwan,
Auckland
↓PHOTOGRAPHER
Charles Howells
↓URL
osborneshiwan.com
↓AGENCY
Osborne Shiwan
↓CLIENT
Atamira Dance Company
↓PRINCIPAL TYPE
Atamira and Neue Haas Grotesk
↓DIMENSIONS
10.7 x 14.6 in. (27.1 x 37 cm)
↓CONCEPT
Atamira Dance Company is New
Zealand's leading Maori contemporary
dance theater creator. Its short works
program showcases three strong
female choreographic voices. Inspired
by the geometric abstractions of
traditional woven tukutuku panels,
the typography is custom, creating a
"weaving" theme within the letters as
well as weaving throughout the bodies
of the dancers. Contrasting color with
monotone imagery creates sculptural
forms. The Maori language, much of
which exists within the everyday New
Zealand lexicon, is used throughout.
The typography represents
mythologies woven in movement.

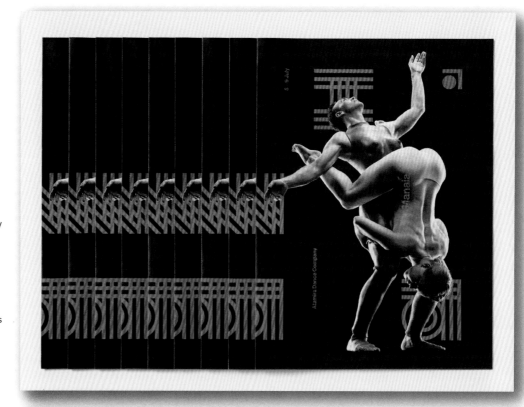

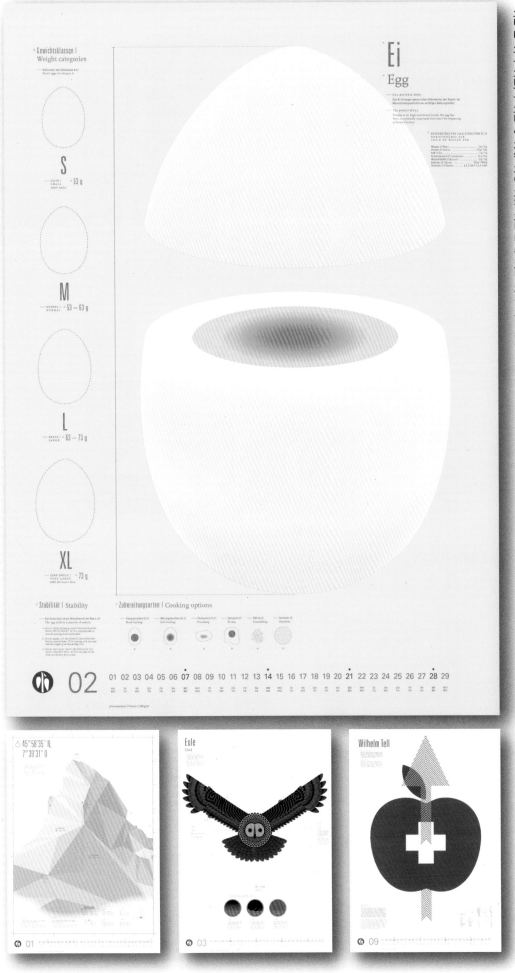

↓DESIGN
Ulla Oberdörffer and Julia Ochsenhirt,
Berlin and Stuttgart
↓CREATIVE DIRECTION
Jochen Rädeker°
↓PROJECT MANAGER AND
PRODUCTION
Jeannette Kohnle
↓PRINT
Meinders & Elstermann GmbH
& Co. KG
↓URL
strichpunkt-design.de
↓TWITTER
@strichpunkt
↓DESIGN AGENCY
Strichpunkt Design
↓CLIENT
Papierfabrik Scheufelen GmbH + Co.
KG, Horst Lamparter, director of sales
and marketing
↓PRINCIPAL TYPE
FF Scala and Univers
↓DIMENSIONS
32.4 x 33.7 in. (82.2 x 85.5 cm)
↓CONCEPT
Perfection is a goal for which many
strive but rarely achieve. However,
the motto suits the thirtieth edition
of the popular Scheufelen wall
calendar perfectly. For 160 years,
this paper factory has been working
on new innovations and continuous
development of its premium paper.
As a result, it commands masters
from art and nature, who achieve
perfection effortlessly: from the silent
flight of the eagle and the brilliance of
a diamond to the unfathomable blue in
the works by Yves Klein. Each month,
the calendar presents an exemplar to
accompany the observer throughout
the year.

↓DESIGN
Katherine Hughes, Boston
↓CREATIVE DIRECTION
Clif Stoltze°
↓URL
stoltze.com
↓TWITTER
@StoltzeDesign
↓DESIGN FIRM
Stoltze Design
↓CLIENT
The Davis Museum at Wellesley
College
↓PRINCIPAL TYPE
Bodoni MT Standard, Didot, and
Swiss 721
↓DIMENSIONS
11 x 14 in. (27.9 x 35.6 cm)
↓CONCEPT
Charlotte Brooks at LOOK 1951–1971
is an oversized, magazine-style
catalog for the eponymous exhibition
at Wellesley's Davis Museum. By
contrasting Brooks's uncropped
original photographs and contact
sheets with thumbnails of the
magazine's layouts, the design
expresses the curator's vision of
Brooks at the vanguard of her
generation's social movements,
curtailed to fit into a general-interest
magazine. Formally, the catalog
references the format of *LOOK*
magazine and incorporates original
title treatments for each referenced
article. The layouts are inspired not
only by the feel of the magazine but
also by the strips of images in the
included contact sheets.

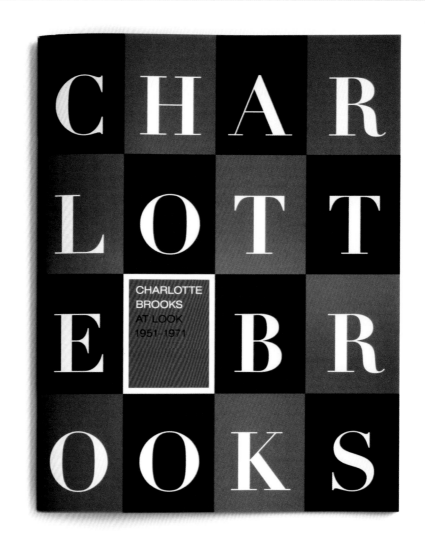

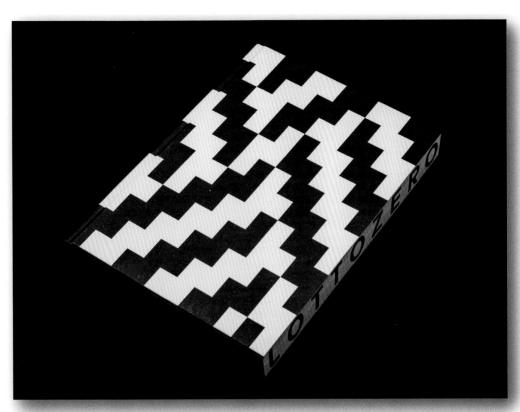

↓DESIGN
Martin Kerschbaumer,
Annelous Konijnenberg,
and Thomas Kronbichler,
Bolzano, Italy
↓ART DIRECTION
Martin Kerschbaumer
and Thomas Kronbichler
↓URL
studiomut.com
↓STUDIO
Studio Mut
↓CLIENT
Lottozero, Arianna Moroder, and
Tessa Moroder
↓PRINCIPAL TYPE
Neuzeit S Bold with customized
letters
↓DIMENSIONS
6.5 x 9.5 in. (17 x 24 cm)
↓CONCEPT
After designing the corporate identity
for Lottozero Textile Lab, Studio Mut
created the catalog for the opening
exhibition, *Inside Lottozero*. The
catalog features thirteen artists,
dealing with textile design, music, and
performance. Its cover shows one
section of a continuous textile pattern,
and only when several copies are
side by side can you see the pattern
unfold. The title of the exhibition is
printed directly on the pages of the
catalog, creating a seemingly closed
or massive object. Only after closer
examination does the object reveal its
nature. The three catalog languages,
English, Italian, and German, are
graphically interwoven too.

↓CREATIVE DIRECTION
Judith Anna Rüther, Dortmund,
Germany
↓EDITOR
Ekkehard Neumann
↓CURATORS
Claudia Rinke and Elly Valk-Verheijen
↓TEXT
Claudia Rinke
↓URL
jac-gestaltung.de
↓DESIGN STUDIO
JAC-Gestaltung
↓CLIENT
Westdeutscher Künstlerbund
↓PRINCIPAL TYPE
Metric
↓DIMENSIONS
8.3 x 10.6 in. (21 x 27 cm)
↓CONCEPT
The exhibition *Expanding
Photography* scrutinizes perceptual
habits in photography in sixteen
works. A large spectrum of various
approaches and forms of behavior
is displayed here and the two-
dimensional limits of photography are
called into question. Just as the artists
fathom out the limitations, the text of
the catalog always moves around the
edges, as if wanting to move beyond
the limits of the medium. But also
within the texts, sections are created
in which the typography swells and
expands beyond its limits by means of
compacting.

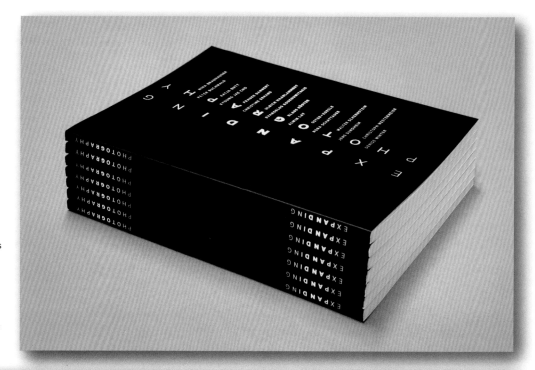

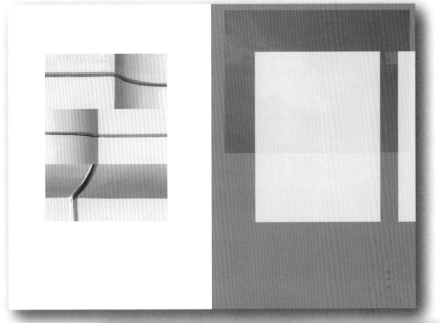

↓DESIGN, ART DIRECTION, AND
CREATIVE DIRECTION
Romain Rachlin and Maxime Tetard,
Paris
↓URL
www.les-graphiquants.fr
↓TWITTER
@lesgraphiquants
↓AGENCY
Les Graphiquants
↓CLIENT
Orient Express
↓PRINCIPAL TYPE
Helvetica
↓DIMENSIONS
8.6 x 12.6 in. (22 x 32 cm)
↓CONCEPT
This is a window to see the world
from the train, passing through all
the landscapes where the mythic
Orient Express follows the rail. We
played with the scales, going from
the large landscape to zooming in
on the fabrics inside the train, so it
is all about distance. This is a way to
relate the poetic journey of the Orient
Express railway road.

↓DESIGN AND CREATIVE DIRECTION
Nancy Campbell°
and Trevett McCandliss°, New York
↓PHOTOGRAPHY
Zoe Adlersberg
↓FASHION EDITOR
Mariah Walker
↓STYLIST
Mariah Walker
↓URLS
earnshaws.com and
mccandlissandcampbell.com
↓INSTAGRAM
@earnshawsmagazine
and @mccandlissandcampbell
↓PUBLICATION
Earnshaw's Magazine
↓PRINCIPAL TYPE
Casey, F37 Bella, Ecuyer DAX,
Orwellian, and Squirrel
↓DIMENSIONS
10.9 x 18 in. (27.7 x 45.7 cm)
↓CONCEPT
Our assignment was to design an
opener for a spring fashion story.
We created a playful look by mixing
various fonts that express the youthful
energy of our model (who was, in fact,
an American in Paris).

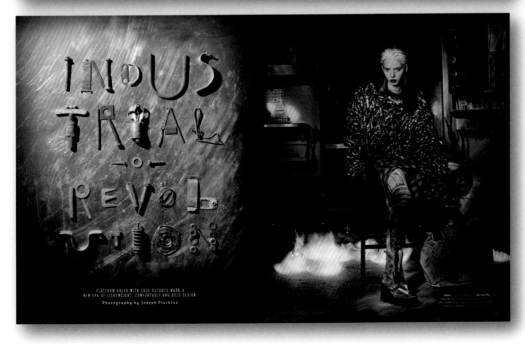

↓DESIGN
Katie Belloff, Nancy Campbell°,
and Trevett McCandliss°, New York
↓CREATIVE DIRECTION
Nancy Campbell
and Trevett McCandliss
↓PHOTOGRAPHY
Joseph Pluchino
↓STYLIST
Edda Gudmundsdottir
↓URLS
footwearplusmagazine.com and
mccandlissandcampbell.com
↓INSTAGRAM
@footwearplus and
@mccandlissandcampbell
↓PUBLICATION
Footwear Plus Magazine
↓PRINCIPAL TYPE
Blaktur, Bureau Grotesque Five One,
and type made out of scrap metal
↓DIMENSIONS
10.9 x 18 in. (27.7 x 45.7 cm)
↓CONCEPT
Our assignment was to design an
opening spread for a story that
featured modern, fashion-forward
footwear for women. The story was
shot one evening at a Brooklyn
workshop. The type was created from
metal pieces gathered from a scrap-
metal yard. A sheet of steel was used
as the canvas.

↓DESIGN
Katie Belloff, Nancy Campbell°,
and Trevett McCandliss°, New York
↓CREATIVE DIRECTION
Nancy Campbell
and Trevett McCandliss
↓PHOTOGRAPHY
Trevett McCandliss
STYLIST
Tara Anne Dalbow
↓URLS
footwearplusmagazine.com and
mccandlissandcampbell.com
↓INSTAGRAM
@footwearplus and
@mccandlissandcampbell
↓PUBLICATION
Footwear Plus Magazine
↓PRINCIPAL TYPE
Hand-drawn type
↓DIMENSIONS
10.9 x 18 in. (27.7 x 45.7 cm)
↓CONCEPT
Our assignment was to design an
opening spread for a fashion story
that featured fall shoes for men. The
model was portrayed as a stylish
intellectual. To emphasize the bookish
mood of the shoot, we handlettered
the typography on the sides of
vintage books.

↓DESIGN AND CREATIVE
DIRECTION
Nancy Campbell°
and Trevett McCandliss°, New York
↓PHOTOGRAPHY
Igor Borisov, Paris
↓FASHION EDITOR
Mariah Walker
↓STYLIST
Mariah Walker
↓URLS
earnshaws.com and
mccandlissandcampbell.com
↓INSTAGRAM
@earnshawsmagazine
and @mccandlissandcampbell
↓PUBLICATION
Earnshaw's Magazine
↓PRINCIPAL TYPE
AT Sackers Gothic Heavy, ITC Stymie
Hairline, Voga Medium, and
our own custom redesign of Bifur
↓DIMENSIONS
10.9 x 18 in. (27.7 x 45.7 cm)
↓CONCEPT
Our assignment was to create an
opening spread for a fall fashion
feature. The young models were
portrayed with dramatic, high-fashion
appeal. We used Art Deco style
fonts to create custom-designed
typography that enhanced the
glamorous mood of the shoot.

Design History faux fur
gilet, **Tommy Hilfiger** suit,
We Love Colors leotard

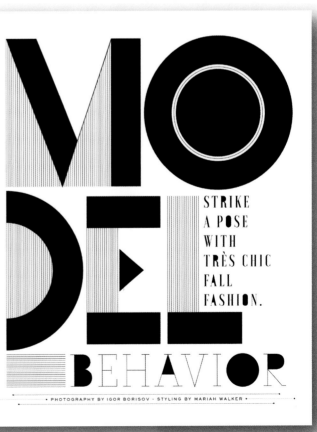

STRIKE
A POSE
WITH
TRÈS CHIC
FALL
FASHION.

BEHAVIOR

• PHOTOGRAPHY BY IGOR BORISOV • STYLING BY MARIAH WALKER •

↓DESIGN
Kai Bergmann and Sebastian Pataki,
Frankfurt
↓ART DIRECTION
Kai Bergmann
↓ILLUSTRATION
Sebastian Pataki
↓URL
bergmannstudios.com
↓TWITTER
@bergmannstudios
↓DESIGN STUDIO
Bergmann Studios
↓CLIENT
Grüne Jugend Hessen
↓PRINCIPAL TYPE
Gill Sans
↓DIMENSIONS
5.8 x 8.3 in. (14.8 x 21 cm)
↓CONCEPT
Schampus is the quarterly member journal of the Green Party's youth league in the federal state of Hesse. This inspiring and somewhat quirky publication is a gentle reminder to stay involved in political activities. Each issue is monothematic: #79 Intoxication (Rausch), #80 25-Years-of (Jubiläum), #81 Summer Recess (Sommerpause). Cornerstones of the visual identity are the typeface, Gill Sans (a variety of its styles), and the use of no more than two spot colors in each issue. Organic, recycled paper; a loud, illustrative, and eclectic graphic language; and a closed A5 format create the appeal of an underground magazine.

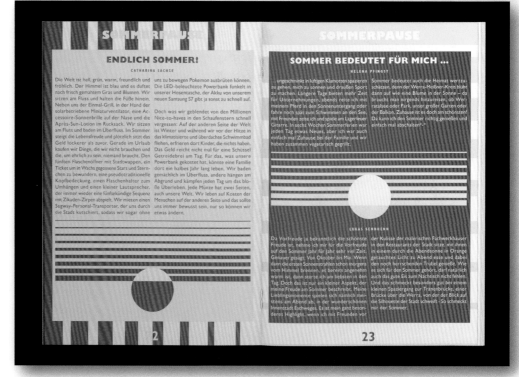

↓ART DIRECTION
Alex Hunting and Jack Saunders,
London
↓URLS
alexhunting.co.uk and jacksaunders.eu
↓TWITTER
@alexhunting1 and @jacksaunderseu
↓CLIENT
Rapha Racing
↓PRINCIPAL TYPE
Adobe Caslon Pro, Mondial Bold, and
Mondial Condensed
↓DIMENSIONS
7.9 x 11.4 in. (20 x 29 cm)
↓CONCEPT
Mondial expands the idea of what
road cycling is and what the sport can
be. We looked extensively at the visual
language used throughout cycling's
history, in particular at early sports
publications such as *Gazzetta dello
Sport* and *Miroir Sprint*. We worked
with Colophon foundry to create a
custom type family that is reminiscent
of early-1900s European woodblock
typography.

FASHION

The current design mania is for 'boro' – centuries-old clothes that were patched and put together by Japan's poorest. These precious scraps of frayed cotton were hand-sewn into the most humble, and beautiful, of garments.

MAPS

The maps we live with now are very different and much more varied from the traditional forms that existed for centuries, and not just because they are mostly digital. The idea that cartography is strictly confined to the mapping of the features and thematic variables associated with terrestrial and celestial objects started to unravel in the 1970s with the advent of the digital age.

PHOTO-ESSAY

PEACE PRIZES

THE SURFER

"You can't control the wind, the size of the waves or the weather, you can only estimate. While you get it right most of the time you work on safety training for peace of mind. Waves this size contain a massive volume of water and have the potential to kill you. I've never been knocked unconscious but I was badly battered by a wave in Portugal when a 50-footer broke on top of me."

ISSUE

004

ARCHITECTURE

Norman Foster points to the chair designs of the Modernist pioneers of the early 20th century such as Marcel Breuer and Ludwig Mies van der Rohe who used bicycle-tubing technology to create their sensual forms. He waxes lyrical about the craft of bike construction; the "elaborate lugs that became cult objects… the refinement of the controls, the shoe clips, the quick releases… When I pick a bike up and take it up the steps, I still get a kick out of the lightness and the hardware." But Foster is reluctant to say if bike design has influenced his architecture.

Rapha.

MONDIAL

PORTRAITS

CIVVIES

H-VAN

Concept cars explore the unproven and often impossible. With the years of research and development required for a road-ready vehicle eschewed in favour of casual fantasy, the concept is glamorous window dressing for a company's more workaday wares. It is often a gateway for new design directions. The brainchild of Citroën's head of advanced design, Carlo Bonzanigo, the Tubik was classic concept fare, unimpeded by real-world practicality. It boasted a vast 'lounge-style' cocoon accessed by a drop-down panel that doubled as a step, much like a private jet.

SILK

The world of the Silk Roads did not lose importance over time. It was to gain access to the trade networks of Asia that led Columbus to sail across the Atlantic; Vasco da Gama found a route around the southern tip of Africa to reach the Persian Gulf and the bustling ports of India. The age of European empire was founded on finding a way to trade with the east – and then taking control. The struggle to dominate Asia was also a central narrative of the 20th century as Britain and Russia, and then the US and USSR, wrestled over Iran, Iraq and Afghanistan, and competed in Pakistan, India and south-east Asia. Today, the countries of the Silk Road still present the greatest opportunities and challenges.

MENTORS

People who like to claim mentorship often over-claim for it. The mentor acquires the status of a Jedi master; the mentee enjoys the reflected glory, but also the mentor's endorsement and, in effect, coronation as the anointed one.

UFC

The Ultimate Fighting Championship was hosting increasingly violent contests as fighters attempted different styles. These were UFC's 'dark ages', when almost anything went in bare-knuckle battles with barbaric results.

↓DESIGN
Mark Denton Esq.°, Andy Dymock,
and Kate Henderson, London
↓ART AND CREATIVE DIRECTION
Mark Denton, Esq.
↓LETTERING
Mike Meyer
↓ILLUSTRATION
Steve Bright
↓CG ILLUSTRATION/CHARACTER
DESIGN
A Large Evil Corporation
↓PHOTOGRAPHY
Oliver Carver, Joe Giacomet,
and Jonnie Malachi
↓TYPOGRAPHY
Andy Dymock and Kate Henderson
↓MAGAZINE PRODUCTION
Kate Henderson
and Juan Coello Hollebecq
↓URL
coy-com.com
↓TWITTER
@Coy_Com
↓DESIGN FIRM
COY! Communications
↓CLIENT
Not Nice Magazine,
A Large Evil Corporation
↓PRINCIPAL TYPE
Various
↓DIMENSIONS
9.4 x 13 in. (24 x 33 cm)
↓CONCEPT
Not Nice Magazine is published
by A Large Evil Corporation, the
very genial animation company
that is not affiliated with any farms,
supermarkets, or fruit and vegetable
growers whatsoever. That's why COY!
Communications wisely chose to
produce this promotional magazine
for them, featuring fresh farm
produce, supermarket fare, and a
variety of fruits and vegetables. It's
rammed full of rude carrots, bitter
lemons, and farting peaches; of
course, there are loads of type in it
too.

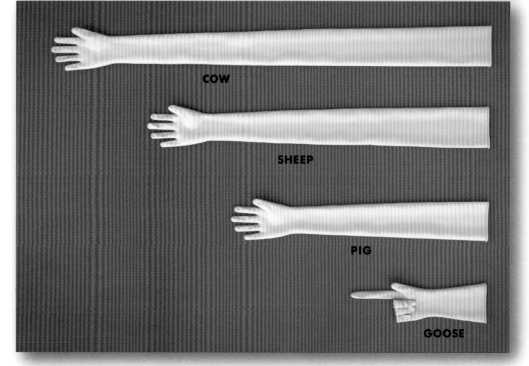

A COMPENDIUM ON SMALL GROUPS THAT CHANGED THE ARC OF HISTORY

↓DESIGN AND CREATIVE
DIRECTION
Lili Li, Laura Vignale,
and Keith Yamashita,
New York and San Francisco
↓PRODUCTION DESIGN
Anne Bodel and Claire Kesson
↓EDITORS
Stephen Friedman, Todd Holcomb,
Lisa Maulhardt, Julia Schweizer, and
Natalie Silverstein
↓WRITERS
Emily Goldstein and Katie Straub
↓CONTRIBUTORS
April Bell, Federico del Nazas,
Vincent Gagliardi, Robert Rollins,
Thomas Winkelmann,
and FLM Graphics
↓RESEARCH EDITOR
Cameron Bird
↓URL
sypartners.com
↓TWITTER
@SYPartners
↓TRANSFORMATION COMPANY
SYPartners, New York
and San Francisco
↓PRINCIPAL TYPE
Bauer Bodoni, LL Calibre, Champion
Gothic, Helvetica Neue, Impact,
and Tiempos
↓DIMENSIONS
9.6 x 12.3 in. (24.4 x 31.1 cm)
↓CONCEPT
There are moments in history when
it's possible to change the arc of
humanity—a flywheel is tripped, and
suddenly once-unimaginable futures
can be realized. Momentum brings
to life the stories of small, committed
groups of people—from different
turning moments in history and
different corners of the globe—who
came together to make progress. We
created this compendium to inspire
and provoke our clients, colleagues,
and broader network about the
impact each of us can make when
we come together around society's
toughest challenges and most hopeful
opportunities.

The pendulum swings from Paris to New York.

Pollock, de Kooning, Rothko, Ginsberg, Kerouac, and the like.

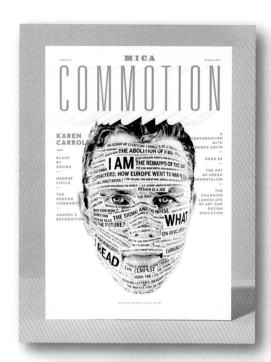

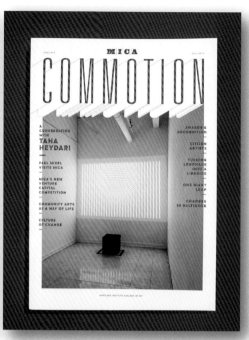

↓ART DIRECTION
Mariela Hsu, Washington, D.C.
↓SENIOR DESIGNER
Lillian Ling
↓CHIEF CREATIVE OFFICER/
CREATIVE DIRECTOR
Pum Lefebure°
↓CEO
Jake Lefebure
↓URL
designarmy.com
↓TWITTER
@designarmy
↓DESIGN AGENCY
Design Army
↓CLIENT
Maryland Institute College of Art
(MICA)
↓PRINCIPAL TYPE
Tiempos Headline, Tomica,
and custom
↓DIMENSIONS
9 x 12.75 in. (22.8 x 32.3 cm)
↓CONCEPT
Located in Baltimore, MICA is one of
the most prestigious art schools. We
developed an interactive magazine
to connect their twenty graduate
programs while uniting students,
alumni, faculty, and prospective
students through news, ideas,
and art. Commotion, the publication's
title, comes from beliefs created
through exploration. Taking inspiration
from a vast scope is chaotic, noisy,
and confusing—but also dynamic
and rewarding. Featuring visually
compelling layouts with bright colors,
bold typography, and custom illustration,
Commotion takes readers on a creative
journey. It has increased graduate
enrollment and seamlessly connected
disparate groups, creating a network
extending beyond college years.

↓COMMENT
Every page of *Commotion* is typographically thrilling. It was
impossible for me to just casually flip through this magazine. (I did
try—I was even prodded to "move on" and judge the next piece!)
I was compelled to look at every single page. Within each page, there
is something new. Whether it is a bold, illustrated text, a slightly
vibrating pattern, or an adventurous color choice, every detail is
completely mesmerizing.

I can only imagine how intimidating it must be for a designer to
represent such a rich, visual community like MICA, but this design is
anything but timid. *Commotion* is aptly named for its riot of color and
typography that erupts page after page in this refreshingly authentic
printed piece. It was impressive to see how different each issue was
and how many ways type and image could be displayed. It sounds
chaotic, but it's not. It's vibrant and energetic, surprising and risky.
It would have been easy to develop a predictable framework and
suitable style sheets and call it a day. What Design Army does
is invite us to get excited about art and design and experience
something in an unexpected way. If you don't know MICA, your
curiosity will be piqued. If you are already a part of the MICA family,
you will be proud to see them keeping up a legacy of creating
something beautiful and sharing inspiring stories.

Commotion confirms what I've always suspected—that MICA
believes in exceptional typography and communication.
Deb Wood

↓DESIGN
Frank Augugliario, Ben Grandgenett,
Chloe Scheffe, and Matt Willey,
New York
↓DESIGN DIRECTOR
Gail Bichler
↓ART DIRECTION
Matt Willey, New York
↓DEPUTY ART DIRECTOR
Jason Sfetko
↓DIRECTOR OF PHOTOGRAPHY
Kathy Ryan
↓PHOTO EDITOR
Christine Walsh
↓PUBLISHER
The New York Times Magazine
↓PRINCIPAL TYPE
Custom
↓DIMENSIONS
8.9 x 10.9 in.
↓CONCEPT
Inspired by the rising skyline of our
city, "The New York Issue: Life Above
800 Feet" was all about altitude. In
print, we rotated the entire magazine
(including the crossword and all the
ads) ninety degrees to make use of
the magazine's tallest dimension,
which enabled stunning vertical
photography and custom type drawn
to fit the height of the new format.

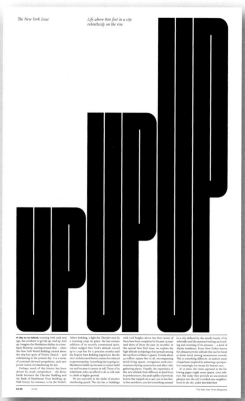

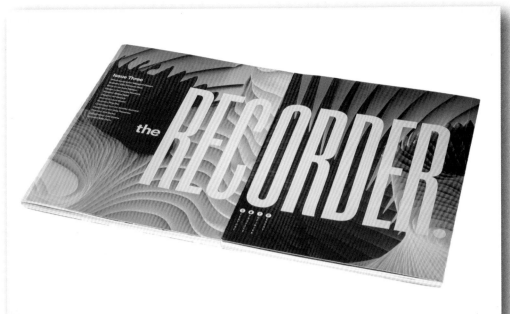

↓DESIGN AND ART DIRECTION
Luke Tonge, London
↓CREATIVE DIRECTION
James Fooks-Bale
↓EDITOR
Emma Tucker
↓URL
monotype.com
↓TWITTER
@monotype
↓DESIGN FIRM
Monotype
↓PRINCIPAL TYPE
Various
↓DIMENSIONS
8.5 x 10.8 in. (21.5 x 27.5 cm)
↓CONCEPT
The idea was to take a fresh look
at typography in all its forms, using
editorial design and illustration to
frame a new conversation around its
role in everyday life and culture.

↓DESIGN
Anna Cairns, Flo Gaertner, and Cécile
Kobel, Karlsruhe, Germany
↓URL
magmadesignstudio.de
↓STUDIO
magma design studio
↓CLIENT
Architekturschaufenster Karlsruhe e.V.
↓PRINCIPAL TYPE
ASF Mono and ASF Sans
↓DIMENSIONS
 8.3 x 11.7 in. (21 x 29.7 cm)
↓CONCEPT
The *ASF Journal 2016* features the
program and exhibition highlights
of the architecture gallery ASF
(Architekturschaufenster), essays, and
other contributions. The publication
is conceived as a collection and
platform for this heterogeneous
material. Several foldout pages
refer to architecture drawings and
large plans. It is held together by a
flexible band, so the publication can
be disassembled and sheets can be
taken out. The constructed typeface is
custom made for the gallery. Diagonal
hatching or section lining is crossing
typography as a formal principle.
Colors and graphic elements reflect
aesthetic terms such as signal, mark,
transparency, visual axes, mirroring,
etc.

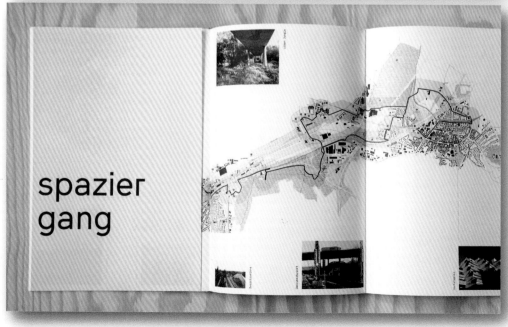

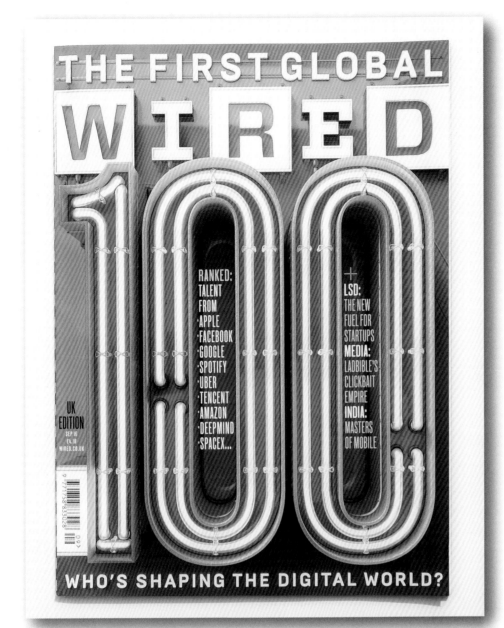

↓DESIGN
Marisa Falcigno and Shantanu Suman,
Muncie, Indiana
↓ART DIRECTION
Mary Lees, London
↓TYPOGRAPHER
Shantanu Suman
↓WRITER
Shradha Sharma
↓URL
opendoordesignstudio.com
↓TWITTER
@sumanshantanu
↓DESIGN FIRM
Open Door Design Studio (ODDS)
↓CLIENT
Condé Nast Publications Ltd.
↓PRINCIPAL TYPE
Hand-drawn Hindi type, Brutal Type,
and New Grotesk Square
↓DIMENSIONS
8 x 10.9 in. (20.3 x 27.6 cm)
↓CONCEPT
When *Wired UK* was planning to
do a feature on Indian startups,
they contacted ODDS to design
the editorial spread introducing the
article. The brief was simple—hand-
painted typography design on a
textured background, created using
Devanagari script. The title of the
article is a Hindi translation of *Wired
India*. Our exploration process led to
the use of vibrant colors, illustrated
motifs, and 3D typographic style
inspired by Indian truck art. Once the
design was finalized, we painted in on
a four-by-four-foot wooden canvas,
which was later photographed and
used as artwork for the magazine.

↓DESIGN
Rob Gonzalez and Jonathan Quainton,
London
↓URL
madebysawdust.co.uk
↓TWITTER
@SawdustStudio
↓STUDIO
Sawdust
↓CLIENT
OFFF Festival
↓PRINCIPAL TYPE
Custom
↓DIMENSIONS
6.8 x 9.2 in. (17.2 x 23.3 cm)
↓CONCEPT
Artwork for the 2016 OFFF book
Archetype—a collection of words,
concepts, ideas, thoughts, images,
and emotions from over a hundred
practicing artists and designers.
Our piece is an extract from a letter
written in 1965 by American artist Sol
LeWitt to fellow artist and close friend
Eva Hesse. During a period of self-
doubt and creative block, Eva received
an emotive and inspirational letter of
advice from Sol, copies of which have
since inspired artists the world over.

July 3, 2016

The Ne... ...Magazi...

GENDER GAMES
For years, international sports organizations have been policing women for
'masculine' characteristics — and turning their Olympic dream into a humiliating nightmare.
By Ruth Padawer

↓DESIGN
Matt Willey, New York
↓DESIGN DIRECTOR
Gail Bichler
↓DIRECTOR OF PHOTOGRAPHY
Kathy Ryan
↓PHOTO EDITOR
Amy Kellner
↓PUBLISHER
The New York Times Magazine
↓PRINCIPAL TYPE
NYT Sans
↓DIMENSIONS
8.9 x 10.9 in. (22.6 x 27.7 cm)
↓CONCEPT
This is a cover about international
sports organizations sex testing
female athletes. The headline was
"Gender Games" and we used XX/XY,
the chromosomal composition used
in sex-determination systems, as the
main graphic.

↓GRAPHIC DESIGN
Minsun Eo and Kyuha Shim, NewYork
↓CREATIVE DIRECTION
Kyuha Shim
↓EDITOR
Kyuha Shim
↓URLS
kyuhashim.com and minsuneo.nyc
↓CLIENT/PUBLISHER
Propaganda
↓PRINCIPAL TYPE
Akkurat Mono, DadaGrotesk, and
NotoSansCJK
↓DIMENSIONS
9.1 x 11.8 in. (23 x 30 cm)
↓CONCEPT
For the special issue of *GRAPHIC
Magazine,* "Intro to Computation,"
which speculates on the future of
programming/computational systems
in graphic design, we applied the
aesthetic of code to format the
content (using indentations). The
cover of the magazine is an index of
interviews that were analyzed and
grouped through text-classification
algorithms.

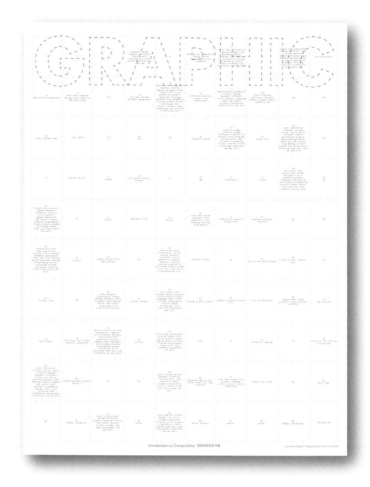

↓DESIGN
Wendy Xu°, West Hollywood,
California
↓DESIGN DIRECTION
Mindy Benham
↓LETTERER AND ILLUSTRATOR
Wendy Xu
↓URL
petitserif.com
↓TWITTER
@petitserif
↓CLIENT
Orange Coast Magazine
↓PRINCIPAL TYPE
Custom lettering
↓DIMENSIONS
8 x 10.5 in. (20.3 x 26.7 cm)
↓CONCEPT
This is a flourished lettering design
with illustrative elements for a fun
feature on ice cream shops.

↓DESIGN AND ILLUSTRATION
Roberto de Vicq°,
Corte Madera, California
↓ART DIRECTION
Chris Curry
↓URL
devicq.com
↓TWITTER
@rdevicq
↓DESIGN FIRM
de Vicq design
↓CLIENT
The New Yorker
↓PRINCIPAL TYPE
Ruritania
↓DIMENSIONS
6.9 x 9.5 in. (17.5 x 24.1 cm)
↓CONCEPT
This portrait of Karl Marx illustrates
an article on his life by Louis Menand
using only the letters of his name and
his most famous book, *Das Kapital*.

↓DESIGN
John Muñoz, New York
↓DESIGN DIRECTOR
Fred Woodward°
↓PHOTO DIRECTOR
Krista Prestek
↓PHOTO EDITOR
Monica Siwiec
↓PUBLICATION
GQ
↓PRINCIPAL TYPE
Eames Century Modern
and hand-drawn
↓DIMENSIONS
15 x 11 in. (38.1 x 27.9 cm)
↓CONCEPT
The idea was for the
February 2016 issue.

↓DESIGN
Andre Jointé, New York
↓DESIGN DIRECTOR
Fred Woodward°
↓PHOTO DIRECTOR
Krista Prestek
↓PHOTO EDITOR
Jolanta Alberty
↓PUBLICATION
GQ
↓PRINCIPAL TYPE
Eames Century Modern and Photo
Composition
↓DIMENSIONS
15 x 11 in. (38.1 x 27.9 cm)
↓CONCEPT
The idea was for the
February 2016 issue.

**My
Life
Saving
Drug**
by
**Eric
Perry**

When a freak brain hemorrhage struck out of nowhere a couple of years ago, I became a little depressed, stuck in a rut, and strangely fearful of DEATH. So when I heard about people (in my neighborhood, even) using hallucinogens to push beyond their preoccupations, to help them live without fear, I decided that was a trip I had to take

↓DESIGN
John Muñoz, New York
↓DESIGN DIRECTOR
Fred Woodward°
↓PHOTO DIRECTOR
Krista Prestek
↓PHOTO EDITOR
Justin O'Neil
↓PUBLICATION
GQ
↓PRINCIPAL TYPE
GT Pressura (modified)
↓DIMENSIONS
15 x 11 in. (38.1 x 27.9 cm)
↓CONCEPT
The idea was for the May 2016 issue.

↓DESIGN
Kristie Bailey, New York
↓DESIGN DIRECTOR
Fred Woodward°
↓PHOTO DIRECTOR
Krista Prestek
↓PUBLICATION
GQ
↓PRINCIPAL TYPE
Bookmania and GT Walsheim
↓DIMENSONS
15 x 11 in. (38.1 x 27.9 cm)
↓CONCEPT
The idea was for the July 2016 issue.

The Loveliest, Sexiest, Madliest of Them All

MERT ALAS &
MARCUS PIGGOTT

Kim Kardashian West has had the same job for a decade now—being Kim Kardashian,
being a bombshell muse for mega-athletes and mad geniuses, being a goddamn physical marvel
with curves dreamed up by God on a drunken bender—and she has never been better at it.
GQ's **CAITY WEAVER** parachutes into the Kimye manse in Bel Air to find out how she keeps it up
(and still finds time to tongue-lash Taylor Swift)

↓DESIGN
Griffin Funk, New York
↓DESIGN DIRECTOR
Fred Woodward°
↓PHOTO DIRECTOR
Krista Prestek
↓PHOTO EDITOR
Michael Allin
↓PUBLICATION
GQ
↓PRINCIPAL TYPE
Century Schoolbook and Whiphand
↓DIMENSONS
15 x 11 in. (38.1 x 27.9 cm)
↓CONCEPT
The idea was for the
November 2016 issue.

↓DESIGN
Selman Design, Brooklyn
↓ART DIRECTION
Andrew Horton
and Ashley Smestad-Velez
↓URL
selmandesign.com
↓TWITTER
@selmandesign
↓CLIENT
The Village Voice
↓PRINCIPAL TYPE
Made with off-the-shelf Police tape.
↓DIMENSIONS
4 x 6 in. (10.2 x 15.2 cm)
↓CONCEPT
The "Police Lies" graphic ran in support
of the cover story for the November
2, 2016, edition of *The Village Voice*.
The story was an in-depth exposé of
a questionable case involving several
Brooklyn police officers, planted
evidence, and vanishing informants.
The piece was one of four illustrations
featured in print.

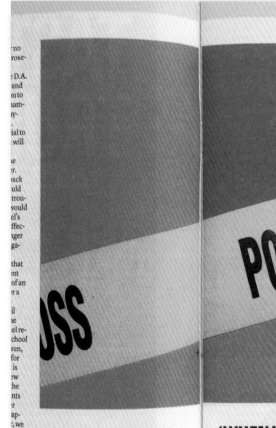

questions about the honesty of a group of NYPD officers. If they were in the clear, why not make that news public, both to rehabilitate the officers' names and to reassure New Yorkers that the system was working?

When the *Voice* asked the D.A.'s office about the news that it was admitting in court it had cleared the police officers, a spokesman confirmed that the investigation was concluded in November of 2015, a year ago: "The investigation involved an extensive review of documents, multi-

'WHEN IT COMES TO POLICE OFFICERS ENGAGING IN QUESTIONABLE BEHAVIOR, IT SEEMS LIKE WE'RE WILLING TO LOOK THE OTHER WAY.' ATTORNEY SCOTT HECHINGER

In fairness, prosecutors generally aren't in the habit of alerting the public when they look into someone's conduct and find no wrong-doing. It might have been courteous to let the public defenders who first flagged this issue know that the investigation was concluded. It might have been thought-ful to alert Herring—who's now suing the police and the city for what happened

↓DESIGN AND PUBLISHER
Kyle Read°, Denver
↓URL
badsonstudio.com
↓TWITTER
@badsonstudio
↓FIRM
Badson Studio
↓PRINCIPAL TYPE
Fern Micro Family and Guilder Family
↓DIMENSIONS
22.5 x 16.5 in. (57.5 x 41.5 cm)
↓CONCEPT
Shoe is a typographically minded
newspaper publication focused
on moving typographic concepts,
themes, ideas, and current issues
to the forefront through presenting
editorial content, illustration, art
direction and lettering to type
professionals and the uninitiated alike.
Issue No. 2 is loosely focused around
the theme of "figurative space."

↓CREATIVE DIRECTION
Katrin Oeding, Hamburg
↓URL
STUDIO-OEDING.COM
↓DESIGN STUDIO
Studio Oeding
↓CLIENT
Essenza—The Essence of Motorcycles
↓PRINCIPAL TYPE
Essenza Asphalt Brush, Essenza
Speedlines, Essenza Tuning, and CA
Oskar Condensed
↓DIMENSIONS
Various
↓CONCEPT
Launched in 2016, the innovative
motorcycle sprint series with
its own design competition
brought international motorcycle
manufacturers and race riders onto
the racetrack. Sixteen racing teams
compete against one another in a
knockout system. The bookazine
visualizes speed and is a tribute to
motorcycling culture, manufacturers,
and race riders but also to the
motorcycle itself. Designed, produced,
and published between two racing
events, within four weeks. The title
of the bookazine shows the logo
of the Essenza brand. Sixteen lines
of the logo represent the sixteen
participants. The "E" symbolizes
the start lines for both participants
in a race.

Bloomberg Businessweek

December 19 — December 25, 2016 | bloomberg.com

BAD SHRIMP

How antibiotic-tainted seafood gets smuggled out of China and onto your table

p38

↓DESIGN
Simon Abranowicz, New York
↓CREATIVE DIRECTION
Robert Vargas
↓DIRECTOR OF PHOTOGRAPHY
Clinton Cargill
↓PHOTO EDITOR
Leonor Mamanna
↓PHOTOGRAPHER
Jamie Chung
↓FOOD STYLIST
Maggie Ruggiero
↓PUBLICATION
Bloomberg Businessweek°
↓PRINCIPAL TYPE
Custom
↓DIMENSIONS
7.9 x 10.5 in. (20.1 x 26.7 cm)

↓ART DIRECTION
Ran Zheng, New York
↓URL
ranzhengdesign.com
↓DESIGN FIRM
Ran Design
↓CLIENT
Maryland Institute College of Art
↓PRINCIPAL TYPE
Neutral and custom
↓DIMENSIONS
Various
↓CONCEPT
"LOOK/HEAR" explores the
relationship between scenes and
soundscapes, looking and hearing.
A system of aural and visual signals
generates shifting typographic forms
and triggers associations about
people and environment.

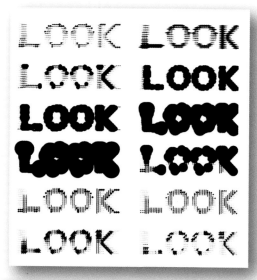

↓DESIGN
David McLeod and Jessica Walsh,
Los Angeles
↓ART DIRECTION
Stefan Sagmeister and Jessica Walsh
↓URL
sagmeisterwalsh.com
↓TWITTER
@sagmeisterwalsh
↓DESIGN FIRM
Sagmeister & Walsh
↓CLIENT
Otium
↓PRINCIPAL TYPE
Custom
↓DIMENSIONS
21.5 x 19.5 ft. (6.6 x 5.9 m)
↓CONCEPT
Otium is a contemporary
restaurant that draws on the rich
culinary heritage of Chef Timothy
Hollingsworth. The name, Otium,
has its roots in Latin; it is a word
that is meant to describe a place in
which time can be spent on leisurely
social activities. In line with this, the
restaurant features an open kitchen
merging indoor and outdoor areas so
that people can socialize and relax
in a casual atmosphere. With custom
lettering composed of shrubs and
plants, it serves as another way to
bring the outside indoors.

↓DESIGN
Caetano Calomino, Travis W. Simon,
and Flavia Zimbardi, Brooklyn
↓ART DIRECTION
Flavia Zimbardi
↓LETTERING AND SIGN PAINTING
Caetano Calomino
↓URL
zimbardicalomino.com
↓TWITTER
@zcstudio
↓INSTAGRAM
@zimbardicalomino
↓STUDIO/AGENCY
ZimbardiCalomino
↓CLIENT
Artists & Fleas
↓PRINCIPAL TYPE
Handlettering
↓DIMENSIONS
317 sq. ft. (29.5 sq. m)
↓CONCEPT
The idea behind the exterior signage
for Artists & Fleas was to capture
the essence of the market with an
emphasis on the wonder, the bizarre,
and the delightful and create an image
as striking and diverse as their core
but also integrated with the building's
architecture. A bottom-heavy script
with a '70s flair was chosen as the
main tone mixed with some freehand
lettering and classic sign-painting
letter styles.

↓DESIGN
Jack Anderson°
and Jay Hilburn, Seattle
↓CREATIVE DIRECTION
Jack Anderson
↓ARCHITECT
Tom Kundig
↓URL
hornallanderson.com
↓DESIGN FIRM
Hornall Anderson
↓CLIENT
Jack Anderson
↓PRINCIPAL TYPE
Neutraface 2 Display Bold, however
the 0 in 110 was custom.
↓DIMENSIONS
5 x 3 x 3.5 ft. (1.5 x .9 x 1 m)
↓CONCEPT
This was the concept of Ben Young
of the landscape architectural firm
Byla Design. This project has taken
a legal requirement (in this case, a
physical address) and turned it into
a piece of art. Drawn from the region
and history of mining, the design is
a contemporary interpretation of an
old mining cart. But the treasures
this cart holds represent three of
the chapters of the homeowners'
lives. From Montana. Work in Seattle.
Live in Sun Valley. Oversized and
stacked, solid, water jet steel numbers
pay homage to each city in which
the homeowners have root—a true
expression of their personality
while also reflecting their home's
physical address.

↓DESIGN
David Blumberg and Andrew
Thomson, Birmingham, Alabama
↓DESIGN DIRECTION
Roy Burns III
↓EXECUTIVE CREATIVE DIRECTOR
Spencer Till
↓ILLUSTRATION
Andrew Thomson and Spencer Till
↓HANDLETTERING/PAINTING
Spencer Till
↓PRODUCERS
George Griswold
and Leigh Ann Motley
↓URL
lewiscommunications.com
↓AGENCY
Lewis Communications
↓CLIENT
Auto & Truck Services
↓PRINCIPAL TYPE
Various
↓DIMENSIONS
Various
↓CONCEPT
Auto & Truck Services views what it
does as an art form. An extension of
the Art of Repair branding campaign,
the exterior building signage playfully,
artfully renders phrases inspired by
the service-driven language of '50s
advertising. Big, bold, hand-painted
letterforms strategically placed
around the building hark back to
the golden age of auto repair while
enlivening the characteristically gritty,
utilitarian space for employees and
patrons alike.

↓DESIGN
Renata Graw and Alexa Viscius,
Chicago
↓ART DIRECTION
Renata Graw
↓URL
thenormalstudio.com
↓DESIGN STUDIO
Normal
↓CLIENT
Mas Studio
↓PRINCIPAL TYPE
Circular
↓DIMENSIONS
Various
↓CONCEPT
MAS Studio curated the exhibition
*BOLD: Alternative Scenarios for
Chicago* as part of the first Chicago
Architecture Biennial. Normal
explored the relationship between
time and line, projecting us into the
future while still being connected
to the present. We extended the
horizontal lines to interrupt the
conventional flow, thus opening
spaces in unexpected places. The
blanks in the typography offer room
for new ideas. Instead of confining the
typography to the boundaries of the
two-dimensional plane, we applied it
to three-dimensional objects within
the exhibition. The reader was invited
to physically move to decipher the
whole.

↓DESIGN
Will Miller and Arjun Harrison-Mann,
Chicago
↓PARTNER AND DESIGN DIRECTOR
Ross Burwell
↓URL
firebellydesign.com/work
↓TWITTER
@firebellydesign
↓DESIGN FIRM
Firebelly Design
↓DIMENSIONS
248 x 101.5 in. (630 x 258 cm)
↓CONCEPT
The studio's seventh Typeforce
title wall was an exercise in
experimentation of concept, powered
by programming, collaboration, and
structure. Designed to reflect an
individual attendee's experience as
their attention shifted focus from
one piece to the next, the installation
centered on a set of hand-built,
Arduino-sequenced LED light bars.
Each bar was programmed to cycle
through seven unique states, rotating
in unison with all others. The effect: a
collection of distinctive points of light
in constant flux, representing both the
emerging talent on display and the
viewer's gaze.

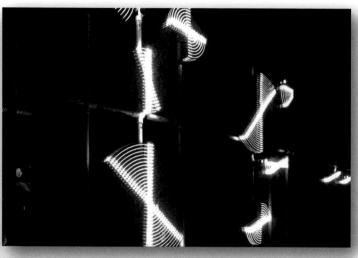

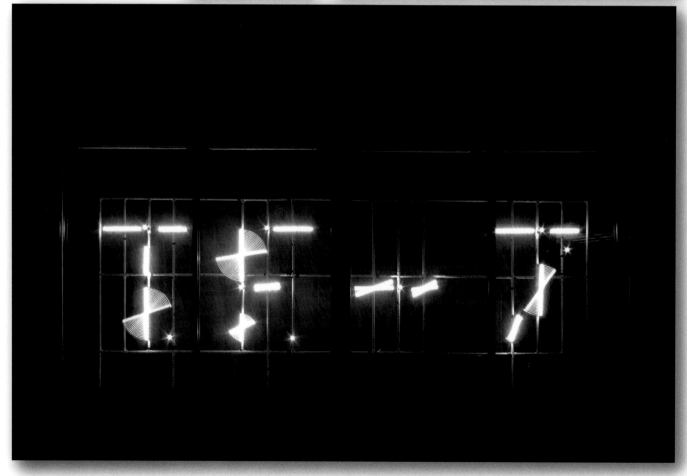

↓DESIGN
Gabriela Luchetta, Lucas Machado,
Flávia Nalon, Fábio Prata, and Helena
Sbeghen, São Bernardo, Brazil
↓ART DIRECTION
Flávia Nalon and Fábio Prata
↓STUDIO
ps.2 arquitetura + design
↓CLIENT
Boldarini Arquitetos Associados and
Planova Planejamento e Construções
↓PRINCIPAL TYPE
Helvetica and custom
↓CONCEPT
Duarte Murtinho Habitacional
Complex is part of an urbanizing effort
conducted by the São Bernardo city
housing department. We were called
on by Boldarini Arquitetos Associados
to create a signage and way-finding
system that could help residents
locate and move around the new
building complex but also to produce
something that would add a sense
of ownership to this group of people.
Our approach was to explore simple
architectural elements, such as the
formation of shadows on the building
walls or the changing perspective
of a stair. These visual interventions
helped create a particular identity
for the building.

↓DESIGN
Gemma O'Brien°, Sydney
↓URL
gemmaobrien.com
↓TWITTER
@mrseaves
↓PRINCIPAL TYPE
Custom
↓DIMENSIONS
Various
↓CONCEPT
This solo exhibition was a hand-painted typographic installation held at the LCAD gallery in Laguna Beach, California. The artworks were inspired by text from password forms, Wi-Fi-connection error messages, and captcha tests: "Remember Me," "Re-establishing Lost Connection," "Prove You're Human," and five iterations of "OK." The appeal was that the language could be so mundane yet also speak to bigger questions of lived experience: relationships, human connection in the digital age, and the desire for legacy and meaning.

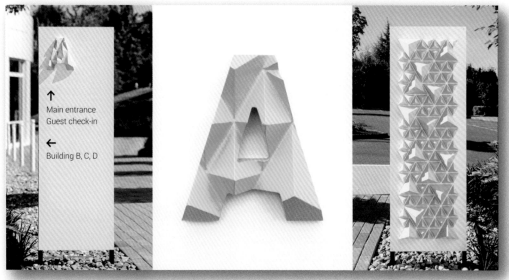

↓DESIGN
Christoffer Hart Hansen,
Scott Ichikawa, Cassie Klingler,
and Kristine Matthews, Seattle
↓FABRICATORS
Trade-Marx
↓URL
studiomatthews.com
↓DESIGN STUDIO
Studio Matthews
↓CLIENT
Google
↓PRINCIPAL TYPE
Roboto
↓DIMENSIONS
Sign panels—18 x 51 in.
(45.7 x 129.5 cm)
↓CONCEPT
When Google's Kirkland campus was
set to dramatically expand, a new
way-finding scheme was needed for
Googlers and visitors. The company's
founders are strong believers in the
Montessori method of learning and
working, which emphasizes using all of
our senses. This inspired the design's
inviting, tactile solution: Each building
can be identified by a different
texture, letter, shape, and color related
to Google's brand. As the light shifts
from day to day and season to season,
the dimensionality of the signs creates
a changing shadow play, making them
highly memorable.

↓DESIGN
Danielle Hall, New York
↓ART DIRECTION
Derek Flynn
↓CREATIVE DIRECTION
Hsien-yin Ingrid Chou
↓TYPOGRAPHY
Derek Flynn and Danielle Hall
↓PRODUCTION
Claire Corey
↓SILKSCREEN CONSULTANT
Tom Black Studio
↓URL
momadesignstudio.org
↓DESIGN STUDIO
Museum of Modern Art (MoMA)
Department of Advertising and
Graphic Design
↓MUSEUM
Museum of Modern Art (MoMA)
Department of Architecture
aand Design
↓PRINCIPAL TYPE
Bespoke Font and Fakt
↓DIMENSIONS
192 x 49 in. (487.7 x 124.5 cm)
↓CONCEPT
A Japanese Constellation highlights a "constellation" of architects that revolves around master architects Toyo Ito and Kazuyo Sejima. The visual identity for the exhibition evokes disparate connectivity, demonstrated in the custom type treatment, formed by a network of nodes and paths. The architects' bios and projects are integrated with the title, creating a constellation that extends into physical space. This motif carries over to the interior walls of the exhibition, where titles, philosophical quotes, and architectural drawings orbit around models and framed artworks. The exhibition concludes with a map representing the relief effort after the 2011 Great East Japan Earthquake.

↓DESIGN
Melissa Baillache, Jason Little°,
and Olivia King, Sydney
↓CREATIVE DIRECTION
Jason Little
↓JUNIOR DESIGNERS
Nick Belshaw and Joy Li
↓WRITERS
Mat Groom, Olivia King,
and Jason Little
↓URL
forthepeople.agency
↓TWITTER
@forthepeopleAU
↓DESIGN FIRM
For The People
↓CLIENT
Adobe
↓PRINCIPAL TYPE
Maison Neue
↓DIMENSIONS
16.4 x 13.1 ft. (500 x 400 cm)
↓CONCEPT
Start-Me-Up Labs was a brand
pop-up shop held at events and
co-working spaces. Created as a
helping hand to startups, it allowed
you to "purchase" a free minimum-
viable brand for your minimum-
viable product. It was a complete
off-the-shelf experience—shoppers
could choose a shape, logotype, and
personality off the rack, pick a name
from an envelope, spin a color palette
wheel, and find their imagery starter
kit. Once they were at the counter,
an SMU technician would take the
basket of items, populate a choice
of templates, and create any number
of branding outcomes. We built over
three hundred of them.

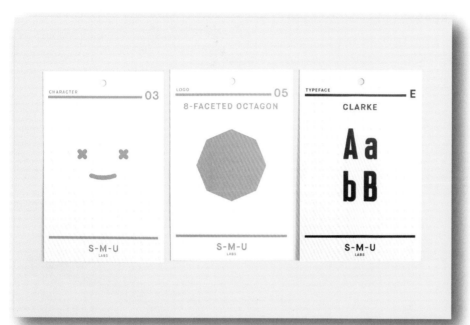

↓GRAPHIC DESIGN
Sunghoon Kim, Seoul
↓URL
sungpaddykim.com
↓PRINCIPAL TYPE
Avenir Next, Sandoll Gothic Neo,
and custom
↓DIMENSIONS
11 x 15.75 in. (27.8 x 40 cm)

↓CONCEPT
By violating the authoritative
typographical rules, Transcendent
Type seeks a way to achieve new and
unique aesthetics of typeface design
that transcends legibility as well as
the language barrier. The barrier
between different languages is a huge
limit of typography besides legibility.
To allow people to read a foreign
language, Korean in this case, a set
of Transcendent Type is presented
as two different versions. Each Latin
alphabet transitions to the Korean
alphabet, Hangul, based on its closest
corresponding phonetic symbol, and
vice versa.

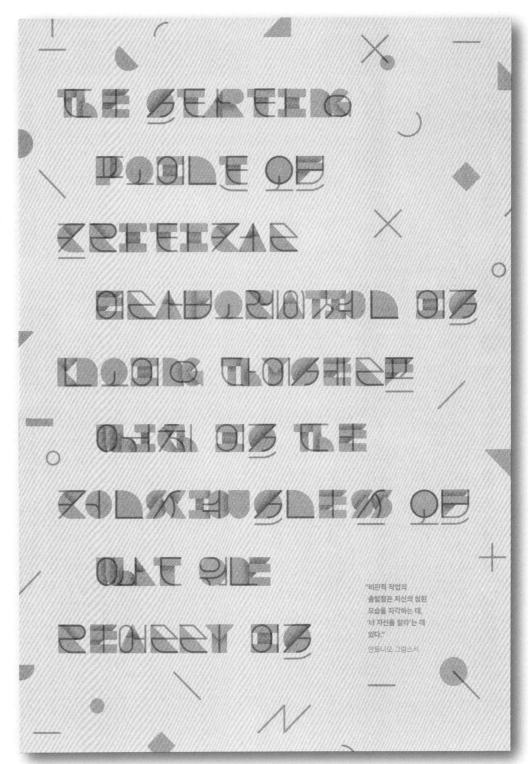

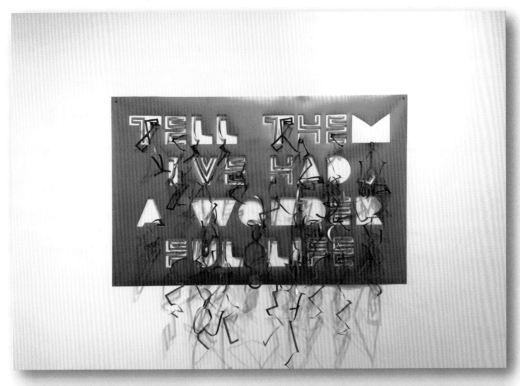

↓ARTISTS
Brian LaRossa° and Allie Rex,
Brooklyn
↓URLS
larossa.co and allierex.com
↓TWITTER
@LaRossa

↓MEDIA
Mylar, acrylic paint, and map pins
↓VENUE
Lorimoto Gallery
↓PRINCIPAL TYPE
Ideoma Liner
↓DIMENSIONS
48 x 30 in. (122 x 76 cm)
↓CONCEPT
The title of the piece is also its most literal description. Ludwig Wittgenstein's last words—carved into, and falling from, a single, unbroken piece of painted Mylar. Wittgenstein once said, "Language is a part of our organism and no less complicated than it." His philosophical writings blur the line between language and existence. This belief imbued his own final words with a special weight. As he fell from being, so do his words fall from the Mylar. The bronze-and-pink palette references the inside and outside of flesh. It is a portrait of the end of someone's language. Side note: Allie and I are married, and at the time that we made this piece we had been together for nineteen years. In all that time of working on our own projects side by side, we never once collaborated on a project until this one.

↓ART DIRECTION
Ran Zheng, New York
↓URL
ranzhengdesign.com
↓DESIGN FIRM
Ran Design
↓CLIENT
Main 0 Gallery
↓PRINCIPAL TYPE
Custom
↓DIMENSIONS
19 x 36 in. (48.2 x 91.4 cm)
↓CONCEPT
The goal was to create a 3D typeface.

↓DESIGN
Kelly Salchow MacArthur,
Ann Arbor, Michigan
↓DESIGN FIRM
elevate design
↓URL
elevatedesign.org
↓PRINCIPAL TYPE
PF Din Text Pro
↓DIMENSIONS
16.5 x 22 in. (41.9 x 55.9 cm)
↓CONCEPT
Tectonic, a five-part poster series,
exploits the capabilities of laser
cutting to create type and image. Five
layers of paper on top of one layer
of wood emphasize the dimension
of solid and void—a conscious
departure from ink and pixel. Planes
progressively shift across the series,
and abstract elements imply the three
tectonic relationships: transformative,
convergent, and divergent.

↓CREATIVE DIRECTION AND
CALLIGRAPHY
Mariana Castellanos°, New York
↓URL
justanotherunicorn.com
↓CLIENT
Just Another Unicorn
↓PRINCIPAL TYPE
Squirt Gothic
↓DIMENSIONS
24 x 38 x 10 in. (61 x 96.5 x 25.4 cm)
↓CONCEPT
These hoodies made for Just Another
Unicorn fuse the cultures of street
art with streetwear to create a
one-of-a-kind piece of wearable
art. They take the self-expression,
legibility boundaries, and handmade
characteristics found in graffiti
and merge them with the material
world. The hoodies use content
from a variety of cultural sources,
transforming them into patterns of
tangible letters that interplay with
the human form. The body of writing
becomes writing on the body. The JAU
hoodies were born out of a quest of
defying expectations to ultimately find
authenticity and uniqueness.

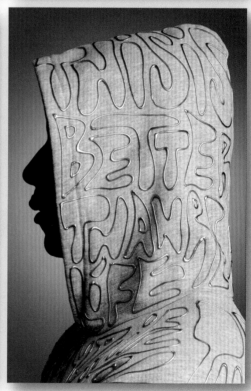

↓DESIGN
Qian Sun°, New York
↓URL
maester.co
↓TWITTER
@CuriousSun
↓INSTAGRAM
@maesterdesign
↓DESIGN FIRM
Maester Design
↓PRINCIPAL TYPE
Custom
↓DIMENSIONS
11 x 17 in. (27.9 x 43.2 cm)
↓CONCEPT
Buildings in New York are full of surprises and stories. Architype: New York was born from my passion toward architecture, typographic lettering, and illustration. The project depicts frozen moments of dancing typography akin to musical notations of melodies. Each piece of Architype starts with wonders and then a research of the architecture, locations, architects, design decision, history, as well as fun facts and secrets.

↓DESIGN AND TYPOGRAPHER
Justin Kowalczuk, Edmonton, Canada
↓URL
justinkowalczuk.com
↓STUDIO
Justin Kowalczuk Design
↓CLIENT
Tegler Youth Centre/Hope Mission
↓PRINCIPAL TYPE
Erotica (modified)
↓DIMENSIONS
33 x 8.5 in. (83.8 x 21.6 cm)
↓CONCEPT
These custom, hand-burned
skateboards were created as a
donation item for a local charity
event. Before the skateboards were
auctioned off, they were used to teach
the youth of the Tegler Youth Centre/
Hope Mission about the importance
of failure and its necessity for success.

↓ART DIRECTION
Qianyi Zhang, Beijing
↓CREATIVE DIRECTION
Yongan Zhou
↓CLIENT
JODU (Zhongshan) Co., Ltd.
↓PRINCIPAL TYPE
Custom
↓DIMENSIONS
Various
↓CONCEPT
The angle is a measure of two intersecting lines. It is the sense of the illumination of the light.

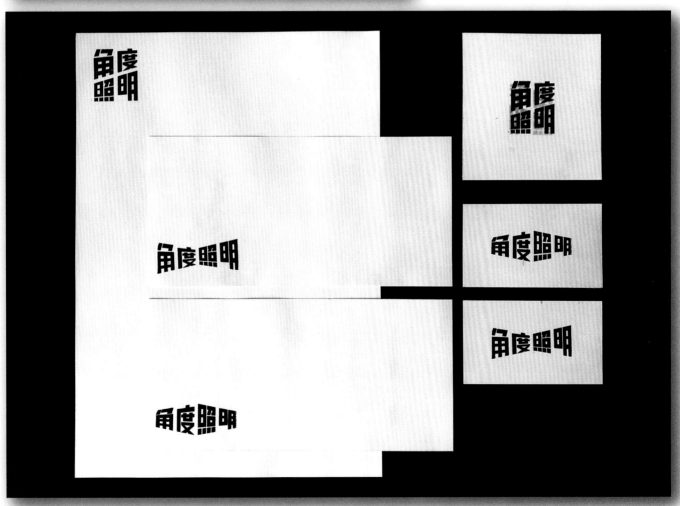

↓DESIGN, LETTERER, AND PAINTER
Stephen Nixon°, Brooklyn
↓TECH CREW
Jonathan Evans, Torin Geller, and
Matt Lau
↓VIDEOGRAPHER
Adam Gundersheimer
↓URL
thundernixon.com
↓INSTAGRAM
@thundernixon
↓CLIENT
One Thousand Birds
↓DIMENSIONS
9 x 11 ft. (2.7 x 3.4 m)
↓CONCEPT
One Thousand Birds is a sound design
studio in Brooklyn, Manhattan, and
Los Angeles that creates soundtracks
for films and commercials. They also
host local music and arts events in
their Williamsburg studio and make
experimental musical instruments,
such as motion-detecting laser harps.
Stephen Nixon and OTB collaborated
to create a mural that can be played
as an instrument: When the black
parts of the letters are touched,
conductive paint carries the signal
and triggers sounds from Arduino
boards made by Bare Conductive. See
it in action at tinyurl.com/otb-mural.

↓DESIGN AND ART DIRECTION
Carlo Alberto Cadenas Gil,
San Antonio de Los Altos, Venezuela
↓URL
behance.net/carlocadenas
↓TWITTER
@cadenas_carlo
↓PRINCIPAL TYPE
Custom
↓DIMENSIONS
7.9 x 7.9 in. (20 x 20 cm) (each one)
↓CONCEPT
This project gave me the opportunity
to establish letters and numbers
in space and composition of
environment to open to a new
path, with a different approach at a
creative level. By alternating color
compositions and shapes, I could
delimit several parameters and follow
the exploratory way of the form to
give life to each one of the symbols.
Every main compound was altered
to seek the desired result through an
experimental process. The Illustrated
Alphabet was created as a personal
project to contribute to the Instagram
challenge "36 Days of Type 2016."

↓DESIGN
Juan Carlos Pagan°, New York
↓URL
carlospagan.com/portfolio/106347
↓PRINCIPAL TYPE
Custom

↓DESIGN DIRECTION
Jules Tardy and Thomas Wilder,
New York
↓CCO
Brian Collins°
↓URL
wearecollins.com
↓TWITTER
@wearecollins
↓DESIGN COMPANY
Collins
↓PRINCIPAL TYPE
Kernit Bold and Kernit Outline
↓CONCEPT

Kernit Display is a custom typeface designed by Collins conceived for an exhibit on the work of Jim Henson. The typeface sought to give the show a voice that is both original and true to Henson's work and unique visual style. We were inspired by the design of the characters that Henson brought to life on screen, as well as the bold typography of the late 1960s and '70s. There are two display weights of the typeface: Kernit Bold and Kernit Outline, which are designed to be used interchangeably, much like the "Anything Muppets" built by Henson's teams for *Sesame Street*.

Kernit Display

Type Specimen

23

24

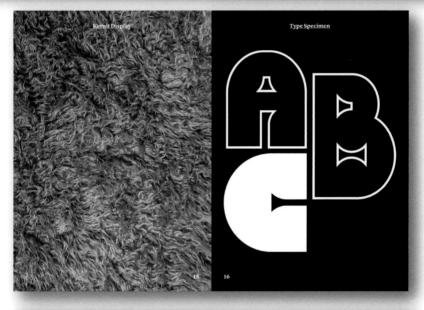

Kernit Display

Type Specimen

15

16

Kernit Display

Type Specimen

19

20

↓DESIGN
Shanyu Gao, Düsseldorf
↓TWITTER
@ShanyuGao
↓TEXT
Dan Wang
↓PROFESSOR
Dominik Lanhenke
↓SCHOOL
University of Applied Sciences
and Arts, Dortmund
↓PRINCIPAL TYPE
Telidon
↓DIMENSIONS
8 x 36 in. (20.3 x 91.4 cm)
↓CONCEPT
This work symbolizes the fusion of
traditional and new media. Wood is
used to represent the old media, as
wood is the main raw material for
papermaking, and thus of books and
newspapers, while solder represents
the new media, as it is used in making
electronic equipment. In order to
combine these two materials, holes
were drilled into the wood and
then filled with solder. These holes
form a kind of pixel font, designed
to create words characterizing
the Internet era: identity, big data,
innovation, digitization, globalization,
dependence, and emotion.

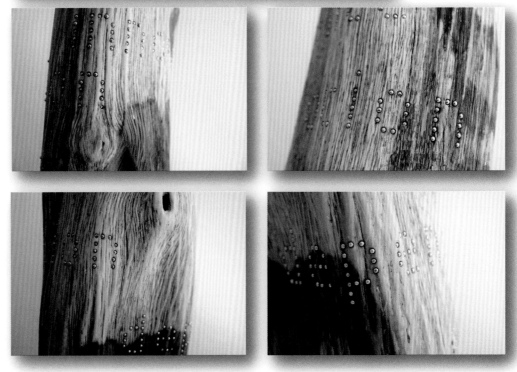

↓SELF-PROMOTION,
ART DIRECTION, AND 3D DESIGN
Alvaro Matas Ferrer, London
↓URL
jenue.net
↓TWITTER
@jenuetypeimage
↓DESIGN FIRM
Jenue
↓PRINCIPAL TYPE
Custom
↓DIMENSIONS
11.7 x 16.5 in. (29.7 x 42 cm)
↓CONCEPT
This is what happens when an
ampersand falls in love with a Bic pen.

↓GRAPHIC DESIGN
François Xavier Saint Georges
and Daniel Robitaille, Montréal
↓ART DIRECTION
Daniel Robitaille
↓PHOTOGRAPHY AND
RETOUCHING
François Xavier Saint Georges
↓URL
bythenorth.com
DESIGN FIRM
Bythenorth—furniture designer
and maker and visual designer
↓PRINCIPAL TYPE
Aperçu
↓DIMENSIONS
Various
↓CONCEPT
Bythenorth has a unique point of
view on furniture—inspired design,
handmade, surrounded by talented
collaborators. Bythenorth is the boreal
forest brought to your home interior.

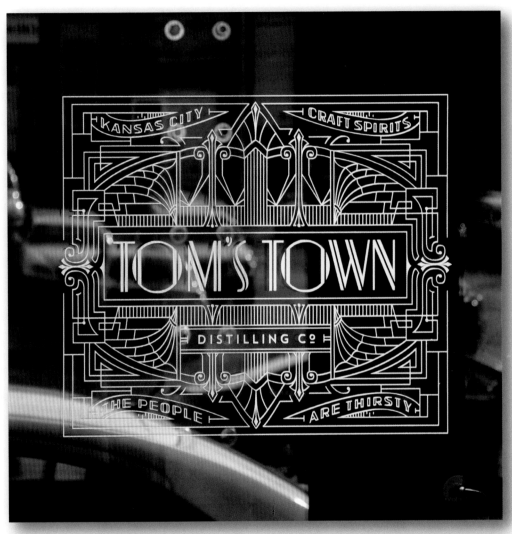

↓DESIGN, ART DIRECTION,
AND LETTERING
Kevin Cantrell°,
Salt Lake City, Utah
↓STRATEGY
Erik Attkisson
↓URL
kevincantrell.com
↓TWITTER
@kevinrcantrell
↓DESIGN FIRM
Kevin Cantrell Studio
↓CLIENT
Tom's Town Distilling Co.
↓PRINCIPAL TYPE
Proprietary Typeface, Verlag, and
custom lettering
↓DIMENSIONS
Various
↓CONCEPT
Tom's Town Distilling Co. is downtown
Kansas City's first legal distillery
since Prohibition. Drawing inspiration
from the country's most polarizing
and corrupt political boss, Tom
Pendergast, Tom's Town brings to
life the glamorous magnetism of
the Gatsby era. Rooted in an Art
Deco optimism, Kansas City flouted
Prohibition under the Pendergast
machine. Today, as Kansas City
experiences its second cultural
rebirth, the people are still thirsty.
Welcome to Tom's Town, where
free spirits reign. KCS created a
comprehensive branding identity
system including a proprietary font,
designed exclusively for Tom's Town.

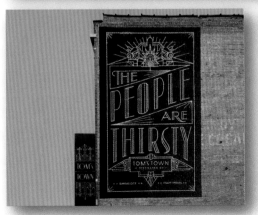

↓CREATIVE AND ART DIRECTION
Mark De Winne°, Singapore
↓DESIGN
Yu May Chua and Mark De Winne
↓LETTERING AND CUSTOM TYPE
Mark De Winne
↓ILLUSTRATION
Yu May Chua
↓PHOTOGRAPHY
Sean Ashley and Dionna Lee
↓URL
parable.sg
↓INSTAGRAM
@parablestudio
↓DESIGN FIRM
Parable Studio Pte Ltd
↓CLIENT
Plentyfull
↓PRINCIPAL TYPE
Infini and Plentyfull Gothic (custom)
↓DIMENSIONS
Variable
↓CONCEPT
Plentyfull is an all-day dining experience incorporating a grocer and bakery, focusing on restoring the soul and body through healthy, hearty food made completely from scratch. The food philosophy of Plentyfull revolves around love for produce—thus its logo was designed as a cheerful, homey script that allows for a secondary lockup containing a series of fresh produce illustrations. Deepening the concept, lush photo compositions of fresh produce were arranged typographically to form Ps. A custom typeface, Plentyfull Gothic, was designed as a display typeface to establish unique textures of the Plentyfull experience and applied across all brand touchpoints.

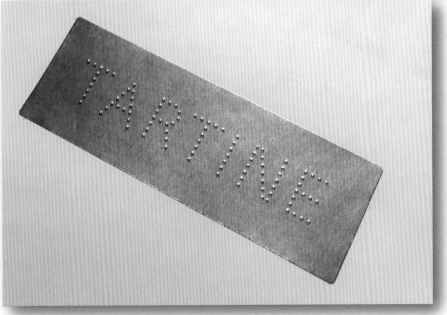

↓DESIGN FIRM
Juliette Cezzar/e.a.d.
↓DESIGN AND ART DIRECTION
Juliette Cezzar, New York
↓DESIGN AND TYPE ASSISTANT
David Klein
↓URL
juliettecezzar.com
↓CLIENT
Tartine, San Francisco
↓PRINCIPAL TYPE
Tartine Thin and Tartine Dots, based
on Neuzeit and a modified version of
Neuzeit S (for body copy)
↓DIMENSIONS
Various
↓CONCEPT
In 2016, Tartine Bakery expanded to
open up Tartine Manufactory in the
Heath Ceramics building. In the run-
up to the new space, all that was really
known was that many things would
happen there, but the specifics would
be unknown and many people would
be deciding on and making design
elements. Embracing this condition,
we based the identity on a single
line modified for its specific use. It
helps to differentiate experiences
while offering some flexibility and
forgiveness when different people
interpret the identity to make both
printed and digital materials on their
own.

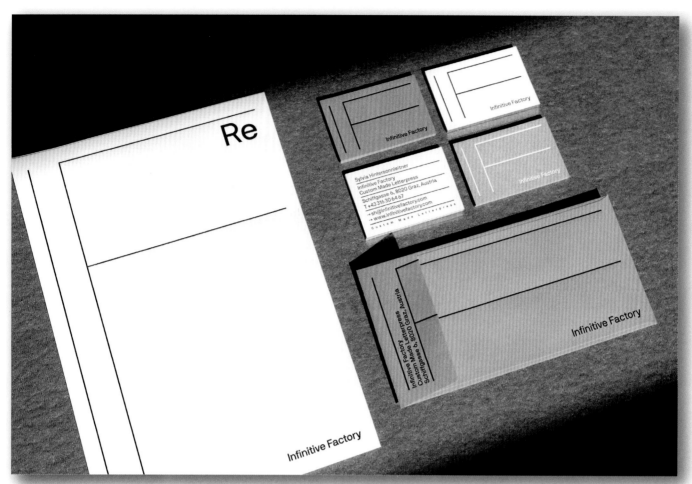

↓DESIGN, ART DIRECTION, AND
CREATIVE DIRECTION
Kurt Glänzer and Josef Heigl
Graz, Austria
↓URL
studiobruch.com
↓DESIGN FIRM
Bruch—Idee&Form
↓CLIENT
Infinitive Factory
↓PRINCIPAL TYPE
NB International
↓DIMENSIONS
Various
↓CONCEPT
Infinitive Factory (IF) stands for high—
quality, custom-made Letterpress.
The company is well known for
experimenting with new ways of
creating overwhelming effects for its
clients. The arranging of the printing
plates was the inspiration to use a
suitable skeleton of the letters "I"
and "F" to create a fine structure that
builds the basis of a highly flexible
branding system that is able to adapt
on every proportion. The simple and
clear composition also functions as a
frame for graphics, illustrations, and
typography to show the countless
possibilities of printing and finishing
with letterpress printing machines.

↓CREATIVE DIRECTION
Daniela Herweg, Alexandros
Michalakopoulos, Jazek Poralla,
Andreas Ruhe, and Marco Schmidt,
Düsseldorf
↓URL
morphoria.com
↓TWITTER
@morphoria_dc
↓INSTAGRAM
@morphoria_design
↓DESIGN STUDIO
The Morphoria Collective
↓CLIENT
Kunsthaus NRW Kornelimünster
Museum, Aachen
↓PRINCIPAL TYPE
Based on Walsheim by Grilli Type;
we expanded the font with one more
weight and 368 ligatures for the
mixture of underlined and crossed
letters
↓DIMENSIONS
Various
↓CONCEPT
With our corporate design for the
museum Kunsthaus NRW we created
a visual language that integrates
itself into a cultural environment
where content is key. By adjusting
the font to the basic principles of
the curation process, we turned the
whole character range into a dynamic
logotype set. As it is fully functional in
every medium and easy to handle for
the user, we were able to brand in the
subtle manner that was required.

↓DESIGN
Rob Alexander, Will Ecke,
and Brittany Waldner, San Francisco
↓CREATIVE DIRECTION
Rob Alexander, Jill Robertson, and
Jason Schulte
↓WRITERS
Dave Eggers and Jill Robertson
↓PRODUCTION ARTISTS
Mimi Chau and Dominique Mao
↓ACCOUNT MANAGERS
Reva Parness and Cindy Wu
↓URL
visitoffice.com
↓TWITTER
@visitoffice
↓DESIGN FIRM
Office
↓CLIENT
826 Valencia
↓PRINCIPAL TYPE
Retro Sans, Rosewood Fill, Trade
Gothic, V Typewriter, and custom
↓DIMENSIONS
Various
↓CONCEPT
826 Valencia is a nonprofit tutoring
center for kids, fronted by King Carl's
Emporium—a store where Carl, a
world-traveling royal puffer fish and
collector, sells his wares to explorers
and navigators of all kinds and from
all lands. Office helped develop
the store's visual identity, products,
packaging, exterior design, and
customer experiences.

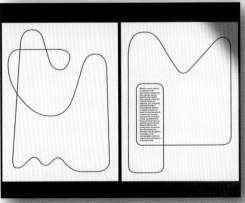

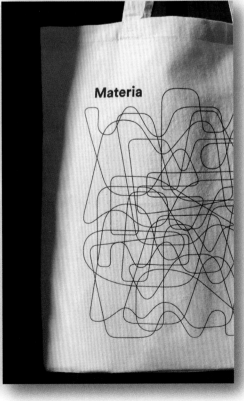

↓ART DIRECTION
Daniel Robitaille, Montréal
↓CREATIVE DIRECTION
Louis Gagnon°
↓URL
paprika.com
↓TWITTER
@PaprikaMontreal
↓DESIGN FIRM
Paprika
↓CLIENT
Centre Materia
↓PRINCIPAL TYPE
Circular
↓DIMENSIONS
Various
↓CONCEPT
Materia is an artist-run center
and exhibition space focused on
promoting and showcasing the
visual arts. To highlight the fine art of
expression, their visual identity had to
be distinctive and dynamic and had to
reflect the diversity of the products
and services offered. Materia's visual
branding platform was developed
to highlight and "frame" images of
contemporary works of art and was
adapted to the following touchpoints:
signage, displays, reusable bags,
invitations, webmail, and more.

↓DESIGN
Ross Burwell, Chicago
↓PARTNER AND DESIGN DIRECTOR
Will Miller
↓DESIGN FIRM
Firebelly Design
↓URL
firebellydesign.com
↓TWITTER
@firebellydesign
↓PRINCIPAL TYPE
FLOR Mono, Pitch Mono, Replica Pro,
and Worchester EF
↓DIMENSIONS
Various
↓CONCEPT
Firebelly partnered with FLOR to
rethink not just the brand for the
eco-conscious retailer of custom
rugs but also the entire consumer
experience. After mapping the ideal-
user journey—from the initial store
visit and creative process to in-home
installation—Firebelly developed a
visual identity, collateral, packaging,
and design tools to facilitate that
experience. Simple, elegant, and
user friendly, the modular identity
system features an ultra-kinetic
custom monospace font that
brings the underlying grid to light
while demonstrating the product's
versatility. A rich suite of brand
elements—broad palette, ownable
marks, and icons—complete the
system, providing FLOR with the
flexibility to keep creating unique,
thoughtful pieces.

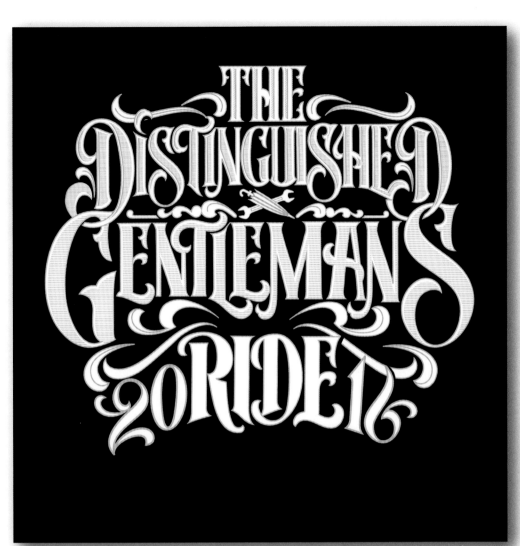

↓DESIGN
Tony DiSpigna° and Luca Ionescu°,
New York and Sydney
↓URL
likemindedstudio.com
↓STUDIO
Like Minded Studio
↓CLIENT
The Distinguished Gentleman's Ride
↓CREATIVE DIRECTION, DESIGN,
AND TYPOGRAPHY
Luca Ionescu/Like Minded Studio,
Tony DiSpigna, NY (Spencerian Script
Posters),
↓CREATIVE DIRECTOR
Chris McMullen
(Client Side/Gentleman's Ride)
↓DESIGNER
Mikey Stojchevski
(Client Side/Gentleman's Ride)
↓FOUNDER
Mark Hawwa
(Client Side/Gentleman's Ride)
↓PRINCIPAL TYPE
Spencerian Script
↓DIMENSIONS
16.5 x 23.4 in. (41.9 x 59.4 cm)
↓CONCEPT
The brief was to develop bespoke
branding for the international charity
event and ride The Distinguished
Gentleman's Ride, including updating
existing branding design. The
updated visual image and collateral
were designed to exude prestige
associated with the ride and its
members, in order to help drive and
motivate contributors to reach a
milestone in donations.

↓DESIGN DIRECTION
Zan Goodman, New York
↓SENIOR DESIGNER
Anthony Cappetta
↓LETTERING AND ILLUSTRATION
Dan Cassaro
↓URL
chandeliercreative.com
↓TWITTER
@chandeliercreative
↓DESIGN FIRM
Chandelier Creative
↓CLIENT
Pappagallo
↓PRINCIPAL TYPE
Euro Sans Pro, Typewriter Elite,
and custom
↓DIMENSIONS
Various
↓CONCEPT
We were approached by the iconic
'60s accessories brand Pappagallo
for a rebrand and identity as they
relaunched for a new generation.
Rather than start from scratch, we
commissioned letterer Dan Cassaro
to redraw one of their original logos
and signature marks while giving
them a modern update. We used the
new mark for packaging patterns and
design features like boxes and zipper
pulls. The name "Pappagallo" is Italian
for "parrot"—thus the logo, which we
found in a dusty shoebox inside their
archive.

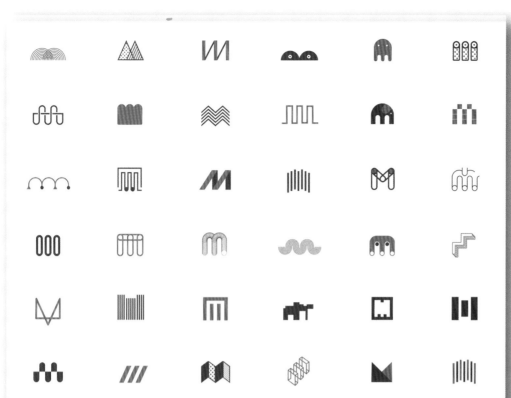

↓CREATIVE DIRECTION
Paul Garbett, Sydney
↓URL
garbett.com.au
↓TWITTER
@garbettdesign
↓DESIGN FIRM
Garbett
↓CLIENT
Manifold
↓PRINCIPAL TYPE
Custom
↓DIMENSIONS
Various
↓CONCEPT
Manifold is a boutique post-production studio specializing in photo retouching and 3D visualization. A philosophy of embracing multiple creative outcomes informed their name and inspired a playful, dynamic identity. The identity consists of around thirty different monograms, all representing an "M" and linked through a simple, bold color palette. The range of monograms is then used as the basis of Manifold's visual language.

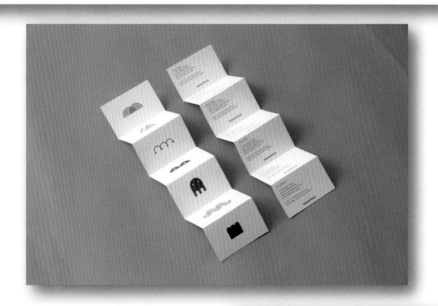

↓DESIGN
Stephie Becker and Ariane Spanier,
Berlin
↓CREATIVE DIRECTION
Ariane Spanier
↓URL
arianespanier.com
↓STUDIO
Ariane Spanier Design
↓CLIENT
Musikalische Akademie des
Nationaltheater Orchesters
Mannheim/Orchestra of the National
Theatre Mannheim
↓PRINCIPAL TYPE
Denver Serial, Larsseit, and custom
↓DIMENSIONS
Various
↓CONCEPT
This is a new visual identity for the
concert series "Academy Concerts" of
the Orchestra of the National Theatre
Mannheim. Each season there are
eight Academy Concerts, which are
numbered from one to eight. The
concert numbers are designed out of
musical notes and give a classical feel
to the orchestra and its concerts.

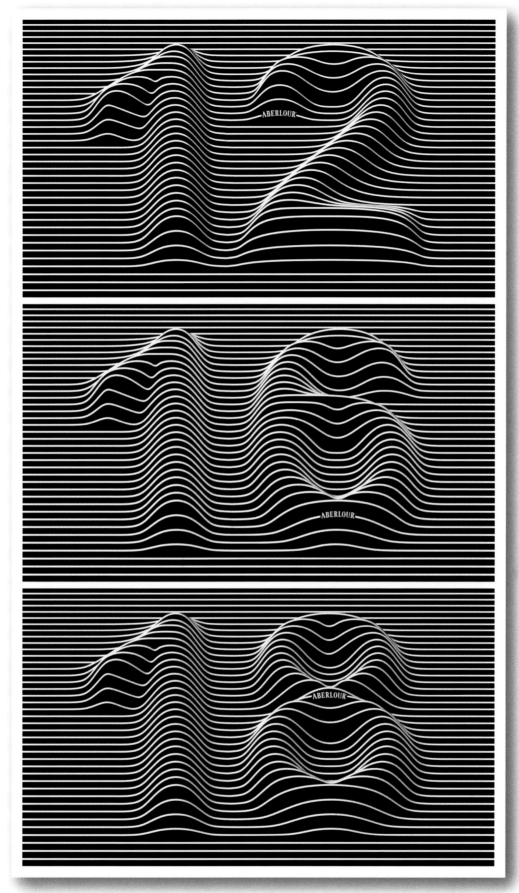

↓DESIGN AND CREATIVE DIRECTION
Juan Carlos Pagan°, New York
↓URL
carlospagan.com
and portfolio/aberlour
↓CLIENT
Ketchum, Ally Mann
↓PRINCIPAL TYPE
Custom
↓CONCEPT
The project's title is "Ages of Aberlour
Whisky." Aberlour single malt whisky is
named after where it's made. It means
"the mouth of the chattering burn" in
Gaelic, and this wild mountain water
stream is part of the Aberlour story.
Each typographic rendering—12, 16,
and 18—is of the ages of whisky in
the Aberlour catalog. Each number
is portrayed as rising from the
famous water source from which its
corresponding whisky is made.

↓CREATIVE DIRECTION
Katrin Oeding, Hamburg
↓URL
studio-oeding.com
↓DESIGN STUDIO
Studio Oeding
↓CLIENT
Essenza –
The Essence of Motorcycles
↓PRINCIPAL TYPE
Essenza Asphalt Brush, Essenza
Speedlines, Essenza Tuning, and CA
Oskar Condensed
↓DIMENSIONS
Various
↓CONCEPT
Launched in 2016, the innovative
motorcycle sprint series with
its own design competition
brought international motorcycle
manufacturers and race riders onto
the racetrack. Sixteen racing teams
compete against one another in a
knockout system. The corporate
design visualizes speed in all its forms.
The logo consists of sixteen lines
representing the sixteen participants
in the sprint. The "E" symbolizes
the start lines for both participants
in a race. The logo design, the
customized type design, the business
equipment, the bookazine, the various
merchandise products, the exhibition
design, the responsive interface
design, and the entire social media
communication were designed.

↓COMMENT
I am not going to lie—I love motorcycles, but I love type just a bit more.
The moment I saw this Essenza identity and all of the elements that
were created for this series of events, I knew it was my judge's pick.

Every component is a distinct and considered mix of typography,
information, and moto-culture. From the intentional black-and-white
implementation of the identity to the impeccably shot and selected
photography, we feel as if we are actually there.

They created three distinct and contrasting typefaces for the
identity: Essenza Tuning, a melding of letterform and motorcycle
parts; Essenza Asphalt Brush, a hand-painted, playfully appropriate,
all-caps brush; and Essenza Speedlines, a multiline face that the logo
is made from with each line representing the number of participants
in the race as well as the markup for the starting blocks.

The translation of these elements into the environmental design
of the bike exhibition area, the letterpressed business cards, and
the visually rich magazine are examples of how an identity should
be done: an end-to-end, complete experience that considers every
viewer touchpoint.

All of this bundled together made me dream of attending an
event that so beautifully combines a love for motorcycles and
typography, executed to perfection.
Xerxes Irani

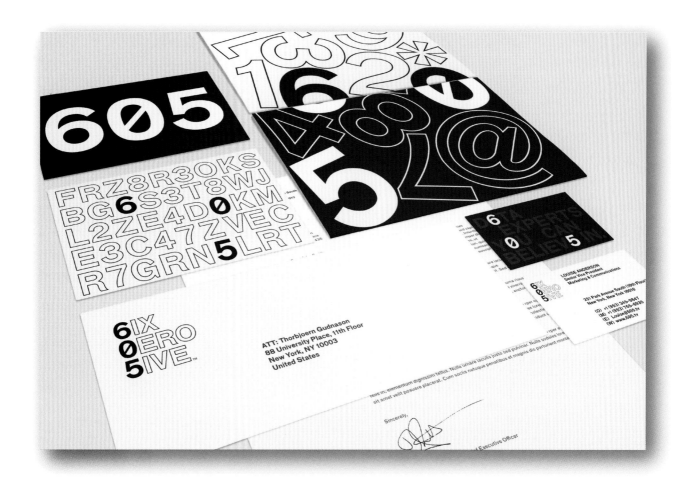

↓DESIGN
Thorbjorn Gudnason, New York
↓CREATIVE DIRECTION
Thomas Wilder
↓CCO
Brian Collins°
↓DESIGN COMPANY
Collins
↓URL
wearecollins.com
↓TWITTER
@wearecollins
↓CLIENT
605—605.tv
↓PRINCIPAL TYPE
Custom 605 F Grotesk
↓DIMENSIONS
Various
↓CONCEPT
605 is a data analytics company
founded on the notion of "radical
transparency." The team—made
up of engineers, analysts, data
scientists, media experts, and
marketing strategists—has pioneered
a movement in the field of TV data
by offering unique, independent
audience-measurement services
to build better marketing and
programming initiatives within the
media and entertainment industries.
The identity we designed focuses
on 605's dedication to transparency
and discovery. The system utilizes
a straightforward, black-and-white
color palette to emphasize that data is
exact—it cannot be shaped, twisted,
or faked. The typography emphasizes
605's no-nonsense approach to data
analysis.

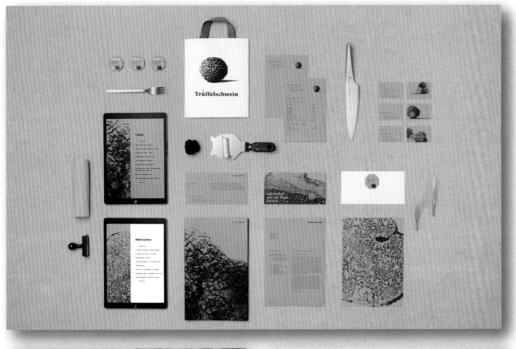

↓CREATIVE DIRECTION
Katrin Oeding, Hamburg
↓URL
studio-oeding.com
↓DESIGN STUDIO
Studio Oeding
↓CLIENT
Restaurant Trüffelschwein
↓PRINCIPAL TYPE
Avenir and Hiroshige
↓DIMENSIONS
Various
↓CONCEPT
The Trüffelschwein restaurant, with Chef Kirill Kinfelt, who was awarded a Michelin star, stands for extraordinary truffle creations. The basis of the corporate design is therefore the truffle in all its facets and varieties. This diversity is illustrated in the entire visual presence with various structures, textures, and abstract forms. The print enhancement with golden hot-foil embossing gives it a special feel.

↓DESIGN DIRECTOR
Tara Lubonivich, New York
↓EXECUTIVE CREATIVE DIRECTOR
Tosh Hall°
↓MANAGING DIRECTOR
Sara Hyman
↓COPYWRITER
Jen Chandler
↓PHOTOGRAPHER
Martin Wonnacott
↓ILLUSTRATOR
Chris Wormell
↓TYPOGRAPHY
Ian Brignell
↓ACCOUNT MANAGER
Josh Griffin
↓URL
jkrglobal.com
↓DESIGN AGENCY
Jones Knowles Ritchie
↓CLIENT
Havana Club
↓CONCEPT
In redesigning the packaging, we wanted to honor the tenacity of the Arechabala family story and resurrect the richness and craft with which the rum is distilled. After an immersion in the Bacardi archives, the team drew inspiration from the vintage labels, which informed many of the design decisions.

↓DESIGN
Erin Dameron and Catherine Wyatt,
New York
↓EXECUTIVE CREATIVE DIRECTOR
Tosh Hall°
↓MANAGING DIRECTOR
Sara Hyman
↓DESIGN DIRECTION
Andy Baron and Daniel D'Arcy
↓ACCOUNT DIRECTOR
Grace Dawson
↓ACCOUNT MANAGER
Vannett Li
↓TYPOGRAPHER
Ian Brignell
↓URL
jkrglobal.com
↓CLIENT
M&M'S
↓DIMENSIONS
24 x 32 in. (61 x 81.3 cm)
↓PRINCIPAL TYPE
Custom
↓CONCEPT
Since 1941, M&M s has been adored
by chocolate lovers around the world.
The brand wanted an ownable logo to
use during the yearlong celebration
of its seventy-fifth anniversary. Many
brands add new visual elements and
clichés to their brand mark during
an anniversary. Our goal was to use
existing iconic equities of M&M's
rather than muddy the symbol with
balloons and birthday cakes. The
belief was that a simple and iconic
symbol integrated into the brand mark
would allow for a flexible system that
would last all year long.

↓DESIGN
Kimberly Mar, San Francisco
↓DESIGN LEAD
Erik Berger Vaage
↓CCO
Matt Luckhurst
↓DIRECTOR OF OPERATIONS
Joanna Hobson
↓SENIOR PRODUCER
Ashley Kasten
↓STRATEGIST
Anna Sternoff
↓VIDEOGRAPHER
Henry Dombey
↓URL
wearecollins.com
↓TWITTER
@wearecollins
↓AGENCY
Collins
↓CLIENT
Summit Public Schools
↓PRINCIPAL TYPE
Summit Display
↓DIMENSIONS
Various
↓CONCEPT
Our assignment was to develop a new brand identity for Summit Public Schools. The organization is experiencing tremendous growth, and it was imperative to create a mark that reflected their values of personalized learning and individualized education. The identity is anchored in a typeface created in collaboration with students from Summit schools. The system responds to the variety of schools and students through color and an avatar tool that allows every student and faculty member at Summit to create their own character. The brand is currently being adapted and implemented across six schools and multiple digital platforms.

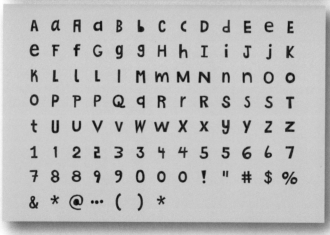

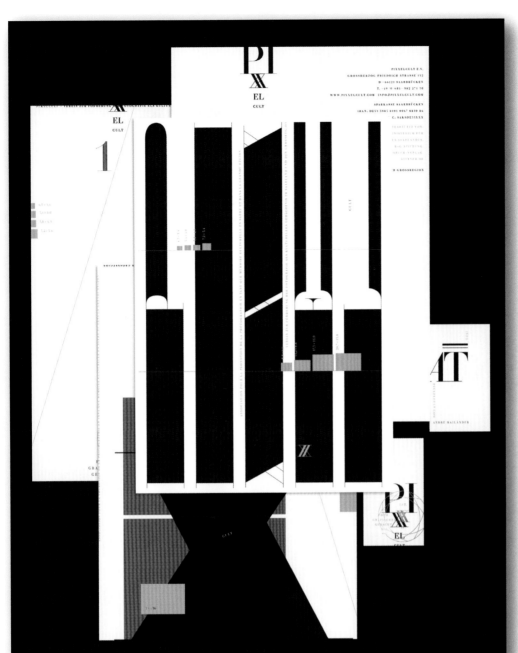

↓DESIGN
Patrick Bittner, Saarbrücken, Germany
↓URL
bittner.de
↓CLIENT
PixxelCult e.V., André Mailänder, and
Thomas Roessler
↓PRINCIPAL TYPE
Custom
↓DIMENSIONS
Various
↓CONCEPT
This is a design for PixxelCult, an
association for the promotion of
photography as cultural memory
in Saarland and the so-called
Grossregion (a cooperation of the
German federal states Rheinland-
Pfalz—Saarland plus the French
region Grand Est, the Grand Duchy
of Luxembourg, and the Belgian
Wallonia). To avoid an early mental
fixation on a particular photographic
image as a benchmark, a purely
typographic appearance was realized.

↓DESIGN
Tom Elsner, Tyrone Lou,
and Hugh Miller, London
↓CREATIVE DIRECTION
Tyrone Lou and Hugh Miller
↓URL
bond-agency.com
↓TWITTER
@london_bond
↓AGENCY
Bond Agency
↓CLIENT
ArtRabbit
↓PRINCIPAL TYPE
Avenir Next and Futura Bold
↓CONCEPT
ArtRabbit is a global digital platform
and mobile app for the promotion,
discovery, and appreciation of
contemporary art. Bond was
approached to refresh the overall
brand identity and realize a more
contemporary logo and visual
language to coincide with the
relaunched website and new app.
Distilling the words "art" and "rabbit"
into a single logotype reveals a simple
and iconic visual metaphor with the
distinctive graphic rabbit head "R"—
turning art on its head!

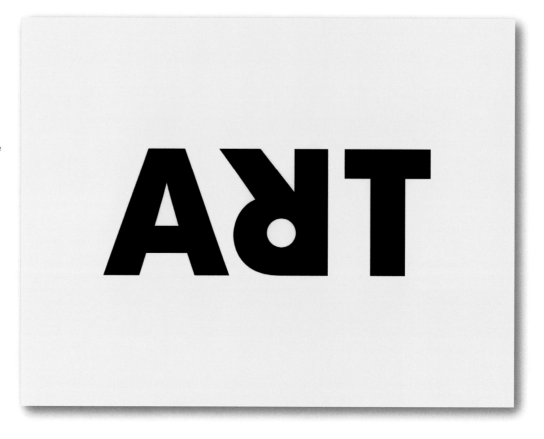

↓DESIGN
Ruth Wood, Leeds, England
↓DESIGN DIRECTION
Rob Skelly
↓EXECUTIVE CREATIVE DIRECTOR
Andrew Lawrence
↓LETTERING AND TYPE DESIGN
Rob Clarke°
↓URLS
elmwood.com and robclarke.com
↓TWITTER
@ElmwoodTweets, @RobClarkeType
↓DESIGN STUDIO
Elmwood
↓CLIENT
22 Street Lane Nursery
↓PRINCIPAL TYPE
Custom
↓CONCEPT
22 Street Lane Nursery is an exclusive day nursery with ambitions to provide excellence in early-years care and education for children between the ages of three months and five years. Children are encouraged to learn through play, and proximity to nature is an important part of the nursery's environment. Equally, there is a strong focus on the learning journey and growth of each child. Our marque seeks to capture this by representing the growth and development of the individual child and the close bond between children and staff.

↓CREATIVE
Jesper Bange
and Marko Salonen, Helsinki
↓URL
bond-agency.com
↓TWITTER
@bondhelsinki
↓AGENCY
Bond
↓CLIENT
Eero Aarnio Originals
↓PRINCIPAL TYPE
Custom
↓DIMENSIONS
Various
↓CONCEPT
Eero Aarnio is the designer and
innovator behind some of the most
recognizable and beloved Finnish
furniture pieces of the last century.
We created the logo for the new
company Eero Aarnio Originals, the
manufacturer of Aarnio's original
designs. The symbol is based on
Aarnio's most iconic design, the Ball
Chair.

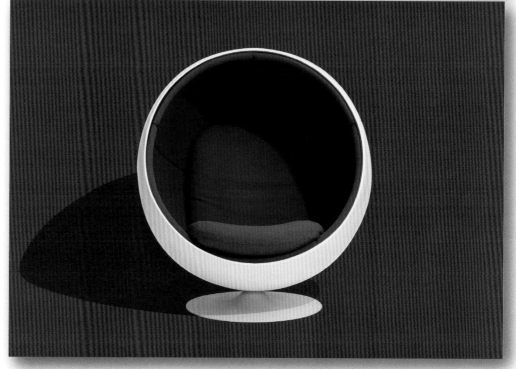

↓DESIGN
Erin Dameron and Catherine Wyatt,
New York
↓EXECUTIVE CREATIVE DIRECTOR
Tosh Hall°
↓MANAGING DIRECTOR
Sara Hyman
↓DESIGN DIRECTION
Andy Baron and Daniel D'Arcy
↓ACCOUNT DIRECTOR
Grace Dawson
↓ACCOUNT MANAGER
Vannett Li
↓TYPOGRAPHER
Ian Brignell
↓URL
jkrglobal.com
↓CLIENT
M&M'S
↓DIMENSIONS
24 x 32 in. (61 x 81.3 cm)
↓PRINCIPAL TYPE
Custom
↓CONCEPT
Since 1941, M&M's has been adored
by chocolate lovers around the world.
The brand wanted an ownable logo to
use during the yearlong celebration
of its seventy-fifth anniversary. Many
brands add new visual elements and
clichés to their brand mark during
an anniversary. Our goal was to use
existing iconic equities of M&M's
rather than muddy the symbol with
balloons and birthday cakes. The
belief was that a simple and iconic
symbol integrated into the brand mark
would allow for a flexible system that
would last all year long.

↓ARTIST AND DESIGN
Ari Weinkle, Boston
↓MUSIC
Dirty Beaches
↓URL
ariweinkle.com
↓TWITTER
@ariweinkle
↓PRINCIPAL TYPE
Custom Copperplate calligraphy
↓CONCEPT
"Growths" is a typographic
experiment juxtaposing the elegance
of copperplate calligraphy with
abnormal organic formations.

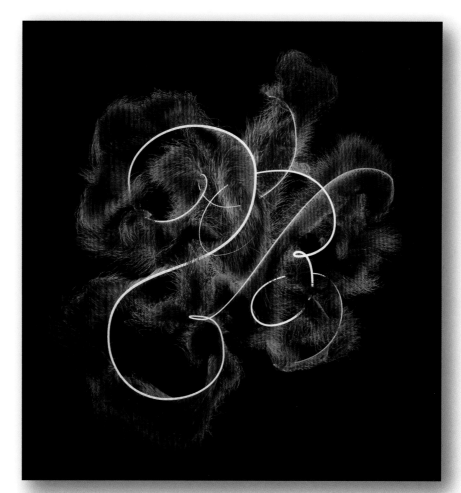

DESIGN AND ART DIRECTION
Kevin Cantrell°,
Salt Lake City, Utah
↓URL
kevincantrell.com
↓TWITTER
@kevinrcantrell
↓DESIGN FIRM
Kevin Cantrell Studio
↓PRINCIPAL TYPE
Custom lettering
↓CONCEPT
The project is inspired by the words
of Paul from the book of Corinthians
in that the negative space of the
overlapping letterforms "hope" and
"love" make up the word "faith,"
suggesting the nature of faith as
being the evidence of things not seen
and the substance of things hoped
for. (Note: The original quote is "faith,
hope, and love," but the order was
switched to emphasize the concept.)

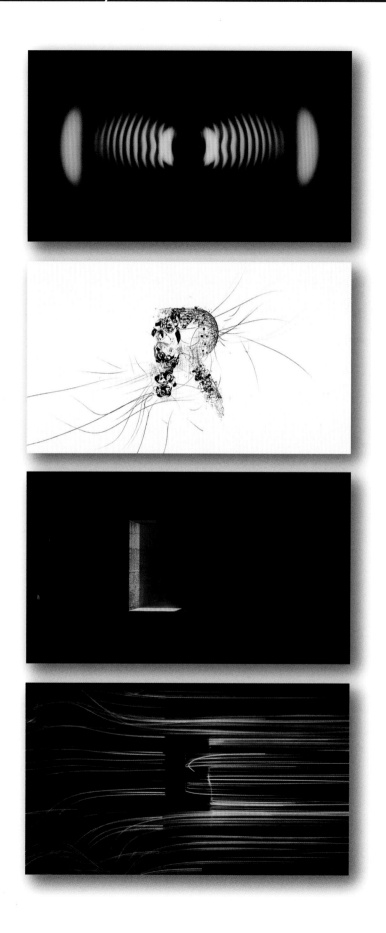

↓CHIEF CREATIVE OFFICER
John Zissimos
↓EXECUTIVE CREATIVE DIRECTOR
Jason Luster
↓VP, GM CREATIVE AND DIGITAL
J.D. Swartz
↓LEAD DESIGNER
Mike Mazza
↓ART DIRECTION
Shirleen Lavalais, San Francisco
↓CREATIVE DIRECTION
Michael Manning
↓DIRECTOR, EXECUTIVE
PRODUCER, BROADCAST AND FILM
Katie Rinki
↓PRODUCER
Marc Hochman
↓BUSINESS MANAGER,
SALESFORCE BRAND
Taylor Hilficker
↓DESIGN FIRM
Salesforce Brand Innovation
↓DESIGN AGENCY
Bonfire Labs
↓URLS
salesforce.com and bonfirelabs.com
↓TWITTER
@salesforce and @bonfirelabs
↓DESIGN AND ANIMATION
Chris Carmichael and Devin Earthman
↓CREATIVE DIRECTION
Phil Spitler
↓PRODUCER
Sheila Smith
↓EDITOR
Robbie Proctor
↓SOUND DESIGN
Conner Jones
↓EXECUTIVE PRODUCER
Mary Mathaisell
↓CLIENT
Salesforce
↓PRINCIPAL TYPE
Salesforce Sans and custom

↓COMMENT
So much typography on film follows generic formulas: from advertising text and production credits to the now ubiquitous video "explainers." In contrast, this piece felt genuinely original, crisp, filmic, and atmospheric. Each letter had a distinct personality; each worked with the others; each told the story of disruptive design the piece intended to communicate. The work was given a synesthetic sparkle of excellence by a charming and imaginative soundscape, which, while not strictly typographic, suggests that the future of type on film may learn more from film than type.
Ben Schott

↓DESIGNER STATEMENT
The second-annual Salesforce Design Leadership Conference, a daylong forum at the de Young Museum, took place in San Francisco on June 13, 2016. The event focused on design disruption— from blindsiding businesses to the advent of the smartphone to revolutionary ride and music services to the new "gig" economy.

The show included talks by an acclaimed UX product designer, a preeminent architect, a *New York Times* best-selling novelist, a biodiversity scientist, and an aviation engineer, among others— all speaking to the subject of disruptive design. In the film, each letterform disrupts the next to convey the conference theme: "World Interrupted: The Remarkable Effects of Disruptive Design."

↓DESIGN
Hui Chiao Chen (Joro Chen),
Valencia, California
↓SOUND DESIGN
Irene, Pin-Hua Chen
↓URL
joro.tv
↓STUDIO
Joro TV
↓PRINCIPAL TYPE
Hand-drawn
↓CONCEPT
Based on the narrative of Myeong
Seok Jeong, a famous poet in South
Korea, the English subtitle is treated
as a typographic element interacting
with the scene to build the experience
of communicating with God through
all things on earth.

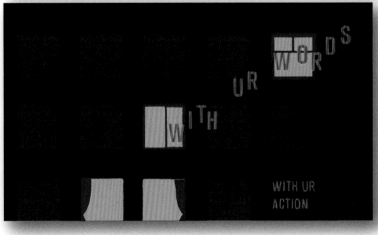

↓DESIGN
Hui Chiao Chen (Joro Chen), Valencia, California
↓SOUND DESIGN
Irene, Pin-Hua Chen
↓NARRATOR
Myeong Seok Jeong
↓URL
joro.tv
↓STUDIO
Joro TV
↓PRINCIPAL TYPE
Akzidenz GroteskBQ
↓CONCEPT
The title sequence uses countdown numbers and photofits as elements to show the multiple personality disorder of Billy Milligan.

THOMAS WRESTLES WITH BEARS SWIMS WITH OTTERS AND LEARNS HOW TO DO NAKED YOGA

VICELAND

WEEDIQUETTE MONDAY 8P
WEEDIQ ETTE MONDAY 8P
WEEDIQ TTE MON AY 8P
WEEDI TE MON AY 8P
EEDI T MON AY 8P
EDI MON 8P
EDI ON N 8P
I N P

NOISEY:	S
MONTREAL	M
EDM	T
	W
	THU. 10:00P
	F
	S

W A V E S

↓BRANDING AGENCY
Gretel
↓URL
gretelny.com
↓TWITTER
@GretelNYC
↓EP, HEAD OF PRODUCTION
Dina Chang
↓EX. CREATIVE DIRECTOR
Greg Hahn
↓CREATIVE DIRECTOR
Ryan Moore
↓PRODUCERS
Haley Klatzkin and Penny Mailander
↓ART DIRECTION
Dylan Mulvaney
↓DESIGN
Caleb Halter and Dylan Mulvaney,
New York
↓LEAD ANIMATOR
Ken Tanabe
↓ANIMATORS
Daniel Clark, Brandon Kennedy, and
Drake Miller
↓EDITORS
Eli Mavros and Bill Saunders
↓CLIENT
Vice, Brooklyn, New York
↓CHIEF CREATIVE OFFICER
Eddy Moretti
↓EXEC. ASST., EDDY MORETTI
Emery Matson
↓CREATIVE SERVICES
COORDINATOR
Louisa Cannell
↓EXECUTIVE DESIGN DIRECTOR
Matt Schoen
↓CREATIVE DIRECTOR
Spike Jonze
↓GENERAL MANAGER
CJ Fahey
↓COORDINATOR
Louisa Cannell
↓VP POST PRODUCTION
Mike Daniels
↓ART DIRECTION
Annie Rosen
↓POST-PRODUCTION SUPERVISOR
VICE TV
Brian Golding
↓DIRECTOR OF POST SERVICES TV
Susan Martin
↓DIRECTOR OF COMMUNICATIONS
Jake Goldman
↓PRINCIPAL TYPE
Helvetica
↓CONCEPT
The VICELAND brand is equal parts
exhibition catalog and street flyer:
Craigslist and couture, generic and
refined. It is simultaneously the
elevated "high" and vernacular "low."
A translation of the VICE sensibility:
It's blunt and raw. It is an exposed
structure, a functional language free
of decoration, artifice, and veneer. The
brand is an objective frame for the
network's content: unstyled, unslick,
and unadorned.

↓COMMENT
VICELAND emerged from a high-quality pool of TDC entries because
of its anti-establishment, no-holds-barred approach to establishing
and communicating a new TV network.

The work is so unique that it made my choice an easy one.
It draws inspiration from brand identity approaches used in music,
culture, and fashion but doesn't mimic or imitate any of them. It feels
completely new. The black-and-white, single-weight typography
gives the design a rebellious, attitudinal feel. It's got emotion,
ironically, using a font that is considered boring. It is bold, dominant,
and unforgiving, but never too much.

Though minimal, with an emphasis on white space, the design
system is energetic and memorable. The simplicity of the typography,
the copywriting, and the interaction of the elements always
complement the content. The system moves effortlessly from print
to animation.

This would have been so easy to get wrong, but they didn't.
It inspires. I really, really wish I'd done this myself.
Stewart Devlin

↓DESIGNER STATEMENT
VICELAND is the new television network by VICE, the most notorious
and innovative youth-media brand in the world. With a focus on
global lifestyle and culture, the network's original content slices
across the cultural spectrum: food, sex, fashion, music, sports,
politics, and more. The challenge was to build a brand that could
punctuate, counterpoint, inform, and whenever possible, step back
from the content. A range of emotion and the impact of the images
had to pass through the brand undiluted. The objective design brings
the personalities, content, and tone of each show to the foreground
while allowing for diversity in composition and messaging and
smooth translation to any platform.

↓DESIGN AND CREATIVE
DIRECTION
Arutza Rico, Bogotá
↓ART DIRECTION
Andrés Dupla
↓LETTERING
Arutza Rico
↓PHOTOGRAPHY
Lucho Mariño
↓URLS
pnglab.co
↓DESIGN FIRMS
Arutza Rico Onzaga and Pnglab
↓CLIENT
AutoMundial: José Miguel Carreira,
Antonio Puerto, and Carolina Puerto
↓PRINCIPAL TYPE
Gotham Bold
↓DIMENSIONS
Various
↓CONCEPT
To celebrate the hundred years of
AutoMundial we did a project that
involves art and technology. The
center of the stand was based on the
unique design of the rubber inspired
by the flowers and the prayer of "The
Virgin of Carmen," who is the patron
for truck drivers.

↓DESIGN
Mattias Amnäs, Anders Bollman,
and Fibi Kung, Stockholm
↓CREATIVE DIRECTION
Perniclas Bedow
↓CALLIGRAPHER
Fibi Kung
↓ILLUSTRATOR
Fibi Kung
↓URL
bedow.se
↓DESIGN FIRM
Bedow
↓CLIENT
Sing a Song Fighter Records
↓PRINCIPAL TYPE
Custom handlettering (Hope Serif)
↓DIMENSIONS
12 x 12 in. (30.5 x 30.5 cm)
↓CONCEPT
The Hope Singers is a Swedish
indie choir consisting of various
artists. They take a spontaneous and
unscripted approach to their music.
The group's record sleeve cover takes
the same unregulated form. Design
started with a set of bird illustrations
using block color and cutout shapes.
The typeface has a rough, hand-
drawn aesthetic with iterations per
letter to provide variation in words.
The cover was screen printed on
unbleached board. The result is
cheerful, individual, and distinctly
crafted. Although rudimentary in form,
the graphics have a distinctive quality
appropriately rooted in the dynamic
and energy of the group.

↓DESIGN
Konstantin Eremenko, Moscow
↓URL
eremenko-vis.com
↓DESIGN FIRM
Eremenko Visual Communication
↓CLIENT
Biotrisse AG
↓PRINCIPAL TYPE
Fedra Sans
↓DIMENSIONS
3.4 x 1.8 x 0.5 in. (8.5 x 4.5 x 1.3 cm)
↓CONCEPT
Biotrisse Filler Cosmetics is a
product line for face care. Four
types of creams are presented with
a systematic approach for pre- and
post-treatment, which consists of
certain sequences of use. The main
aim of packaging development was
to create quick and easy recognition
of the whole product line. Each box
contains two tubes. Outer boxes for
1/2 and 3/4 sets are the same and
could be used as a temporary stand.
A difference consists in the inner tube
holder, which allows you to see which
cream set is packed inside. Moreover,
the inner holder has an information
leaflet function.

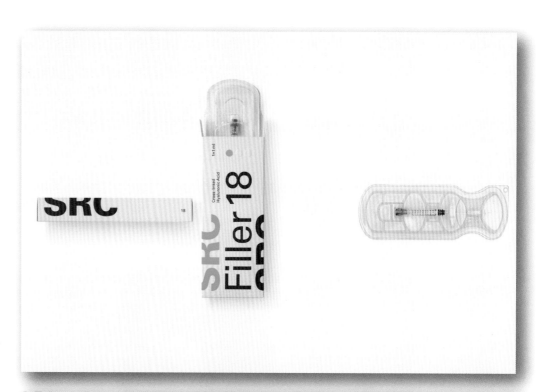

↓DESIGN AND LETTERING
Kevin Cantrell°, Salt Lake City, Utah
↓ART DIRECTION
Kevin Cantrell
↓STRATEGY
Erik Attkisson
↓URL
kevincantrell.com
↓TWITTER
@kevinrcantrell
↓DESIGN FIRM
Kevin Cantrell Studio
↓CLIENT
Tom's Town Distilling Co.
↓PRINCIPAL TYPE
Proprietary typeface, Verlag, and
custom
↓DIMENSIONS
Various
↓CONCEPT
Tom's Town Distilling Co. is downtown
Kansas City's first legal distillery
since Prohibition. Drawing inspiration
from the country's most polarizing
and corrupt political boss, Tom
Pendergast, Tom's Town brings
to life the glamorous magnetism
of the Gatsby era. Rooted in Art
Deco optimism, Kansas City flouted
Prohibition under the Pendergast
machine. Today, as Kansas City
experiences its second cultural
rebirth, the people are still thirsty.
Welcome to Tom's Town, where
free spirits reign. KCS created a
comprehensive branding identity
system including a proprietary font,
designed exclusively for Tom's Town.

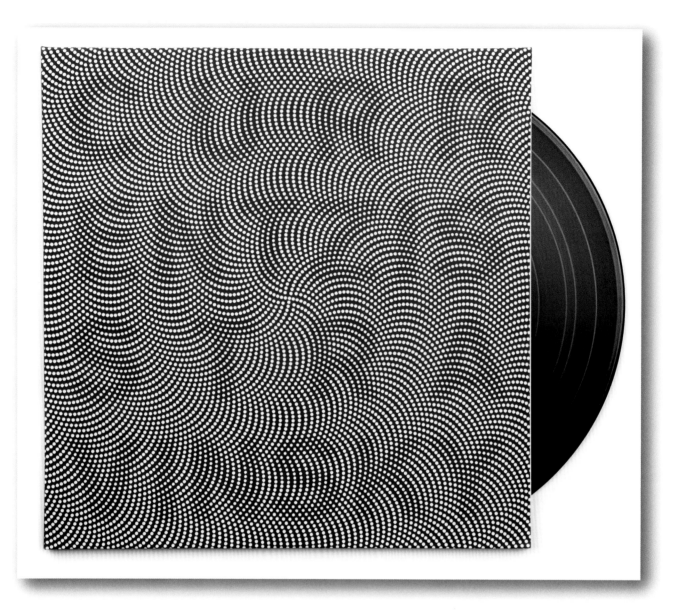

↓DESIGN
Fons Hickmann° and Lizzy Onck,
Berlin
↓ART AND CREATIVE DIRECTION
Fons Hickmann°
↓URL
m23.de
↓TWITTER
@fonshickmannm23
↓STUDIO
Fons Hickmann m23, Berlin
↓CLIENT
Sony Classical Music, Berlin
↓DIMENSIONS
12 x 12 in. (30.5 x 30.5 cm)
↓PRINCIPAL TYPE
Akzidenz Grotesk
↓CONCEPT
After the spectacular production
of the Mozart trilogy by Teodor
Currentzis, we started with the
artwork for "Le Sacre du Printemps"
by Stravinsky. For the design of the
vinyl, we used Op Art techniques and
transformed it into a typographic play.

↓DESIGN AND CREATIVE DIRECTION
Ross Clodfelter and Shane Cranford, Winston-Salem, North Carolina
↓URL
WeAreDevice.com
↓TWITTER
@wearedevice
↓DESIGN FIRM
Device Creative Collaborative
↓CLIENT
Sutler's Spirit Co.
↓PRINCIPAL TYPE
Custom
↓DIMENSIONS
3.75 x 10.5 in. (9.5 x 26.7 cm)
↓CONCEPT
Sutler's Spirit Co. produces spirits that blend audaciousness with subtlety—just like its historic namesakes. Sealed with old-school corks and topped with textured seals, the company's initial offering is housed in opaque ceramic bottles aglow with the luster of screen-printed text and rich with historicity. Inspired by the minimalist, inscrutable ceramic vessels used for housing gin during times past, and rebelling against the clear glass standards of today, these striking bottles are designed as modern-day objets d'art—as collectible as they are functional.

↓DESIGN AND CREATIVE
DIRECTION
Michael Hester, Oakland, California
↓ILLUSTRATOR
Dave Stevenson
↓PHOTOGRAPHER
StudioSchulz
↓URL
pavementsf.com
↓DESIGN STUDIO
Pavement
↓CLIENT
Cooperstown Distillery
↓PRINCIPAL TYPE
Nomah Script, Triumph, and custom
↓DIMENSIONS
5 x 11.5 x 2.5 in. (12.7 x 29.2 x 6.4 cm)
↓CONCEPT
When Cooperstown Distillery created
Cooper's Classic, it was deemed
the finest, smoothest whiskey to
come from their distinctive line of
handcrafted, artisanal spirits. The
branding of this whiskey also needed
to reflect the company's deep
appreciation for American history
and more than a passing admiration
for a local boy made good: author
James Fenimore Cooper. The name
pays homage to the author, while the
gold embossed lettering, deep indigo
blue background, and classic design
on each individually numbered bottle
speak to American craftsmanship at
its highest levels. This is the debut of
a new American classic.

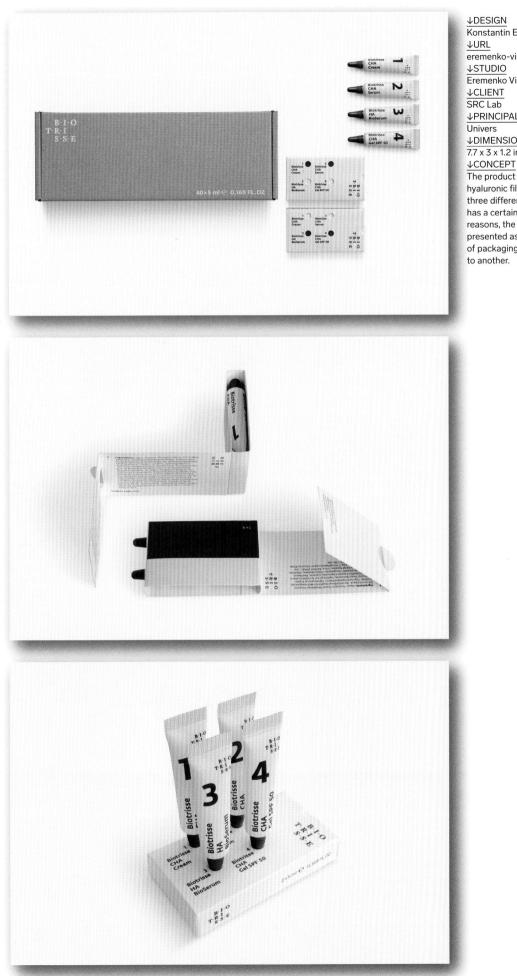

↓DESIGN
Konstantin Eremenko, Moscow
↓URL
eremenko-vis.com
↓STUDIO
Eremenko Visual Communication
↓CLIENT
SRC Lab
↓PRINCIPAL TYPE
Univers
↓DIMENSIONS
7.7 x 3 x 1.2 in. (19.5 x 7.5 x 3 cm)
↓CONCEPT
The product line of intradermal hyaluronic fillers by SRC consists of three different positions. Each of them has a certain density. For marketing reasons, the brand should be presented as a real physical sequence of packaging continually passing one to another.

↓DESIGN
Augustus Cook, New York
↓DESIGN DIRECTION
Daniel D'Arcy and Paul Sieka
↓EXECUTIVE CREATIVE DIRECTOR
Tosh Hall°
↓MANAGING DIRECTOR
Sara Hyman
↓COPYWRITER
Jen Chandler
↓PHOTOGRAPHER
Martin Wonnacott
↓TYPOGRAPHY
Ian Brignell
↓ACCOUNT MANAGERS
Phil Buhagiar and Josh Griffin
↓URL
jkrglobal.com
↓DESIGN AGENCY
Jones Knowles Ritchie
↓CLIENT
Budweiser
↓PRINCIPAL TYPE
The Budweiser Script
↓DIMENSIONS
12 fl. oz.
↓CONCEPT
There are few brands that conjure
up an image of Americana quite like
Budweiser. And summer 2016 was
the most American summer ever: the
buildup to a presidential election,
human achievement redefined at the
Olympics in Rio, and the U.S. National
Soccer Team winning the hearts
of the nation at the Copa America
Centennial. It was a time when our
national identity was debated, re-
evaluated, and celebrated. Ultimately,
the America packaging was about
making an impossible-to-ignore
statement: to literally hold America in
your hand.

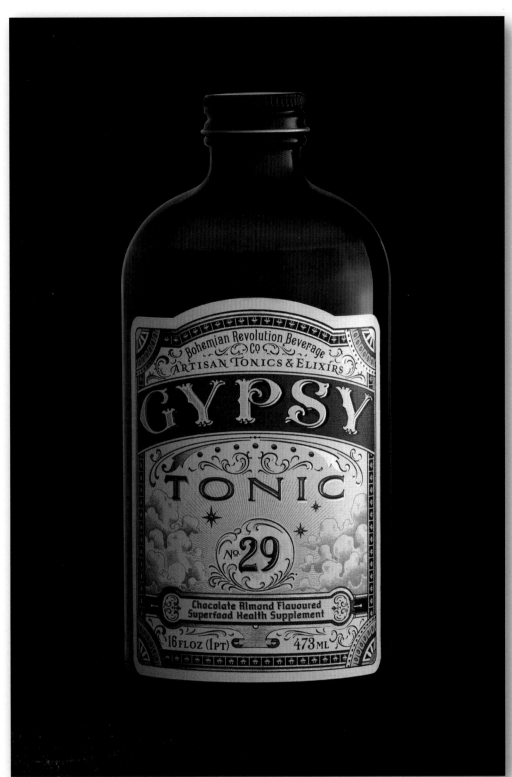

↓DESIGN, ART DIRECTION,
ILLUSTRATION, AND LETTERING
Tom Lane, Liverpool
↓URL
gingermonkeydesign.com
↓TWITTER
@gingermonkey_tl
↓CLIENT
Brandon Johnson—Bohemian
Revolution Beverage Company
↓PRINCIPAL TYPE
Custom
↓DIMENSIONS
3.2 x 3.9 in. (8.1 x 10 cm)
↓CONCEPT
Brandon Johnson, founder of the
Bohemian Revolution Beverage
Company, tasked me with bringing to
life his new health food drink Gypsy
Tonic. He had a vision—it was to make
the package label feel at home with
the 1800s apothecary scene while
keeping a modern edge. The artwork
was designed by hand in the initial
phase to help draw out an authentic
handmade quality. It was then
redrawn digitally in order to make it
easier to manage for print.

↓DESIGN
David Heasty and Stefanie Weigler,
Brooklyn
↓URL
triborodesign.com
↓DESIGN FIRM
Triboro
↓PRINCIPAL TYPE
Custom
↓DIMENSIONS
45 x 58 in. (114.3 x 147.3 cm)
↓CONCEPT
Our fascination with the New York
City subway began when we moved
to Brooklyn sixteen years ago. Our
first attempt to design a map for the
system, in 2010, became the One-
Color Subway Map. The Wrong Color
Subway Map is the next evolutionary
leap. One color has expanded into
multitudes—and they are all totally
wrong. Subway lines have traded
their familiar shades for vibrant
alternatives. All elements of the map
have been created from scratch with
an eye toward information hierarchy
and visual harmony. The map includes
bespoke typefaces created in
collaboration with Kevin Dresser.

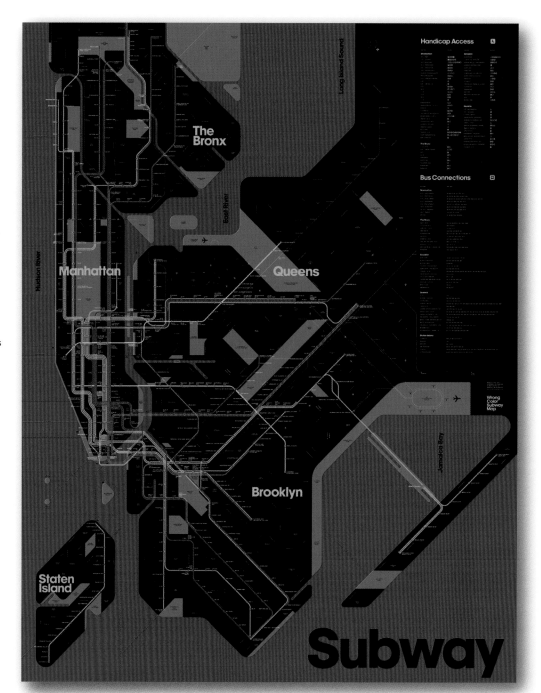

↓DESIGN
Fidel Pena, Toronto
↓CREATIVE DIRECTION
Claire Dawson and Fidel Pena
↓URL
underlinestudio.com
↓DESIGN FIRM
Underline Studio
↓CLIENT
Advertising & Design Club of Canada
↓PRINCIPAL TYPE
Druk and NB International
↓DIMENSIONS
Main Poster: 19.7 x 27. in. (50 x 70 cm)
Series Posters: 15.75 x 19.7 in. (40 x 50 cm)
↓CONCEPT
The ADCC (Advertising & Design Club of Canada) hosted Design New York in Toronto in November 2016. Guest speaker and curator Paula Scher°, creative director at Pentagram New York, curated the work from six of New York's top studios. Underline Studio designed a campaign to promote the event that included a logo, online advertising, and posters. Exploring the work of the six studios, Underline developed a typographic campaign that represents New York as a condensed, crazy city full of energy and elegance.

↓DESIGN
Joshua Hardisty, Minneapolis
↓CHIEF EXECUTIVE OFFICER
Krista Carroll
↓EXECUTIVE CREATIVE DIRECTOR
Jason Strong
↓ACCOUNT EXECUTIVE
Heather M. Bonn Tomas
↓WRITER
Jeremy Carroll
↓PRINTER
Burlesque Design
↓URL
latitudeelevates.com
↓TWITTER
@LatitudeForGood
↓AGENCY
Latitude
↓CLIENT
Latitude Realty
↓PRINCIPAL TYPE
Andes and Sentinel
↓DIMENSIONS
11 x 17 in. (27.9 x 43.2 cm)
↓CONCEPT
Latitude Realty is a full-service real estate firm that invests fifty percent of its profits back into the communities it serves locally or around the world chosen by the buyer or seller. To communicate this impact, we designed a screen-printed poster that was beautiful enough to hang at home and inspiring enough to help us spread the word. The custom, multicolored, geometric typeface brought our brand campaign to life, while the playful composition of symbols signified our investment efforts. Each poster was embossed with a label showing the number of homes sold and what we've invested in to date.

↓DESIGN
Sascha Lobe° and Sven Thiery,
Stuttgart
↓URL
l2m3.com
↓STUDIO
L2M3 Kommunikationsdesign GmbH
↓CLIENT
Werkbundarchiv—Museum der Dinge,
Berlin
↓PRINCIPAL TYPE
Folio BQ and custom
↓DIMENSIONS
35.2 x 50.4 in. (89.5 x 128 cm)
↓CONCEPT
This is a poster for an exhibition on
material education recounting the
story of learning with, about, and
through materials. Letters of different
shapes are arranged like items in
an object lesson box, which is the
centerpiece of the exhibition.

↓DESIGN
Lucas Blat, Anna Bühler, Stephanie Hamelin, Nina Odzinieks, Pit Stenkhoff, and Katerina Trakakis, Berlin
↓URL
neuegestaltung.de
↓DESIGN FIRM
Neue Gestaltung GmbH
↓CLIENT
Staatstheater Mainz GmbH
↓PRINCIPAL TYPE
Suisse Works, Suisse Int'l, and handwritten fonts by Neue Gestaltung
↓DIMENSIONS
33.1 x 46.8 in. (84.1 x 118.9 cm)
↓CONCEPT
In a marked departure from convention, a wide range of striking illustrative and photographic techniques and typography are employed to create a series shaped by its bold use of an unusually broad palette of visuals. Specifically designed to raise people's awareness of the artistic richness offered by a multi-genre repertory theater, every poster aims to embrace a given production's particular flair and focus, with only the theater's characteristic star logo referencing the series' origin.

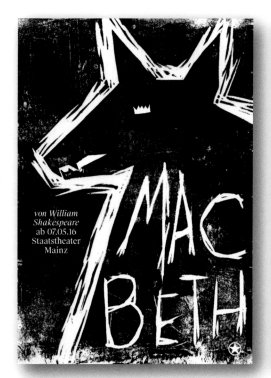

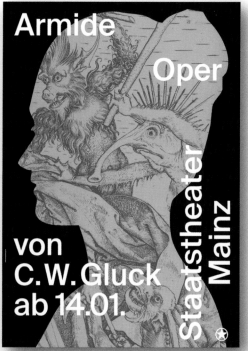

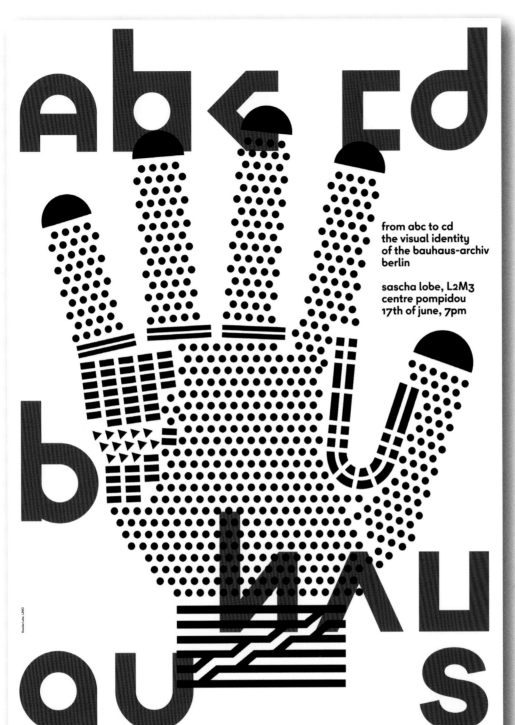

from abc to cd
the visual identity
of the bauhaus-archiv
berlin

sascha lobe, L2M3
centre pompidou
17th of june, 7pm

↓DESIGN
Sascha Lobe°, Stuttgart
↓URL
l2m3.com
↓STUDIO
L2M3 Kommunikationsdesign GmbH
↓CLIENT
Centre Pompidou
↓PRINCIPAL TYPE
Bauhaus Glyphs and Bayer Next
↓DIMENSIONS
33.1 x 46.8 in. (84.1 x 118.9 cm)
↓CONCEPT
This poster announces a lecture
held by Sascha Lobe at the Centre
Pompidou about the visual identity of
the Bauhaus Archive Berlin, which he
created in 2014. The artwork depicts
in a placative scheme the subjects
of identity, designing with grids, and
solid craftsmanship.

↓CREATIVE DIRECTION
AND LETTERING
Angelos Ntinas, Thessaloniki,
Macedonia, Greece
↓COPYWRITER
George Mantzouranedes
↓URL
fotone.gr/anxel.gr
↓TWITTER
@AngelosNtinas
↓DESIGN FIRM
Fotone
↓CLIENT
Taratsa International Film Festival
(taratsaiff.com)
↓PRINCIPAL TYPE
Custom (numbers), Fedra,
and Gotham
↓DIMENSIONS
19.6 x 27.5 in. (50 x 70 cm)
↓CONCEPT
The Taratsa IFF poster series
was designed as a part of a visual
system in which typography takes
the spotlight. The posters feature
bespoke numbering, as well as
bespoke typography in the main
poster (lettering with a great height
symbolizes the rooftops that the
festival takes place under). The visual
identity is designed to evoke interest
and bring out the elegance and
prestige of the festival.

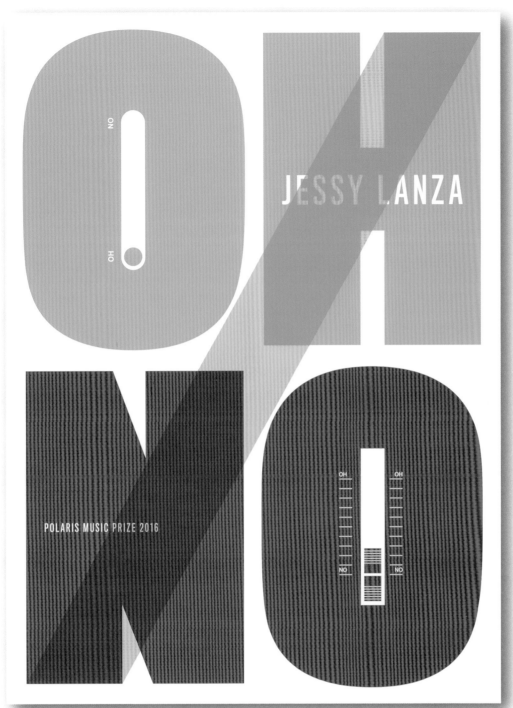

↓DESIGN AND
CREATIVE DIRECTION
Stéphane Monnet, Toronto
↓SILKSCREEN PRINTER
Kid Icarus
↓URL
monnet.ca
↓DESIGN FIRM
Monnet Design
↓CLIENT
Polaris Music Prize
↓PRINCIPAL TYPE
Titling Gothic
↓DIMENSIONS
17.75 x 24 in. (45 x 61 cm)
↓CONCEPT
The poster celebrates the Jessy
Lanza album *Oh No*, one of the ten
albums shortlisted for the 2016
Polaris Music Prize. Within the type,
we incorporated switches inspired by
those found on the Roland SH-101, a
synthesizer used to create the album's
unique sound.

↓DESIGN
Niklaus Troxler°, Willisau, Switzerland
↓STUDIO
Niklaus Troxler Design
↓CLIENT
bau 4, Altbüron
↓PRINCIPAL TYPE
Custom
↓DIMENSIONS
35.4 x 50.4 in. (90 x 128 cm)
↓CONCEPT
This is a visualization of the
improvisation "just with lines."

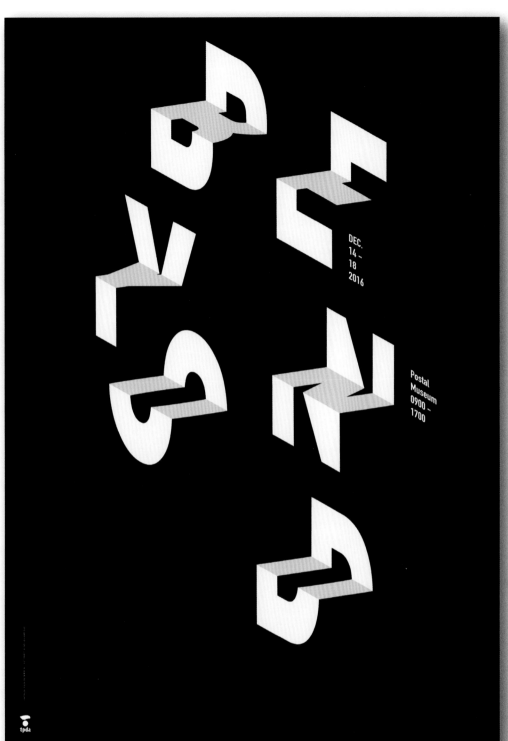

↓DESIGNER AND PROFESSOR
Chun-liang Leo Lin, Taipei
↓DESIGN FIRM
Leo Lin Design/NTNU
↓CLIENT
Taiwan Poster Design Association
↓PRINCIPAL TYPE
Custom
↓DIMENSIONS
27.6 x 39.4 in. (70 x 100 cm)
↓CONCEPT
This was designed for the annual topic
of TPDA, "Beyond." The image of a
ladder is represented with type, which
indicates being more progressive
than yesterday. "Beyond" is stable
progress, one step at a time.

DEC.
14 –
18
2016

Postal
Museum
0900 –
1700

tpda

↓DESIGN
Mark Fox and Angie Wang,
San Francisco
↓DESIGN FIRM
Design is Play
↓URL
designisplay.com
↓TWITTER
@DesignisPlay
↓PRINCIPAL TYPE
Oblong
↓DIMENSIONS
18.75 x 22.5 in. (47.6 x 57.2 cm)

↓COMMENT
The judging for this competition took place the weekend after
the U.S. presidential inauguration, the same weekend the nation
was dealing with the fallout from the immigration ban that had
just been enacted. Because of this context, and because of the
thoughtful execution of this poster, it provoked a conversation
unlike any other entry in the competition. Additionally, it
demonstrated that typography can (and should) extend beyond
formal and aesthetic considerations and can very powerfully
communicate the spirit of its content, even if that purpose is to
agitate and make a political statement.
Spencer Charles

↓DESIGNER STATEMENT
Trump 14K Gold-Plated and Trump 24K Gold-Plated are
unauthorized presidential campaign posters we designed for
Donald J. Trump as an exercise in free speech. Four gold, rotating
letter Ts suggest qualities projected by Trump, among them
success, wealth, and revolutionary (i.e., impolitic) speech.
The counter-form suggests a conflicting narrative, however:
namely, that Donald Trump's careless and divisive rhetoric is
creating negative spaces in the fabric of American society.
These spaces—fracture lines, really—snake through the design's
square silhouette to reveal a swastika. And while the swastika is
historically a symbol of dynamism and cyclical renewal associated
with the sun, in this context it evokes hate speech and nationalist
demagoguery. Since the election, we have been selling our
remaining posters to raise money for the ACLU and Planned
Parenthood.

↓DESIGN
Sven Lindhorst-Emme°, Berlin
↓URL
lindhorst-emme.de
↓STUDIO
studio lindhorst-emme
↓CLIENT
blankposter
↓PRINCIPAL TYPE
Wilhelm Klingspor Gotisch and
custom based on Akzidenz Grotesk
↓DIMENSIONS
33.1 x 46.8 in. (84.1 x 118.9 cm)
↓CONCEPT
For the topic of an exhibition about
the decay of the German language, I
used an old quotation from Goethe in
the center surrounded by a sentence
with the same meaning in ordinary
youth language. I also used a metallic-
bronze color mixed with brown to get
a color that looked a bit more like scat
because this word—Scheiße (scat)—
is mainly used in the surrounding
youth language text.

TEMPOGARAGE

Ausstellung 29. 7. — 14. 8.

Vernissage am 29. 7.
ab 18 Uhr
Finissage am 14. 8.
ab 14 Uhr

Tempogarage
Fischerhäuserstrasse 61
8200 Schaffhausen

zwisc⊢enraum

zwischenraum-sh.ch

↓DESIGN
Sven Lindhorst-Emme°, Berlin
↓URL
lindhorst-emme.de
↓STUDIO
studio lindhorst-emme
↓CLIENT
zwischenraum-sh, Schaffhausen,
Switzerland
↓PRINCIPAL TYPE
ITC Avant Garde Gothic Bold and
Eurostile Bold Extended
↓DIMENSIONS
33.1 x 46.8 in. (84.1 x 118.9 cm)
↓CONCEPT
For the Tempogarage 2 poster for a
group exhibition, I wanted to use the
effect of dimensionality. Paper sheets
lay over one another; together they
build up the big "2" and the title. It is
like a puzzle, and it fits only if you have
all the papers—like at the exhibition,
it was important to have all the artists
there to complete the exhibition in
its best way. For the poster, I made
analog tests at a wall and I scanned
many different paper structures to
use them.

↓ART DIRECTION
Ran Zheng, New York
↓URL
ranzhengdesign.com
↓DESIGN FIRM
Ran Design
↓CLIENT
Shenzhen Poster Festival
↓PRINCIPAL TYPE
DIN and Times New Roman
↓DIMENSIONS
24 x 33 in. (61 x 83.8 cm)
↓CONCEPT
This project addresses environmental
issues in Beijing.

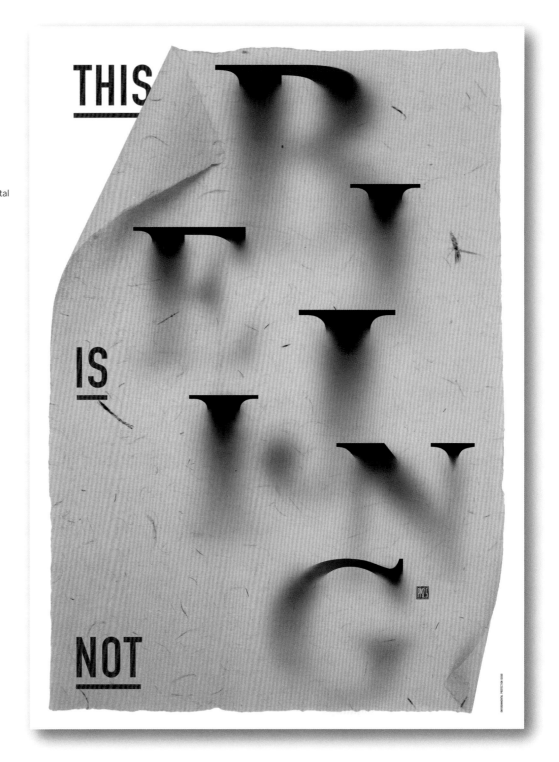

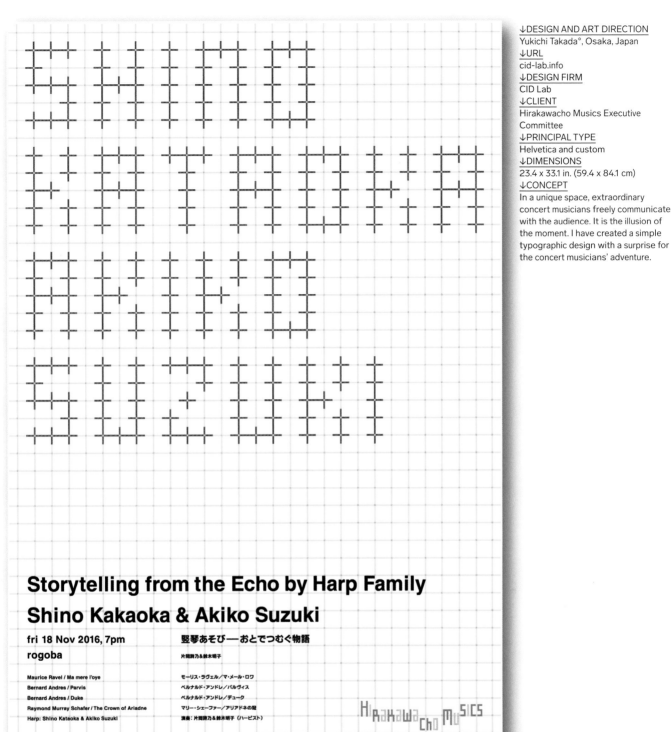

Storytelling from the Echo by Harp Family
Shino Kakaoka & Akiko Suzuki

fri 18 Nov 2016, 7pm
rogoba

竪琴あそび──おとでつむぐ物語

片岡詩乃＆鈴木明子

Maurice Ravel / Ma mere l'oye
Bernard Andres / Parvis
Bernard Andres / Duke
Raymond Murray Schafer / The Crown of Ariadne
Harp: Shino Kataoka & Akiko Suzuki

モーリス・ラヴェル／マ・メール・ロワ
ベルナルド・アンドレ／パルヴィス
ベルナルド・アンドレ／デューク
マリー・シェーファー／アリアドネの冠
演奏：片岡詩乃＆鈴木明子（ハーピスト）

Hirakawacho Musics

↓DESIGN AND ART DIRECTION
Yukichi Takada°, Osaka, Japan
↓URL
cid-lab.info
↓DESIGN FIRM
CID Lab
↓CLIENT
Hirakawacho Musics Executive
Committee
↓PRINCIPAL TYPE
Helvetica and custom
↓DIMENSIONS
23.4 x 33.1 in. (59.4 x 84.1 cm)
↓CONCEPT
In a unique space, extraordinary
concert musicians freely communicate
with the audience. It is the illusion of
the moment. I have created a simple
typographic design with a surprise for
the concert musicians' adventure.

↓DESIGN
Fons Hickmann°, Raúl Kokott,
and Björn Wolf, Berlin
↓ART AND CREATIVE DIRECTION
Fons Hickmann°, Raúl Kokott,
and Björn Wolf, Berlin
↓URL
m23.de
↓TWITTER
@fonshickmannm23
↓STUDIO
Fons Hickmann m23, Berlin
↓CLIENT
Biennale Wiesbaden
↓PRINCIPAL TYPE
Dynamo and Favorit
↓DIMENSIONS
23.6 x 33.1 in. (60 x 84 cm)
↓CONCEPT
“This is not Europe” is the new motto
of the Theater Biennale initiated by
Staatstheater Wiesbaden. For the
corporate design, we smeared golden
paint on all of their media, such as
posters, books, and digital media. The
long tradition of the festival is getting
lost in a changing Europe that is
longing for its former glory and ideals.

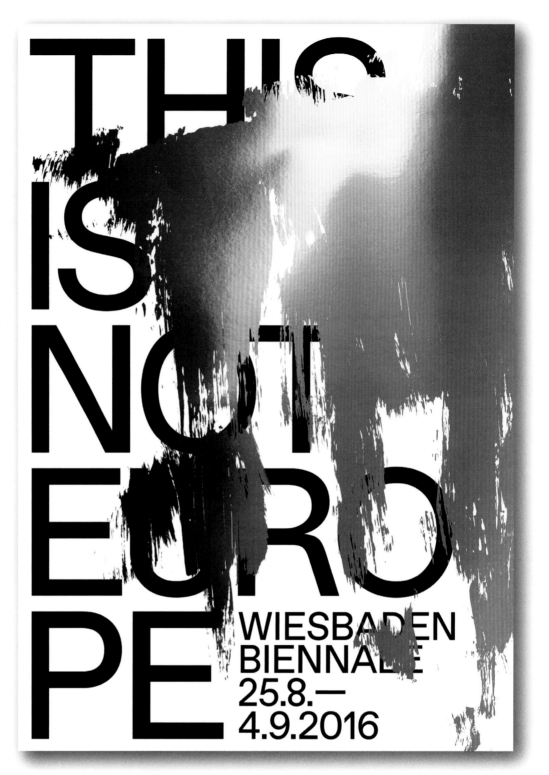

Tot està per fer

Valèncía, Capital de la República

(1936-37)

Centre Cultural La Nau
Universitat de València
Sala Acadèmia
Del 7 de novembre de 2016
al 19 de febrer de 2017

↓DESIGN
Ibán Ramón, Valencia
↓URL
ibanramon.com
↓TWITTER
@ibanramon
↓STUDIO
Ibán Ramón, diseñador
↓CLIENT
Universitat de Valencia
↓PRINCIPAL TYPE
Handmade
↓DIMENSIONS
26.7 x 38.6 in. (68 x 98 cm)
↓CONCEPT
This is a poster for the exhibition that contains photographs, posters, and documents from the period in which Valencia was the seat of the government of the Republic during the civil war (1936–37). Among the materials, elements of anarchist propaganda abound with illustrations and typographic signs of Art Deco style. The proposal alludes to the signs used by anarchist unions of the time in their logos and posters, in which simple geometric forms replace elements of typography.

↓DESIGN
Vincent Vrints, Amsterdam
↓ART DIRECTION
Liza Enebeis
↓URL
studiodumbar.com
↓TWITTER
@studiodumbar
↓STUDIO
Studio Dumbar
↓CLIENT
Amsterdam Sinfonietta
↓PRINCIPAL TYPE
Helvetica Neue
↓DIMENSIONS
33.1 x 46.8 in. (84.1 x 118.9 cm)
↓CONCEPT
We created a distinctly modern
identity driven by a bold logotype
and typographic palette, the
implementation of which remains
consistent across all communications.
Beyond these core elements, the
identity is free to evolve, with color
palettes and illustrations reflecting
the ensemble's diverse repertoire, as
well as the rich and varied nuances
of music in general. With each
poster responding graphically to the
performance's musical themes, this
award-winning series continues to
produce remarkable imagery while
retaining a signature style.

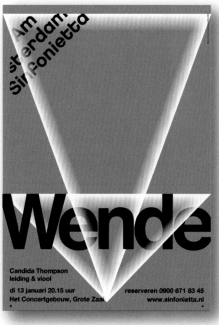

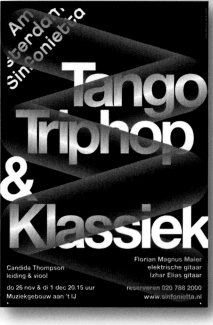

↓DESIGN
Zipeng Zhu, New York
↓ART DIRECTION
Jessica Walsh
↓CREATIVE DIRECTION
Stefan Sagmeister
↓3D MODELING
Liron Ashkenazi
↓URL
sagmeisterwalsh.com
↓TWITTER
@sagmeisterwalsh
↓DESIGN FIRM
Sagmeister & Walsh
↓CLIENT
Visionaire
↓PRINCIPAL TYPE
Custom
↓DIMENSIONS
25 x 39 in. (63.5 x 99.1 cm)
↓CONCEPT
We designed this "free" poster as part
of a poster issue for the legendary—
and usually very expensive—fashion
magazine *Visionaire* that was given
away for free at Art Basel, Miami.

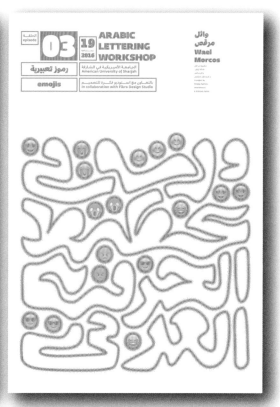

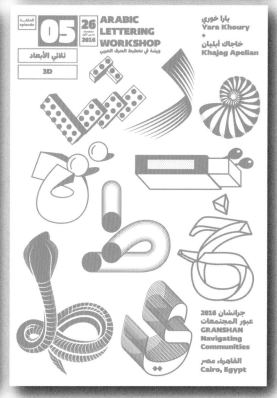

↓DESIGN
Khajag Apelian, Lara Balaa,
Yara Khoury, Wael Morcos°,
and Kristyan Sarkis,
Beirut, Lebanon, New York,
and Amsterdam
↓URLS
debakir.com, maajoun.com,
mohtaraf.com, waelmorcos.com,
and tptq-arabic.com
↓TWITTER
@debakir, @larabalaa, @yarakhoury,
@waelmorcos, @KristyanSarkis,
and @TPTQArabic
↓INSTAGRAM
@khajag, @maajounstudio,
@yarakhouryn, @waelmorcos,
and @kristyansarkis
maajoun.com
↓GRAPHIC DESIGN
Lara Balaa
↓URL
maajoun.com
↓TWITTER
@maajoun, @larabalaa
↓INSTAGRAM
@maajounstudio
↓EDUCATOR
Yara Khoury

↓COMMENT
Good typography will often bridge languages; great typography
can express and emote without the viewer even being able to
understand the letterforms. These posters for the Arabic Lettering
Workshop do just that.

Being from Argentina, I speak my native language and English.
I am constantly trying to work on this visual translation between
languages in my design and when I create type for the global
designer. I love these posters because they communicate a very
clear meaning and emotion without the viewer having to know
the language.

The variety of styles and the unique voice of each of the posters
in this series are impressive; to accomplish this with one spot color
is remarkable. The expressive variety of visuals, clearly unique voice
for each workshop, and incredible use of the page while keeping
the series contemporary and modern make this set of posters
my judge's choice.

These posters really do represent the best that typography
has to offer.
Alejandro Paul

↓DESIGNER STATEMENT
The Arabic Lettering Workshops teach the participants about
the expressive potential of Arabic script. We devised a series of
educational workshops to explore the relationship between the
shape of the word and its meaning. We introduced a different
subject every time keeping it thematically focused. The workshop
title is redesigned by the workshop leaders every time. The subject
of the poster has a constant structure where the details stack to the
sides leaving the center empty. While some participants are more
comfortable with drawing by hand, others prefer to sketch digitally,
but most of them are pleasantly surprised by how much there is to
learn about the script.

↓ART DIRECTION
Sha Feng, Florence
↓DESIGN FIRM
SoFeng Design Studio
↓CLIENT
Nanjing University of the Arts
↓PRINCIPAL TYPE
Custom
↓DIMENSIONS
27.6 x 39.4 in. (70 x 100 cm)
↓CONCEPT
The idea behind the poster is to
"bring salvation to all living things."

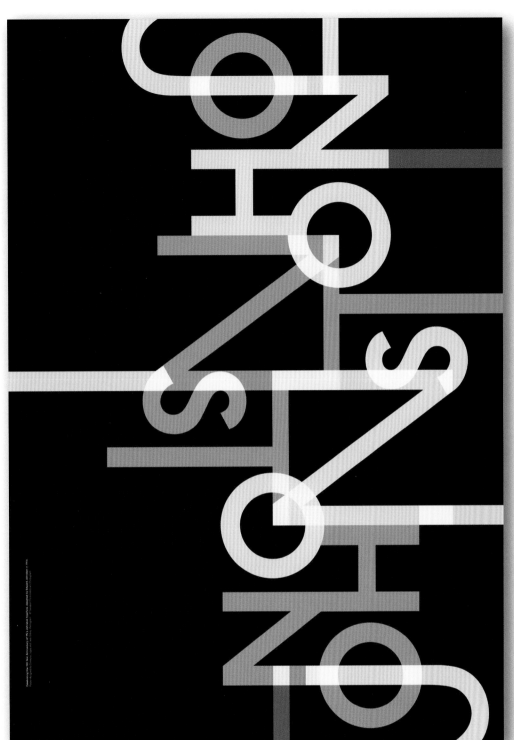

↓DESIGN
Jack Gilbey and Domenic Lippa°,
London
↓PARTNER
Domenic Lippa
↓DESIGN COMPANY
Pentagram Design
↓CLIENT
Transport for London
↓PRINCIPAL TYPE
New Johnston Book and New
Johnston Medium
↓DIMENSIONS
23.3 x 33.1 in. (59.4 x 84.1 cm)

↓CONCEPT
This is a poster designed to celebrate
a hundred years of the London
Underground's Johnston typeface,
referencing its ubiquity throughout
the network and the important role it
plays in helping passengers navigate
the transit system's lines
and intersections.

↓DESIGN AND ART DIRECTION
John Clark°, El Segundo, California
↓PROJECT COORDINATORS
Laurie Burruss, John Clark,
Haven Lin Kirk, and David Mayes
↓PHOTOGRAPHER
Donald Miller
↓URL
looking.la
↓DESIGN STUDIO
Looking
↓CLIENT
AIGA Los Angeles
↓PRINCIPAL TYPE
Haarlemmer Sans
↓DIMENSIONS
19 x 28 in. (48.3 x 71.1 cm)
↓CONCEPT
The In Type LA Event brings together
student/mentor participants from
ten of the region's design programs.
The intent of this event is to have
each participant create a typographic
poster that represents one of the
over 120 identified neighborhoods
of Los Angeles, essentially beginning
the creation of a Los Angeles
"typographic mosaic." This call-to-
participate poster was intended to
tease potential participants into
bringing their individual voices to
the definition of our typographic
culture. The poster calls for them to
complete the statement "In Type:
_____", with their own
neighborhood filling in the blank. The
result was, in fact, a highly expressive
representation of the very diverse
neighborhoods throughout the region:
affluent, poor, hip, and everyday.

↓DESIGN AND LETTERING
Stephen Nixon°, New York
↓CONSULTATION
Krissi Xenakis
↓URL
thundernixon.com
↓INSTAGRAM
@thundernixon
↓PRINCIPAL TYPE
Handlettering
↓DIMENSIONS
11 x 14 in. (27.9 x 35.6 cm)
↓CONCEPT
I worked with design lead Krissi Xenakis to bring together creatives from the many different teams working in our office for an hour of enjoying beer and drawing letters. To promote this, I created three posters referencing the layout and lettering styles from the signage of midcentury lounges and dive bars. To emphasize the subject of the event, I used pencil and marker and created three distinct variations along the central theme, with a wide variety of letterforms. Additionally, layering lettering and calligraphy allowed me to create a promotional GIF by mixing and matching the layers.

↓DESIGN AND ART DIRECTION
Masayuki Terashima, Sapporo, Japan
↓URL
tera-d.net
↓DESIGN FIRM
Terashima Design Co.
↓PRINCIPAL TYPE
Engraver
↓DIMENSIONS
28.7 x 40.6 in. (72.8 x 103 cm)
↓CONCEPT
This poster announces an
international conference on the role
of the sea in Japanese religious
history, held at the University of
California, Santa Barbara, in June
2016. I designed the characters for
"Japan" (Nihon) based on a traditional
pattern representing waves.

SUZIE KUROIWA with JAZZ

↓DESIGN AND ART DIRECTION
Masayuki Terashima, Sapporo, Japan
↓URL
tera-d.net
↓DESIGN FIRM
Terashima Design Co.
↓CLIENT
Day by Day
↓PRINCIPAL TYPE
Custom
↓DIMENSIONS
28.7 x 40.6 in. (72.8 x 103 cm)
↓CONCEPT
This is a poster for jazz singer Suzie Kuroiwa. Using a typography based on musical notes, I tried to create an unprecedented design.

↓DESIGN
Gemma O'Brien°, Sydney
↓URL
gemmaobrien.com
↓TWITTER
@mrseaves
↓CLIENT
Adobe Creative Cloud
↓PRINCIPAL TYPE
Custom
↓DIMENSIONS
16.5 x 23.4 in. (42 x 59.4 cm)
↓CONCEPT
Adobe Creative Cloud invited a group
of designers to create an artwork
using the iPad Pro, Apple Pencil, and
Adobe Mobile Apps. The group was
taken to the music festival Outside
Lands in San Francisco as a starting
point for the piece. My alphabet
poster was inspired by the beautiful
surroundings of Golden Gate Park:
the mysterious winding pines, the
scattered baby daisies, and the ever-
present Karl the Fog.

↓DESIGN
2xGoldstein+Fronczek,
Rheinstetten, Germany
↓URL
2xgoldstein.de
↓CLIENT
INMM—Institut für Musik und
Musikerziehung Darmstadt
↓PRINCIPAL TYPE
Compacta and custom
↓DIMENSIONS
27.6 x 39.4 in. (70 x 100 cm)
↓CONCEPT
The design creates motion based on
the title BODY SOUNDS. This motion
was not generated with a digital filter
but on a copier—so to say, in the
old-fashioned way. The design refers
to the word BODY in the title as well
as to the subtitle: Aspects of the
Physical in New Music.

↓DESIGN LEAD
Erik Berger Vaage, San Francisco
↓CCO
Matt Luckhurst
↓DIRECTOR OF OPERATIONS
Joanna Hobson
SENIOR PRODUCER
Ashley Kasten
↓STRATEGIST
Anna Sternoff
↓URL
wearecollins.com
↓TWITTER
@wearecollins
↓AGENCY
Collins
↓CLIENT
Summit Public Schools
↓PRINCIPAL TYPE
Summit Display
↓DIMENSIONS
24 x 36 in. (61 x 91 cm)
↓CONCEPT
Our assignment was to develop
a new brand identity for Summit
Public Schools. The organization is
experiencing tremendous growth, and
it was imperative to create a mark that
reflected their values of personalized
learning and individualized education.
The identity is anchored in a typeface
created in collaboration with students
from Summit schools. The system
responds to the variety of schools
and students through color and an
avatar tool that allows every student
and faculty member at Summit to
create their own character. The brand
is being adapted and implemented
across six schools and multiple digital
platforms.

↓DESIGN
Qiushuo Li, New York
↓URL
sva.edu
↓INSTRUCTOR
Gae Savannah
↓SCHOOL
School of Visual Arts, New York°
↓PRINCIPAL TYPE
Custom font inspired by
ACME Studios
↓CONCEPT
This was a self-initiated project. The
project is inspired by ACME Studios,
applying the color in its logo and
geometric shapes. The collage of each
layer creates rhythm and movement in
the composition.

↓DESIGN
Fenghe Luo, New York
↓INSTRUCTOR
Steven Heller
↓SCHOOL
School of Visual Arts°, New York
↓PRINCIPAL TYPE
Colt Soft
↓CONCEPT
WTF NYC is a souvenir brand that captures the true personality of New York City. The visual of the brand intends to present the quirkiness, the humor, and the quality of the products. Instead of creating a bold visual, I adopt a more elegant approach to the visual language, in contrast to the intense graphics and the aggressive brand name, which also emphasizes the sarcastic character of the brand itself.

↓DESIGN
Heeyoung Jun, New York
↓INSTRUCTOR
Eric Baker
↓SCHOOL
School of Visual Arts, New York°

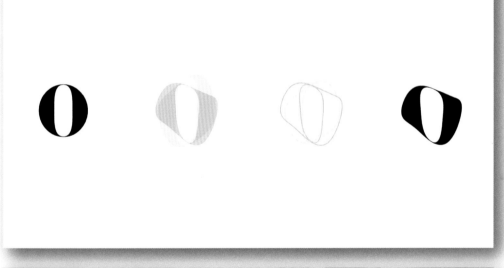

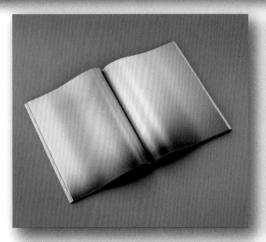

↓DESIGN
Liron Ashkenazi, New York
↓URL
Lirona.me
↓INSTRUCTORS
Tim Goodman and Jessica Walsh
SCHOOL
School of Visual Arts, New York°
↓PRINCIPAL TYPE
Abril Fatface, Blanch, Bodoni,
Circular, and Sofia
↓DIMENSIONS
8.3 x 5.8 in. (21 x 14.8 cm)
↓CONCEPT
This is a typographic zine featuring
Gertrude Stein's poem "As a Wife Has
a Cow: A Love Story." Stein's poem
self-consciously messes up/messes
with language, and the zine matches
the concept with a structural form.
Not only is the "meaning" behind the
poem obscured by the primary layer of
Stein's playfulness with language, but
the fundamental presentation of the
typography mirrors this action. The
viewer may read the typography in the
zine, but it would be very difficult to
follow through and the viewer is likely
to be distracted by the intensity of the
typography and get immersed in it.

↓DESIGN
Miles Barretto, New York
↓URL
milesbarretto.com/non-place
↓TWITTER
@milesbarretto
↓INSTRUCTOR
E Roon Kang
SCHOOL
Parsons the New School of Design
↓PRINCIPAL TYPE
Helvetica Neue
↓DIMENSIONS
4.5 x 6.9 in. (11.4 x 17.4 cm)
↓CONCEPT
In an era of fast-paced globalization
and corporate internationalization,
there has been a rise in the number of
sterile, homogeneous spaces—which
anthropologist Marc Auge refers to
as "non-places." These spaces are
defined by their lack of individual
identity, interaction, and history. To
further investigate this topic, I created
booklets with stickers based on
common visual elements associated
with three non-places in New York:
ATM vestibules, supermarkets, and
parking lots. The final outcome is
a response to the lack of identity,
history, and interaction within these
non-places by recontextualizing their
common visual associations.

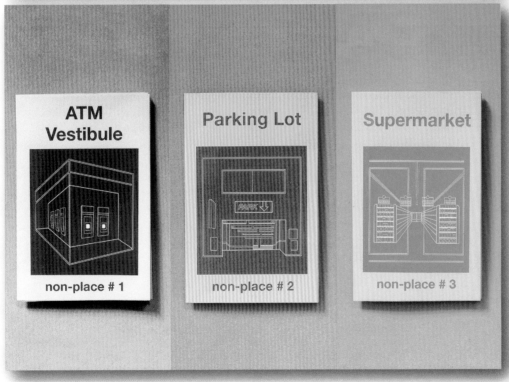

JOSE NEVES X SVA PRESENTS
THE SMOKE PRINTER

↓FIRST PLACE STUDENT

↓DESIGN
Jose Maria Almeida Neves, New York
↓PHOTOGRAPHY
Leonid Urossov
↓INSTRUCTOR
Nigel Sielegar
↓SCHOOL
School of Visual Arts°,
Advertising BFA
↓PRINCIPAL TYPE
Bebas Font and SmokePrinterType
↓CONCEPT
This was a project for my
Communication Graphic Design
class: To Design in Temporal Context.
The challenge was to experiment
with media that are affected by
time to defy the conventional notion
that graphic design is a constant
replication of flat surfaces. Often,
graphic design can be designed
to incorporate a certain degree of
interactivity and/or transformation
that is affected by time while still
maintaining the main function as a
communication tool. My idea was
an ashtray that could create, with
smoke, a message for smokers to see
after they put out their cigarettes—
something profoundly captivating.

↓SECOND PLACE STUDENT

↓DESIGN
Miriam Rieger, Munich
↓PROFESSORS
Sybille Schmitz and Tobias Wühr
↓SCHOOL
Mediadesign Hochschule München
↓PRINCIPAL TYPE
Suisse International Book, Medium,
and Bold
↓DIMENSIONS
8.3 x 11.8 in. (21.2 x 30 cm)
↓CONCEPT
Each human being perceives different
sensory impressions simultaneously.
But what happens if one sense
is stimulated and, in addition to
the normal perception, the brain
automatically adds another sense?
Only a few people have this special
kind of perception—it's called
synesthesia. The first book of the
work shows actual scientific findings
and thematic relations in art and
design. A second book contains
an experimental poster series, in
which synesthesia becomes the
metaphorical stylistic device. The aim
is the pulsating of the senses and
the activation of the mind in order to
reach a new level of perception.

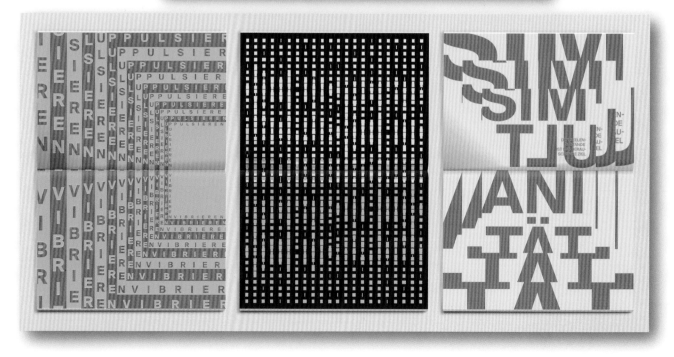

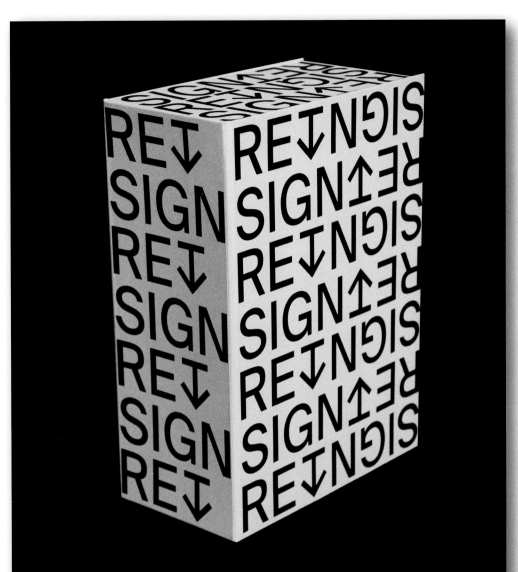

↓THIRD PLACE STUDENT

↓DESIGN
Kevin Kremer, Munich
↓URL
kevinkremer.design
↓PROFESSOR
Sybille Schmitz
↓SCHOOL
Mediadesign Hochschule München
↓PRINCIPAL TYPE
Suisse Int'l
↓DIMENSIONS
6.1 x 8.2 in. (15.5 x 21 cm)
↓CONCEPT
"RE SIGN" creates a redraft of
typographic shapes. It describes
the systematic deconstruction of
present-day letter shapes and their
subsequent reconstruction in order
to explore new ways of expressing
alphabetic characters.

↓DESIGN
Qiushuo Li, New York
↓URL
sva.edu
↓INSTRUCTOR
Kevin Brainard
↓SCHOOL
School of Visual Arts, New York°
↓PRINCIPAL TYPE
Custom
↓DIMENSIONS
Various
↓CONCEPT
Fisher Wave is a retailing-based
surfing club located in Australia. It
is owned by the Fisher couple, who
are devoted to enhancing the value
of surfing culture. The design was
inspired by the glamour of waves.
The letters in Fisher and Wave flux
into one another, creating a gesture
of shifting and a form of consistency.
As a result, the logo, which can be
applied by stretching, pressing, and
combining, is as fluid as water.

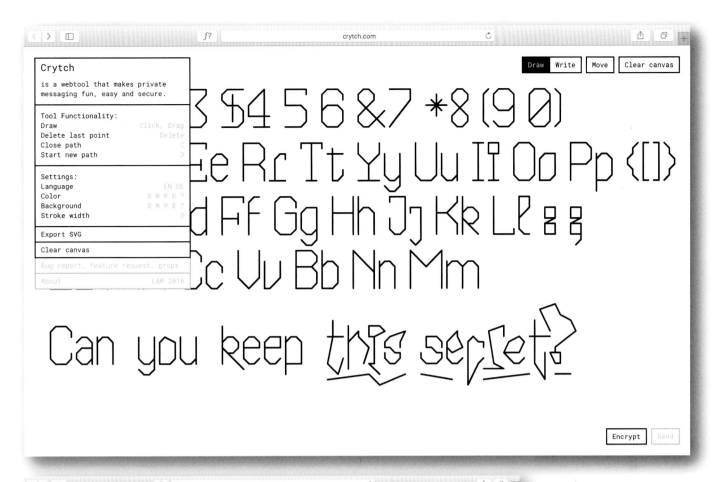

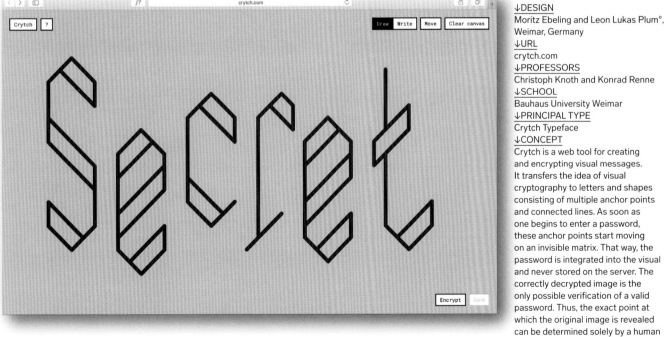

↓DESIGN
Moritz Ebeling and Leon Lukas Plum°,
Weimar, Germany
↓URL
crytch.com
↓PROFESSORS
Christoph Knoth and Konrad Renne
↓SCHOOL
Bauhaus University Weimar
↓PRINCIPAL TYPE
Crytch Typeface
↓CONCEPT
Crytch is a web tool for creating
and encrypting visual messages.
It transfers the idea of visual
cryptography to letters and shapes
consisting of multiple anchor points
and connected lines. As soon as
one begins to enter a password,
these anchor points start moving
on an invisible matrix. That way, the
password is integrated into the visual
and never stored on the server. The
correctly decrypted image is the
only possible verification of a valid
password. Thus, the exact point at
which the original image is revealed
can be determined solely by a human
observer.

↓DESIGN AND ANIMATION
Anne Zeygerman, New York
↓INSTRUCTOR
Ori Kleiner
↓SCHOOL
School of Visual Arts, New York°
↓PRINCIPAL TYPE
Aver, Bodidota, Futura, Apple
Garamond, and Leitura

↓CONCEPT
This was a school project for an After
Effects Pro class. I used a minimalist
approach consisting of a limited
color palette with strong yet delicate
graphic cues to communicate the
subject matter to the viewer. I used
hairlines as a digital paintbrush in
order to highlight each individual
segment, thus helping the eyes follow
each movement of the animation.

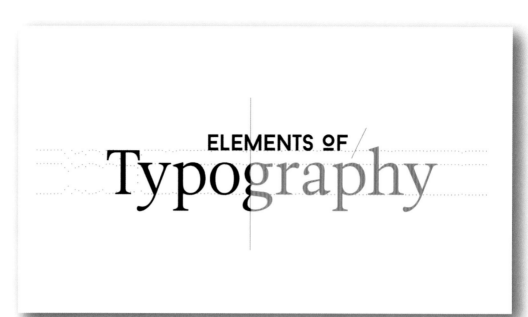

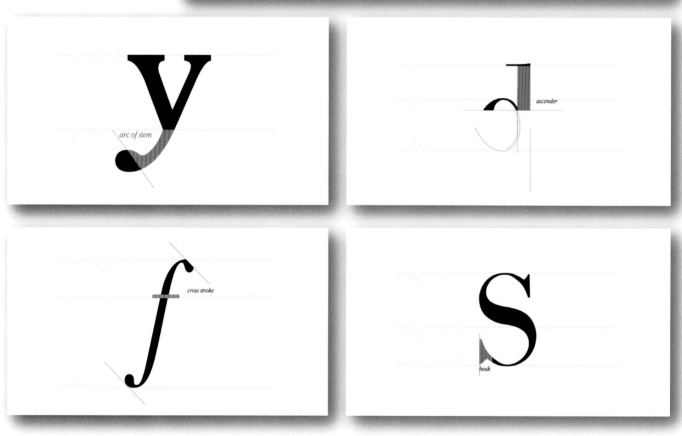

↓DESIGN
Petra Dočekalová, Prague
↓URL
petra-d.com
↓TWITTER
@docekalovapetra
↓PROFESSOR
Karel Haloun
↓SCHOOL
Academy of Arts, Architecture
and Design
↓PRINCIPAL TYPE
Narrow script written with a flat
marker; Italic written with a flat
marker; casual handwritten script;
and Monolinear script
↓DIMENSIONS
27.8 x 37.4 in. (70 x 100 cm)
↓CONCEPT
This is a sign-painting project dealing
with the Czechoslovak calligraphy and
new lettering forms.

↓DESIGN AND ANIMATION
Lemon Sanuk Kim, New York
↓URL
sanuk.kim
↓BEHANCE
behance.net/lemonsanukkim
↓MUSIC
"Dokidoki (kidkanevil Remix)" by
Laura J. Martin, First Word Records
↓SCHOOL
School of Visual Arts, New York°
↓PRINCIPAL TYPE
Druk
↓CONCEPT
In this self-promotional video, the
concept of a "jack-of-all-trades"
multidisciplinary designer is
explored through the combination
of typography, photography, 3D,
illustration, and moving images.

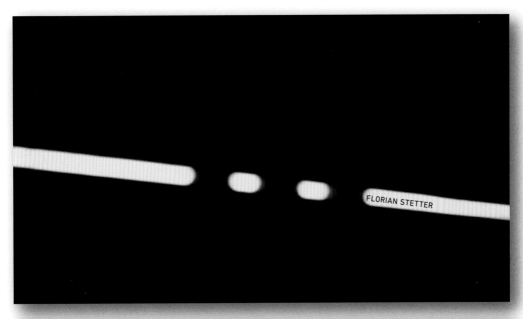

↓DESIGN
Yeryung Ko, New York
↓INSTRUCTOR
Ori Kleiner
↓SCHOOL
School of Visual Arts, New York°
↓PRINCIPAL TYPE
DIN Next Pro Italic
and DIN Next Pro Regular
↓CONCEPT
The film takes place at the end of
World War II at the concentration
camp Buchenwald, where a three-
year-old boy is smuggled into the
camp in a suitcase by his dad. The title
sequence is meant to portray the little
boy's vantage point as he is being
locked in the suitcase and able to see
only through a thin hole.

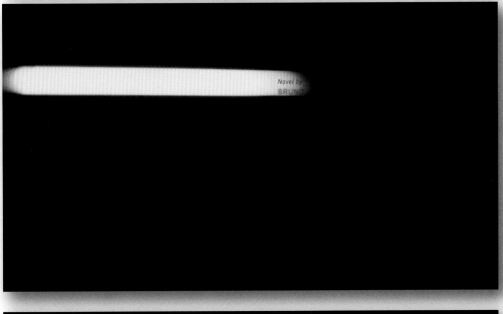

↓DESIGN
Tzu-Yi, Su, Kaohsiung City, Taiwan
↓INSTRUCTOR
Shin Ling-Hung
↓SCHOOL
National Taiwan Normal University
Department of Design
↓PRINCIPAL TYPE
世界之聲
↓CONCEPT
Such gradual changes are like doors.
We should open them one after
another and dismantle them to see
our selves that have not been seen.
We can find out the selves that cannot
be shaken by the environment and
inner selves in their simplest forms.

↓DESIGN
Huan Nguyen, Long Beach, California
↓URL
huan-nguyen.com
↓TWITTER
@Huan_Nguyen
↓INSTRUCTOR
Andrew Byrom
↓SCHOOL
California State University,
Long Beach
↓PRINCIPAL TYPE
Copper Display
↓DIMENSIONS
5 x 7 in. (12.7 x 17.8 cm)

↓CONCEPT
This project was done for an
Advanced Type class at California
State University, Long Beach. The
objective was to design an original
set of display numbers and create
them in three-dimensional form.
The numbers play with the retro
look of Art Deco and the dramatic
composition of '80s neon aesthetic.
Each was painstakingly bent (by
hand) from a single continuous copper
wire, polished, then coated with clear
enamel to keep it from being oxidized.

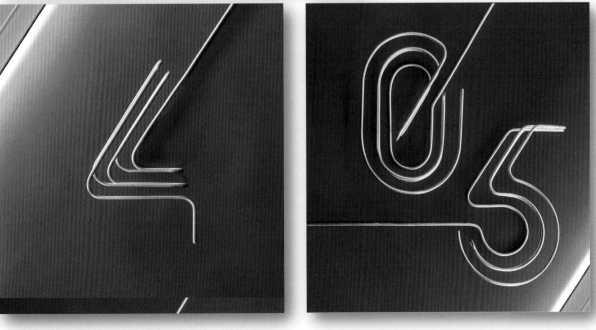

↓DESIGNER AND ASSISTANT
PROFESSOR
Riem Ibrahim, Dubai,
↓URL
mobius-studio.com
↓SCHOOL AND STUDIO
American University of Sharjah +
Mobius Design Studio
↓PRINCIPAL TYPE
Based on Akzidenz Grotesk
↓CONCEPT
The project challenges the familiar
static nature of typefaces and
questions the potential expansion of
communication through the possible
transformation of letterforms over
time. It looks into the formal qualities
of the Latin letters and explores how
their possible change over time may
bear and/or expand meaning and how
the interaction between a written
word and the motion of its letterforms
influences the viewers' reading and
interpretation. The investigation
is therefore both a formal and a
conceptual experimentation of and
with letterforms through different
manual processes over time. A
prototype tool was created to help
preview the four kinetic typefaces that
resulted from this process.

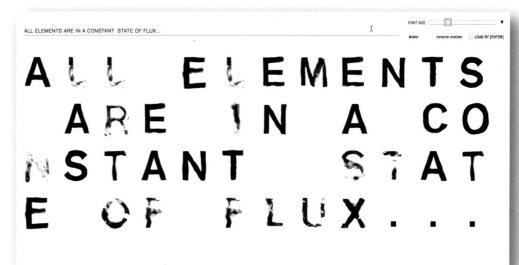

↓DESIGN
Chris Allen, Dennis Kung,
Robyn Makinson, Blake Rutledge,
and Lauren Van Aswegen,
New York
↓DESIGN DIRECTION
Lucas Camargo
↓CREATIVE DIRECTION
Abe Baginsky, Bastien Baumann,
and Chris Rowson
↓CHIEF CREATIVE OFFICERS
Corinna Falusi and Alfonso Marian
↓ARTIST IN RESIDENCE
Justin Au and Weston Doty
↓APPLICATION DEVELOPER
Joseph Laquinte
↓CREATIVE TECHNOLOGY
DIRECTOR
Kaare Wesnaes
↓URL
typevoice.net
↓AGENCY
Ogilvy New York
↓CLIENT
The Webby Awards, NYC
↓PRINCIPAL TYPE
Custom
↓CONCEPT
To celebrate The Webby Awards
People's Voice twentieth anniversary,
we created Typevoice, the first
fontshop that allows anyone to
create their own typeface using their
voice. Scream, shout, or sing and
Typevoice will generate a customized
font based on your unique sound
wave. We created an algorithm that
measured pitch, volume, and time
lapsed, allowing each letter to react in
real time (using two independent SVG
animation timelines). Share animated
GIFs of your font or even download
the typeface of your whole alphabet
to use in your design projects. Visit
typevoice.net for the full experience.

↓ART DIRECTION
Kengo Tatsuzawa, Tokyo
↓URL
future.h-mp-recruit.jp
↓STUDIO
Hakuhodo Inc./Hakuhodo DY Media
Partners Inc.
↓PRINCIPAL TYPE
Helvetica and custom
↓CONCEPT
What we set as a goal of this project
is to make visitors feel how work in
the advertising trade is changing
dramatically and imagine it as their
future, which is amplified boundlessly.
It was realized by visualizing many
predictions in public with dynamic
motions of WebGL. Categories of
those predictions are sectioned by
different colors so that visitors can
expect what is going on in their future
by seeing the contrast of black and
vivid colors on the back.

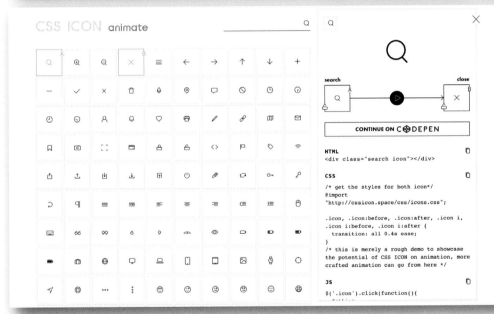

↓DESIGN
Wenting Zhang°, New York
↓URL
github.com/wentin
↓TWITTER
@DesignJokes
↓PRINCIPAL TYPE
Futura PT

↓CONCEPT
Can graphics such as letterforms
and icons be completely designed
with code, without the help of design
software? CSS ICON is a set of icons
and letterforms drawn, animated, and
made interactive by pure CSS code.
By using code as a design tool, it frees
the project from the limitations of
design software. Instead, the project
embraces CSS's limitations and
tries to push the boundary of web
standards. CSS ICON is also an open-
sourced library consisting of 512 icons
and letterforms and a free learning
platform for anyone who wants to
learn CSS.

↓DESIGN
Grant Gold, Chris Ladd, Aura Seltzer,
and Bethany Snyder , New York
↓DIGITAL DESIGN
The New York Times
↓CREATIVE DIRECTOR
FOR NYT COOKING
Barbara de Wilde
↓PRINCIPAL TYPE
NYT Cheltenham, NYT Franklin, and
NYT Karnak
↓DIMENSIONS
Desktop, iPad, and iPhone
↓CONCEPT
NYT Cooking is part of *The New
York Times*. NYT Cooking is a cross-
platform, searchable database of
recipes published by *The New York
Times*. In addition to recipes, NYT
Cooking is a tool that helps users save
and organize their recipes from *The
Times* as well as other sources into a
digital recipe box.

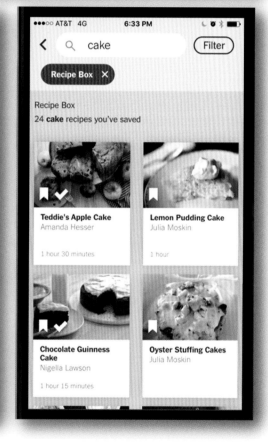

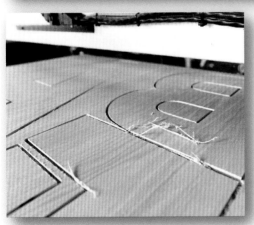

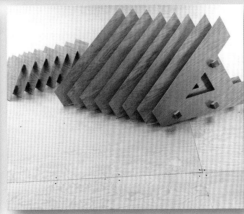

↓ARTIST AND DESIGN
Ben Johnston, Toronto
↓CREATIVE DIRECTION
Chris Unwin
↓PRODUCER
Olga Kisza
↓PARTNER MANAGER
Denym Dupont
↓URL
benjohnston.ca
↓DESIGN FIRM
Ben Johnston Design
↓CLIENT
Free
↓DIMENSIONS
62 x 59.3 x 14 in.
(150.5 x 157.5 x 35.5 cm)
↓CONCEPT
Free is a Toronto-based Creator
Studio designed to empower creative
entrepreneurs. Their studio, Free
Space, acts as a hub for a community
of photographers, filmmakers, and
influencers. As part of Canon's title
sponsorship of Free's production
studio Canon Creator Lab, Free
tasked designer and art director
Ben Johnston with developing a
custom typographical installation as
Canon's signage in the production
area. Johnston took tonal references
from Free Space's minimalist palette,
utilizing laser cuts of raw wood to
bring his typographic sculpture to life
in all its Instagram-friendly glory.

↓DESIGN
Dejan Djuric and Jeff Watkins, Toronto
↓ART DIRECTION
Dejan Djuric, Lisa Greenberg, and Jeff
Watkins
↓CREATIVE DIRECTION
Lisa Greenberg
↓CHIEF CREATIVE OFFICER
Judy John
↓GROUP CREATIVE DIRECTOR
Ryan Crouchman
↓PHOTOGRAPHER
Arash Moallemi, Fuze Reps
↓PRINTING COMPANY
Webnews Printing Inc.
↓URL
leoburnett.ca
↓TWITTER
@LeoBurnettTor
↓AGENCY
Leo Burnett, Toronto
↓CLIENT
Smith Restaurant + Bar, Renda Abdo
↓PRINCIPAL TYPE
Chronicle Display and Hudson
↓DIMENSIONS
22.75 x 34 in. (57.8 x 86.4 cm)
↓CONCEPT
Smith is a restaurant that creates
a unique experience for every new
and returning visitor. They have an
ever-changing menu and a collection
of plates and cutlery gathered from all
over the world. The odds of eating off
the same plate twice are pretty slim.
This inspired us to design a dinner
menu series that, when combined,
became as eclectic as the plates
you ate from. The new brunch menu
showcased on the cover brunch items
in their raw form and revealed the
delicious possibilities on the inside.

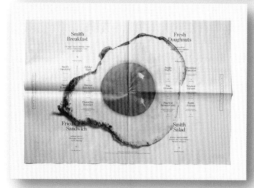

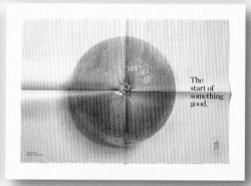

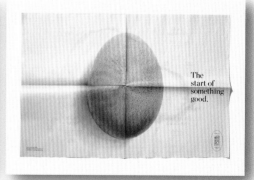

↓DESIGN DIRECTION
Sarah Newitt, London
↓URL
kikuobata.com
↓DESIGN STUDIO
Kiku Obata & Company
↓CLIENT
Jazz St. Louis
↓PRINCIPAL TYPE
Bee Four, Century Schoolbook,
Futura, and Venus
↓DIMENSIONS
Various
↓CONCEPT
Jazz St. Louis is a nonprofit
organization whose mission is to
advance the art of jazz through live
performance and education. We
were asked to design the invite for
their 2016 fundraising gala, "New
York, New York." Our design is a
contemporary take on the vernacular
of classic jazz graphics, using a mix
of typefaces and modernized with a
bright palette of neons. The intent was
to create a sophisticated yet fun set
of pieces that appeals to a cultured
audience without falling into the trap
of clichéd jazz graphics.

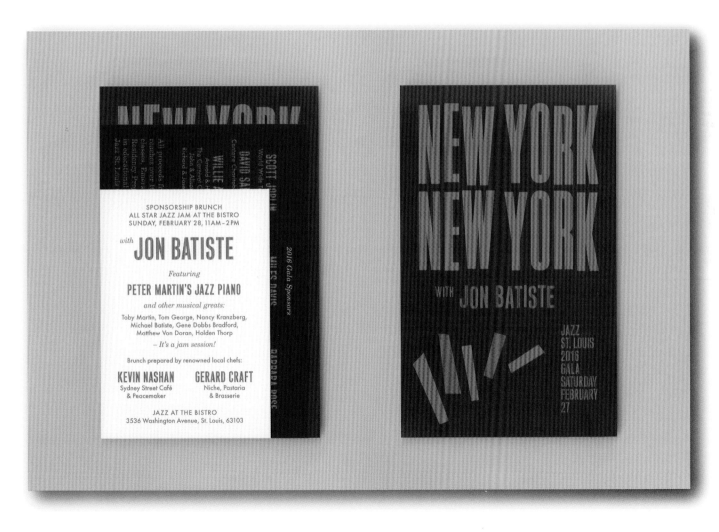

↓DESIGN
Tim Belonax, San Francisco
↓TWITTER
@timbelonax
↓CLIENT
San Francisco Center for the Book
↓PRINCIPAL TYPE
Ambroise, DIN, Futura, Georgia,
Tahoma, Tangent, and Univers
↓DIMENSIONS
12 x 19 in. (30.5 x 48.3 cm)
↓CONCEPT
"The Punctuation Party "is San
Francisco Center for the Book's
annual fundraiser. Each year a new
piece of punctuation is used as the
"grand marshal" of the event. For
2016, the exclamation point was
given that distinction. I designed a
flexible identity for the event and its
printed materials, which were meant
to communicate the excitement and
festive attitude of the party.

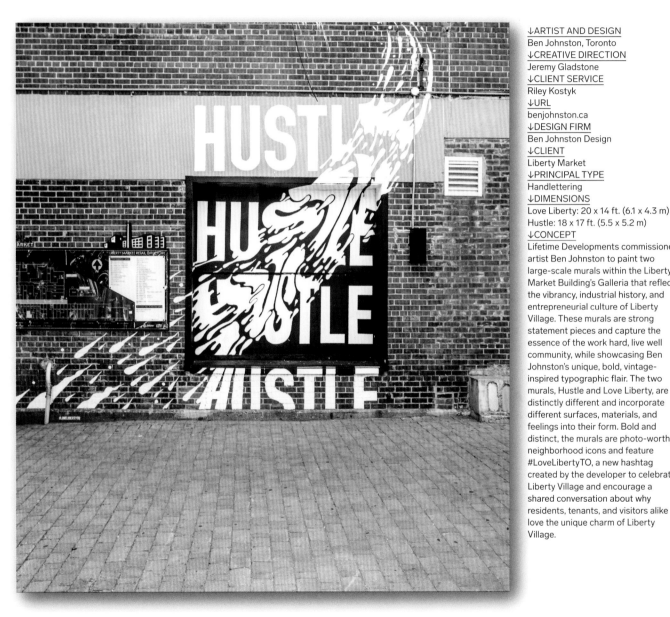

↓ARTIST AND DESIGN
Ben Johnston, Toronto
↓CREATIVE DIRECTION
Jeremy Gladstone
↓CLIENT SERVICE
Riley Kostyk
↓URL
benjohnston.ca
↓DESIGN FIRM
Ben Johnston Design
↓CLIENT
Liberty Market
↓PRINCIPAL TYPE
Handlettering
↓DIMENSIONS
Love Liberty: 20 x 14 ft. (6.1 x 4.3 m);
Hustle: 18 x 17 ft. (5.5 x 5.2 m)
↓CONCEPT
Lifetime Developments commissioned
artist Ben Johnston to paint two
large-scale murals within the Liberty
Market Building's Galleria that reflect
the vibrancy, industrial history, and
entrepreneurial culture of Liberty
Village. These murals are strong
statement pieces and capture the
essence of the work hard, live well
community, while showcasing Ben
Johnston's unique, bold, vintage-
inspired typographic flair. The two
murals, Hustle and Love Liberty, are
distinctly different and incorporate
different surfaces, materials, and
feelings into their form. Bold and
distinct, the murals are photo-worthy
neighborhood icons and feature
#LoveLibertyTO, a new hashtag
created by the developer to celebrate
Liberty Village and encourage a
shared conversation about why
residents, tenants, and visitors alike
love the unique charm of Liberty
Village.

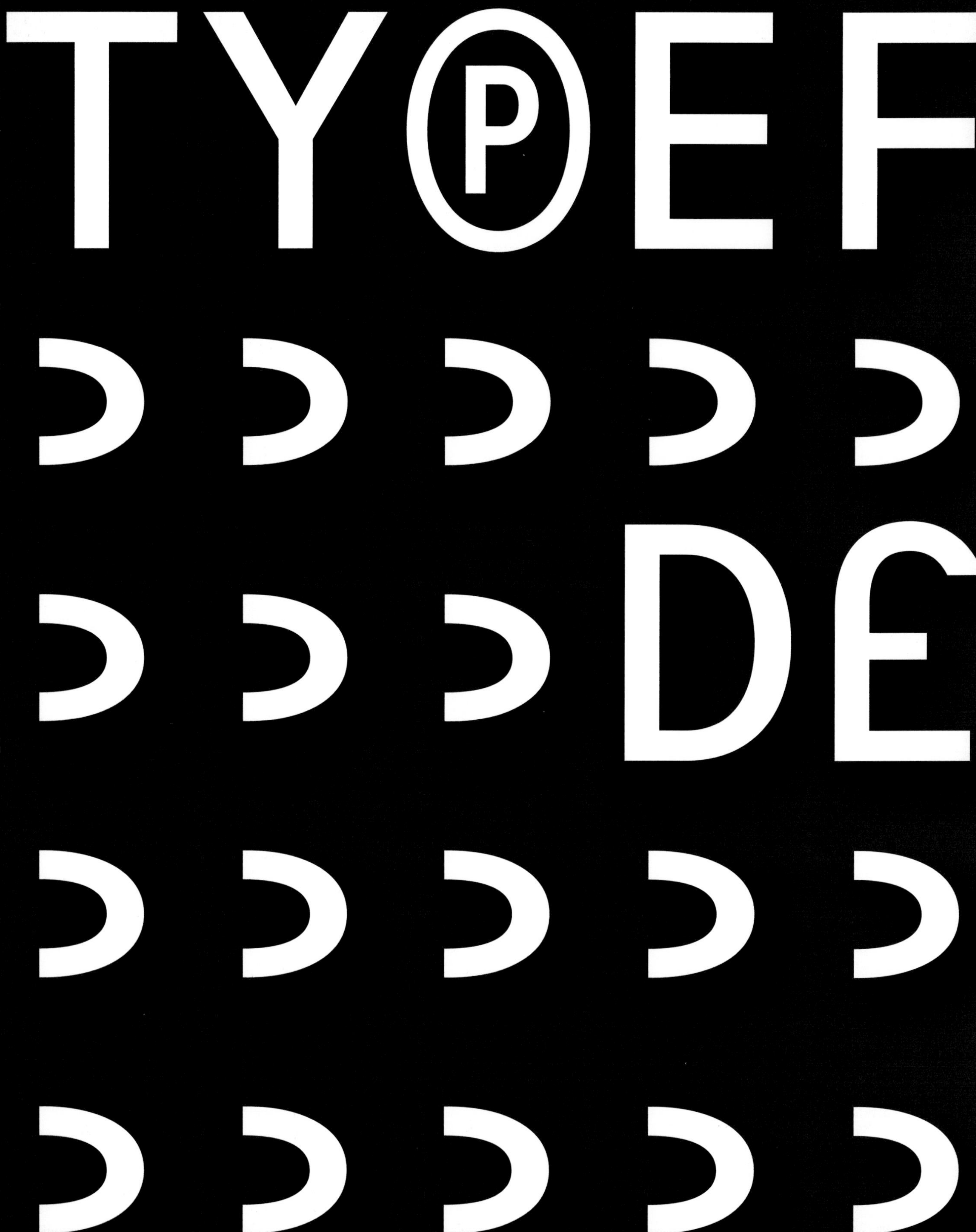
TYPEF
DE

ACE

SIGN

2017

→DAN
RHATIGAN

This year was the first time I watched the proceedings of the TDC typeface competition firsthand. After observing the scrutiny of the judges, and listening to their debates about this year's entries and the field in general, I am more impressed than ever with the competition winners. Recognition comes after a long process of comparison, debate, and nitpicking, and it doesn't come easily.

The entries selected this year rose to the top after a day during which our judging panel worked through 230 typeface families submitted from over 40 countries, with commentary from external advisors when necessary. Each judge brought their unique perspective to the table, and when there was disagreement about a design, the judges had some rousing discussions to try and build consensus.

Gathering a panel of judges with diverse and critical opinions is part of the challenge of a competition chair, and I was so pleased by what each of this year's judges contributed to the discussions. Alice, Berton, Brendán, and Ksenya come from different countries, each with different professional paths and areas of expertise, but they share a seriousness of purpose when it comes to typography. They were committed to looking for skill and creativity: not just pretty typefaces, but ones that push the boundaries of the craft a little further outward.

This year we saw even more new designs for typefaces supporting more writing systems from around the world. The growing interest in type development for more languages hints at a promising future for designers and readers who haven't yet been spoiled by a dizzying array of type choices for their own scripts. Appropriately, Maxim Zhukov's support for our judges become even more essential. As more non-Latin entries arrive each year, he gathers more feedback from a team of specialists and native speakers. His thick dossier of commentary for our judges is a now a vital part of the overall process, a detail that shows that the competition is committed to excellence not just of form but also of function.

Our judges and advisors help the Type Directors Club recognize work that pushes the boundaries of our craft into ever newer territory, and we're VERY grateful.

¡KING KONG! The Movie

MOVIE MONSTER *(1933 film)*

KING KONG is a giant movie monster, resembling a colossal gorilla, that has appeared in various media since 1933.

The Giant Gorilla

The character first appeared in the 1933 film King Kong, which received universal acclaim upon its initial release and re-releases.

1933*

The character first appeared in the 1933 film King Kong, which received universal acclaim upon its initial release and re-releases. The film was remade in 1976 and once again in 2005.

The character has become one of the world's most famous movie icons, having inspired countless sequels, remakes, spin-offs, imitators, parodies, cartoons, books, comics, video games, theme park rides, and even a stage play.[2]

Monday.5
26 - CREWS & BIKES   NUMBERS - LETTERS - FOR THE DISPLAY N.2 $45
$95/SEW:
MC. LORIMER/SUMMER ¡OK! 36
NEW.$73:
SMALL CAPS (REG)- WORKING AT 12 POINTS - LET'S MAKE A TEST WITH THE DISPLAY   THIS CURRENCY RATES TABLE LETS YOU COMPARE AN AMOUNT
NEW YORK- ¿WHEN? - ¡SEEMS SOON!

N.Y.

The earliest historical description of Long Island, in Daniel Denton's "A Brief Description of New York, formerly called *New Amsterdam*," published in London in 1670, remarks that "the greatest part of the Island is very full of timber, as Oaks, white and red, Walnut-trees, Chestnut-trees, which yield stores of Mast, etc.

—WOLVES, FOXES & RACCOONS (NY).

"For wild beast there is Deer, Bear, Wolves, Foxes, Raccoons, Otters, Musquashes, and Skunks. Wild fowl there is a great store of, as Turkeys, Heath-hens, Quails, Partridges, Pigeons, Cranes, Geese of several sorts, Brants, Widgeons, Teal, and divers others. Upon the south side of Long Island in the winter lie store of Whales and Grampusses, which the inhabitants begin with small boats to make a trade, catching to their no small benefit. Also, an innumerable multitude of seals, which make an excellent oyle; they lie all the winter upon some broken Marshes and Beaches or bars of sand before mentioned, and might be easily got were there some skilful men would undertake it."

↓TYPEFACE
Salvaje
↓DESIGN
Cristian Vargas, Brooklyn
↓URL
typozon.com
↓TWITTER
@Typozon
↓FOUNDRY
Typozon
↓CLIENT
Type and Media, Royal Academy
of Art, The Hague
↓MEMBERS OF TYPEFACE FAMILY/
SYSTEM
Salvaje Display No.1, Salvaje Display
No.2, Salvaje Text, and Salvaje Text
Italic

↓COMMENT

Salvaje is a compelling typeface. What I like most about it is how it explores the boundaries of contrast (the relationship of thick vs. thin) and how this contrast works with its different styles as a family.

Salvaje was inspired by the "Birds of Paradise," and its display styles use an unconventional letterform model to support its exuberant details. Its display styles are reverse-contrast, which means that the thicks and thins of its letterforms are switched— opposite to what you'd find in a traditional typeface. The way Salvaje pairs this model with swooping terminals and serifs is a skillful execution of concept and form. The display's italics takes this model a step further by literally twisting its weight around itself, pushing it into new, unexpected territory.

As striking as Salvaje's display styles are, what impressed me most about this typeface is its range as a family. Its display and text occupy opposite ends of a spectrum but maintain a consistent relationship to each other. In many typefaces, their display counterparts can easily overshadow text styles, but in this case I find both to have an equal amount of character and charm.

Opposite to the display, Salvaje's text styles have more of a conventional contrast. Despite this difference, Salvaje's text and display still feel related, with its text referencing just the right amount of its display's expressiveness. The text is interesting not so much in its individual details but more in its overall texture: nuanced, consistent in color, and distinct without being distracting to read. Technical details aside, Salvaje is just a beautiful typeface. It shows what Peter Verheul, a former teacher of mine, would call "a love of form." I could tell there was a lot of sketching, iteration, and testing. There are no wasted gestures but also no missed opportunities—an overall solid typeface from a practiced hand.
Berton Hasebe

↓DESIGNER STATEMENT

Salvaje is a typeface family consisting of four styles, two for display and two more for text. The inspiration for this typeface comes from the "Birds of Paradise," which are birds that live in only one part of the world (New Guinea/Australia). The appearance of these birds is extra particular because they have evolved in a visual way: with big feathers, bright colors, and extreme shape transformation. As with the birds, this typeface emulates the same behavior; there is a lower-contrast text version (more neutral, quiet, and readable) and a high-contrast display version (more dynamic, loud, and extreme).

↓TYPEFACE
Lingering Fonts
↓DESIGN
Zhang Weimin, Shenzhen, China
↓URL
zwm98.com
↓CLIENT
WESUN Culture Communication
↓CONCEPT
Lingering Fonts takes inspiration
from the great Chinese poet Li Bai's
poem "Sauvignon Blanc" (everlasting
longing). The strokes wind, hug,
cuddle, and sometimes stretch.

↓COMMENT
If life is divided into a binary of elements that are hard vs. soft, most
everything in my quotidian experience fits in the former: all sounds,
East Coast nature, West Coast nature, logic, architecture, and every
typeface I've ever drawn. Weimin's glyphs end up as a balance on the
other side, amid tactile visceral pleasure—a realm of soft nostalgia,
melty Mickey T-shirts, skin, fur, gallium, and modeled virtual reality.

The design judging process is an experience of observing
elements fall apart under closer scrutiny. Was the full typeface
shown? Did we spot a maladapted kern pair? Does the specimen
wording pantomime the banal? Weimin's constructions, however,
refuse to stay within the constraints of established expectation.
Instead, the typeface calls for our suspension of disbelief. The glyphs
draw us into their reality—seducing toward a pop cultural pinprick of
wrangling gesticulation, into a happy place of pure emotion and raw
movement.

If you're intending to purchase, this is not a font that'll stay limited
to the pages or posters it starts out on. Anticipate it to pivot at night,
to finger-tut up the walls and across the ceiling of your bedroom, to
swell to the size of a gallery before it leaps out its window, only to
shrink back down to size and scatter about while giggling wildly.
Ksenya Samarskaya

Unmathematically *Supercarbonization*
Lighthousekeeper *Acquaintanceships*
Photomacrograph *Thermodynamical*
Quintessentialize *Demutualizations*

ȷ ABCDEFGHIJKL
MNOPQRSTUVW
XYZ & abcdefghijk
lmnopqrstuvwxyz
☛ 1234567890 ☚

AÀÁÂÃÄÅĀĂĄÆBCÇĆĈĊČDĎÐĐEÈÉÊËĒĔĖĘFGĜĞĠĢĜGHĤHIÌÍÎÏĨĪĬĮIJJĴKĶĸĹĻĽŁLL
ŁMNÑŃŅŇŊŇOÒÓÔÖÕŌŎŐQØŒPQRŔŘŖŖŜSŚŜŞŠŠŞŠŞSSBTŢŤŢŢŢTUÙÚÛÜŨŪŬŮŰŲVW
ẀẂŴẄXYÝŶŸYZŹŻŽ3ŠÐÞƏ‖AÀÁÂÃÄÅĀĂĄÆBCÇĆĈĊČDĎÐĐEÈÉÊËĒĔĖĘFGĜĞĠĢGHĤHI
ÌÍÎÏĨĪĬĮIJJĴKĶĸĹĻĽŁLLMNÑŃŅŇŊŇOÒÓÔÖÕŌŎŐQØŒPQRŔŘŖŖŜSŚŜŞŠŠŞŠŞSSBTŢŤŢŢTUÙÚÛ
ŨŪŬŮŰŲVWẀẂŴẄXYÝŶŸYZŹŻŽ3ŠÐÞƏ‖aàáâãäåāăąæbcçćĉċčdďđeèéêëēĕėęfgĝğġģĝgh
ħĥiìíîïĩīĭįiıjȷjĵkķĸĺļľłŀl·lmnñńņňŋňn'nŋoòóôöõōŏőǫøœpqrŕřŗŗŝsśŝşšşšịsßtţťţţtuùúûüũū
ůúųvwẁẃŵẅxyÿýŷÿyzźżž3šðþǝ‖bfffhhĥjkķĸĺ|l|ll'l·þ‖fbffffhfifjfkflftffbffhffiffjffkfflfftijíjŪŬ‖ǒ
ǒọ̣ǫǫ̂ǫ́ọ̀ȯȯ̃ȯ̈ộọ̈ǫ̂ọ̌ọ̃‖123456789012345678901234567890123456789⁰ ¹²³⁴⁵⁶⁷⁸⁹ ₁₂₃₄₅₆₇₈₉₀
/¼½¾⅓⅔⅛⅜⅝⅞⅐⅑⅒⅕⅖⅗⅘⅙⅚Y¹³⁸⁄₂₄₇ ‖.,:;…·!?_'"‹'"‚„‛'"*†‡°ªº&¶§¶※*©®℗™ℓℯ/\|¦‖----()[]{}‹›
«»@¡¿‖----()[]{}‹›«»@¡¿‖+-±÷×=<>¬~µπ#%‰$¢£¤¥€ƒ←↑→↓↖↗↘↙☛☜☝☞□■□◻▪

↓TYPEFACE
Nordvest
↓DESIGN
Nina Stössinger°, Brooklyn
↓URL
ninastoessinger.com
↓TWITTER
@ninastoessinger
↓FOUNDRY
Monokrom Type Foundry, Oslo,
Norway
monokrom.no/@monokromfonts
↓MEMBERS OF TYPEFACE FAMILY/
SYSTEM
Nordvest Regular, Nordvest Regular
Italic, Nordvest Medium, Nordvest
Medium Italic, Nordvest Bold,
Nordvest Bold Italic, Nordvest Black,
Nordvest Black Italic
↓CONCEPT
Nordvest is an uncommon serif text typeface whose horizontals are just slightly thicker than its verticals. This gentle reversal of the conventional weighting of thick and thin strokes started as a mistake and continued as an experiment in subtle rule breaking. It lends the typeface a unique voice and texture, causing lines of text to strongly band together. The regular weights have been carefully optimized to be readable first and interesting second, while the heaviest weights are best suited to eye-catching display use. This versatile family of eight styles thus aims to be useful, for instance, in editorial, branding, or packaging design. Nordvest started as a graduation project in the TypeMedia program at KABK The Hague and was published by Monokrom in 2016.

↓COMMENT
At the end of Pixar's movie *The Incredibles* there's a short called *Boundin'* by Bud Luckey. While the lead actor is a naked, high-steppin' lamb, the true stars are the banjo-plucking team of Bud Luckey and his animators. Bud and his team steal the show from the highly polished *Incredibles*—not for the short's storyline, characters, or cinematography, but for its pure simplicity ... the evident love of their craft and the fresh, unbounded joy of what the team was making.

Nordvest stood out among a field of exacting and finely tuned sans and serif specimen sheets by figuratively bounding off the table, singing, and dancing with its shy and honest pluck.

In a time of digital pretension, Nordvest is modest, unassuming, and authentic. To this judge, its imperfect perfection and humor set it apart from a field of worthy competitors. In Nordvest's roman form, one can see a hint of the Playbill tactile wood type of Western newsprint and the comedic genius of Mr. Magoo. In the italic form, Nordvest has an Eastern European '50s influence. And perhaps therein lies its appeal.

Nordvest harks back to an earlier era that is more "man" than machine and more wood than metal. Its creative roots lie in its soul, melody, and rhythm. From the serendipity and appreciation of its accidental flaws to its blue-collar mass appeal, Nordvest steps high but doesn't take itself too seriously.
Brendán Murphy

↓TYPEFACE
Qandus
↓ARABIC TYPEFACE DESIGN
Kristyan Sarkis, Lebanon and
Amsterdam
↓LATIN TYPEFACE DESIGN
Laura Meseguer, Barcelona
↓TIFINAGH TYPEFACE DESIGN
Juan Luis Blanco—Zumaia, Spain
↓CURATOR
Khatt Foundation khtt.net—
Amsterdam
↓TYPE FOUNDRIES
Multiscript Family: TPTQ Arabic
TPTQ-Arabic.com—The Netherlands
Latin: Type-Ø-Tones type-o-tones.
com—Spain
↓CONCEPT
Qandus is a multiscript typeface
system that explores a conceptual
relationship between three writing
systems: Arabic, Latin, and Tifinagh.
Although it started as an homage
to the work of brilliant calligrapher
Al-Qandusi, it expanded to become a
study of the unique mixture of Arabic
constructions (solid vs. fluid) in the
Maghribi calligraphic style, and an
exploration of how to disseminate
this feature of duality of forms into
the other two scripts. The concept
was to design three styles that go
beyond the difference in weight and
highlight the mixture of solid and fluid
forms differently depending on the
intended texture, overall character,
and available space. From Regular to
Dark, letterforms change drastically
in structure, proportions, contrast
behavior, and the writing/drawing
ratio involved. The Qandus multiscript
family was developed as part of the
Typographic Matchmaking in the
Maghrib project.

↓COMMENT
This collaborative work is an ambitious and lively attempt at
developing a typeface family covering three writing systems: Arabic
(following the Maghribi calligraphic style), Tifinagh, and Latin.
Although these three scripts feature very different structures and
rhythm, the designers managed to inject a homogeneous feel to the
family, while preserving each script's specificities and respective
identity.

The Maghribi style, which has rarely been adapted
typographically, beautifully influenced the fluidity of the Latin and
Tifinagh letterforms. The design brings out some audacious decisions
and striking features, such as very recognizable lowercase letters
"a" and "y" in the Latin. Whereas existing Tifinagh typefaces usually
emphasize the geometric aspect of the script, Qandus proposes
a softer and refreshing alternative, which I am looking forward to
seeing in use.

The progression from one weight to another is also remarkable:
The text version leans toward a warm yet more restrained and
functional design, while the darker weight is flamboyant and
immediately recognizable. Achieving all this requires great mastery,
and the result is a generous and highly recognizable design that is a
pleasure for the eye.
Alice Savoie

↓TYPEFACE
Bely
↓DESIGN
Roxane Gataud, Paris
↓FOUNDRY
TypeTogether
↓URL
type-together.com/bely
↓TWITTER
@RoxaneGataud
↓CONCEPT
Bely is Roxane Gataud's venturesome text family paired with a fearless display in the French style. Built upon classical proportions to capitalize on reading familiarity, Bely's four text weights combine comfortable reading with an admirable texture. Bely Display pushes the logic of the text weights to their extreme, resulting in adventurous forms for unforgettable packaging and headlines.

Blossom &

Pomegranate juice and fresh Basilic

printemps

DE LA MONTAGNE FLEURIE

autrichien

les baleines bleues dans les nuages

jolie fleur du jardin

RAWNALD GREGORY ERICKSON THE SECOND — STRFKR 2009

Flying Butterflies & Needles

HUILE D'OLIVE

Radios Albrechtsberger
Hendrix Sharp Grotesk
Invisible Queensrÿche
Delfonics Frutieger
Beangrowers Kendrick
Shostakovich Gyptian
Mendelssohn Mogwai

↓TYPEFACE
Sharp Grotesk
↓DESIGN
Lucas Sharp, New York
↓ASSISTANTS
Wei Huang, Ben Kiel, Chantra Malee,
and Octavio Pardo
↓DESIGN FIRM
Sharp Type Co.
↓URL
sharptype.co
↓TWITTER
@SharpTypeCo
↓INSTAGRAM
@sharp_type
↓CONCEPT
Swiss styling collides with the
unexpected construction and wonky
imperfectionism of nineteenth-
century American woodtype in Lucas
Sharp's monument to Adrian Frutiger:
Sharp Grotesk. With its exuberant
personality, ink traps, and incredible
range of moods, Sharp Grotesk is a
brand-new and uniquely American
perspective on the genre of the
multi-width neo-grotesk. Originally
beginning as hand-drawn poster
lettering in 2011, Sharp Grotesk
eventually grew to encompass a
massive range of 21 widths in
7 weights of roman and italic, for a
total of 249 fonts.

↓TYPEFACE
Qingyu Lishu
↓DESIGN
Han-yi Shaw, Seattle
↓TWITTER
@hanyis
↓DESIGN FIRM
HYS Design
↓CONCEPT
This typeface is a modern revival and reinterpretation of a long-lost Chinese calligraphy style once favored by China's Qianlong Emperor during the Qing Dynasty (1644–1912) and seen on only a few of the remaining emperor-commissioned imperial treasures from the eighteenth century. Based on a venerable, millennia-old clerical script (*lishu* is Chinese; *reisho* is Japanese), this typeface reimagines, accentuates, and standardizes key aesthetic qualities to broaden its appeal for modern print and screen. The essence of these aesthetic attributes has also been further applied to Japanese hiragana and katakana for a broader audience with a common East Asian cultural heritage.

世申乾京人修儀再冬凰前創力千勝北南博
博原臺台名吾國国園圓坂城堂夏夕外夜奎
好如妹学字安宮寶宝寺対導小尾山建往御
心必情愛成我抱故散新方旅日明景書月朝
本東案業楼樓橋武步步歷殿母氣気永池河
治海清港港漢漢灯無物独猫発盛秀私秋竹
築簬紀約紅緑緒美考聞自色茶華葉虎行袋
見観詩語警實赤輩迎道遠邵都銀録長院陽
隆隷隷雁響風飛高麗鳳龍あいうえおかき
くけこさしすせそたちつてとなにぬねの
はひふへほまみむめもやゆよらりるれろ
わをんアイウエオカキク 1234567890%

清朝　盛世　乾隆　御詩　臺北　北京　故宮博物院
隷書　隷書　雁尾　漢字　漢詩　華麗　京華　圓明園
台北　新竹　臺中　台南　高山茶　建築　旅行　散步
東京　池袋　秋葉原　赤坂　新橋　迎賓館　銀行　海港
京都　東寺　鳳凰堂　龍安寺　東山　紅葉　秋風　紀行
長安　青龍寺　華清池　名勝　夜月　飛雁　茶道　華道
樓臺　宮殿　風儀　心儀　成長　美景　景色　夕陽紅
新聞　創業　朝日　必勝　前景　無限　秀麗　河山
美華書館　東方見聞録　春夏秋冬　山外青山樓外樓

台北の名勝を注く、
故宮の国宝を観る。
紅葉めぐりの秋旅、
日本の美を再発見。
名前はまだ無い。
吾輩は猫である、

Astounding Stories
QUARTERLY
Le meilleur des mondes

#MACHINERY #QUALITY @DAILY_LIFE #20THCENTURY #SKILLS

König der Roboter №137

¶ Het principe van de *oneindige-onwaarschijnlijkheidsaandrijving* is gebaseerd op KWANTUMMECHANICA. Sneller dan licht[216] reizen?

2017 CEĻU ZĪMES & KARTE
Gigantische Maschinen, übergroße Raumschiffe!

↓TYPEFACE
Pilot
↓DESIGN
Aleksandra Samuļenkova,
Berlin and The Hague
↓FOUNDRY
Bold Monday
↓URL
boldmonday.com
↓TWITTER
@boldmonday
↓MEMBERS OF TYPEFACE FAMILY/
SYSTEM
Pilot Light, Pilot Light Italic, Pilot
Regular, Pilot Regular Italic, Pilot
SemiBold, Pilot SemiBold Italic, Pilot
Bold, Pilot Bold Italic, Pilot Black, and
Pilot Black Italic
↓CONCEPT
Condensed by design, Pilot is an
informal jobbing typeface for short
texts and striking display use—e.g.,
headlines, posters, book jackets, or
packaging. The angular design and
handmade character contributes to a
slightly nostalgic feel reminiscent of
sign-painter-style lettering. Latvian-
born Aleksandra Samuļenkova started
the design in 2012 during her studies
in the TypeMedia program at the
KABK in The Hague. The result is a
family of ten styles—five weights with
corresponding italics. Bringing Pilot
full circle, it is one of the very few
contemporary typefaces that are also
available as metal type.

↓TYPEFACE
Gräbenbach
↓DESIGN
Wolfgang Schwärzler, Leipzig
↓FOUNDRY
Camelot Typefaces
↓URL
camelot-typefaces.com
↓TWITTER
@camelot_type
↓MEMBERS OF TYPEFACE FAMILY/
SYSTEM
Regular, Regular Italic, Medium,
Medium Italic, Bold, Bold Italic, Black,
Black Italic
Gräbenbach Mono—Light, Regular,
Medium, Bold, and Black
↓CONCEPT
Gräbenbach is inspired by early
grotesque typefaces and borrows
details from brush-painted signs. The
typeface combines the sharpness
of the digital design process with
the warmth of hand-drawn type.
Gräbenbach consists of four weights
in roman and italic, accompanied by
five monospaced weights.

CAMELOT

Parallel School belongs to no one.
Parallel School has no location —
Parallel School is not teaching;
Parallel School is learning!

312

BEAUSAGE—beauty through usage. *It's not patina.*
Patina usually refers to *environmental degradation of*
metal that happens without use, but beausage *requires*
use. It happens in high quality things generally made
of natural materials. *Use it, don't abuse it.* Remember,
it's pronounced byoo-sij; rhymes with blue midge.

Regular
Regular Italic
Medium
Medium Italic
Bold
Bold Italic
Black
Black Italic

Edukację
CALIFORNIA
Regulators
L'écologie
CATALOGUE
Bağımsız
FRANÇAISE
Przeszłość
Netværk!
Craftsman
VERKRATZT
Maikäfer.

Light
Regular
Medium
Bold
Black

BRUTALIZE
Magnetic
Obergärig
DISPLACE
Albertina
GENERALLY
Natures
MYSTIQUES
Painting
Gymnasial
Capitées
ZEITGEIST
rejecting
Espiègle
BUILDINGS

Gräbenbach

↓TYPEFACE
Lalezar
↓DESIGN
Borna Izadpanah°, London
↓URL
borna.design
↓TWITTER
@Bornalz
↓CLIENT
Google Fonts
↓CONCEPT
During the 1960s and 1970s, a genre of filmmaking known as FilmFarsi emerged in Iran. The main focus of the films produced in this period was on popular subjects such as romances, musicals, and unrealistic heroic characters. The movie posters designed to represent these films were also intended to exaggerate these elements through the use of provocative imagery and a particular type of display lettering. Lalezar is an attempt to revive the appealing qualities in this genre of lettering and transform them into a modern Arabic display typeface and a Latin companion.

↓TYPEFACE
Laica
↓DESIGN
Alessio D'Ellena, Rome
↓URL
alessiodellena.com
↓TWITTER
@_superness
↓SCHOOL
TypeMedia master's program at KABK
Royal Academy of Arts, The Hague
↓CONCEPT
"Laica" is the Italian translation for
"Laic." Laica is a slightly conflicting
type family, with a lot of hidden
details, often not completely
compatible. There are three weights:
Regular, Bold, and Italic, which are
designed explicitly for running texts
covering the size range of 9-12 points.

Prière d'insérer.

Dans son nouveau roman, traité avec le brio qui lui est propre, le célèbre romancier X, à qui nous devons déjà tant de chefs-d'œuvre, s'est appliqué à ne mettre en scène que des personnages bien dessinés et agissant dans une atmosphère compréhensible par tous, grands et petits. L'intrigue tourne donc autour de la rencontre dans un autobus du héros de cette histoire et d'un personnage assez énigmatique qui se querelle avec le premier venu. Dans l'épisode final on voit ce mystérieux individu écoutant avec la plus grande attention les conseils d'un ami, maître ès dandysme. Le tout donne une impression charmante que le romancier X a burinée avec un rare bonheur.

Onomatopées.

Sur la plate-forme, pla pla pla, d'un autobus, teuff teuff teuff, de la ligne S (pour les sons, s'entend) qui sifflent sur), il était environ midi, ding din don, ding din don, un ridicule éphèbe, proût proût, qui avait un de ces couvre-chefs, phui, se tourne (virevolte, virevolte) soudain vers son voisin d'un air de colère, rreuh, rreuh, et lui dit, hm hm : «vous faites exprès de me bousculer, monsieur.» Et toc. Là-dessus, vroûm, il se jette sur une place libre et s'y assoit, boum.

Ce même jour, un peu plus tard, ding din don, ding din don, je le revis en compagnie d'un autre éphèbe, proût proût, qui lui causait bouton de pardessus (brr, brr, brr, il ne faisait donc pas si chaud que ça...).

Et toc.

26

Insistance.

Un jour, vers midi, je montai dans un autobus presque complet de la ligne S. Dans un autobus presque complet de la ligne S, il y avait un jeune homme assez ridicule. Je montais dans le même autobus que lui, et ce jeune homme, monté avant moi dans ce même autobus de la ligne S, presque complet, vers midi, portait sur la tête un chapeau que je trouvai bien ridicule, moi qui me trouvais dans le même autobus que lui, sur la ligne S, un jour vers midi.

Ce chapeau était entouré d'une sorte de galon tressé comme celui d'un fourragère, et le jeune homme qui le portait, ce chapeau —et ce galon— se trouvait dans le même autobus que moi, un autobus presque complet parce qu'il était midi ; et sous ce chapeau, dont le galon imitait une fourragère, s'allongeait un visage suivi d'un long, long cou. Ah! qu'il était long le cou de ce jeune homme qui portait un chapeau entouré d'une fourragère, sur un autobus de la ligne S, un jour vers midi.

La bousculade était grande dans l'autobus qui nous transportait vers le terminus de la ligne S, un jour vers midi, moi et ce jeune homme qui plaçait un long cou sous un chapeau ridicule. Des heurts se produisaient qui résultaient soudain d'une protestation, protestation qui émana de ce jeune homme qui avait un long cou sur la plate-forme d'un de la ligne S, un jour vers midi.

Il y eut une accusation formulée d'une voix mouillée de dignité blessée, parce que sur la plate-forme d'un autobus S, un jeune homme avait un chapeau muni

27

Exercices de style by Raymond Queneau —1947

RANDO

↓TYPEFACE
Rando
↓DESIGN
Maurice Göldner, Leipzig
↓URL
camelot-typefaces.com
↓TWITTER
@camelot_type
↓FOUNDRY
Camelot Typefaces
↓MEMBERS OF TYPEFACE FAMILY/ SYSTEM
Regular, Regular Italic, Medium, Medium Italic, Semibold, Semibold Italic, Bold, Bold Italic, Black, and Black Italic
Rando Display—Regular, Medium, Semibold, Bold, and Black
↓CONCEPT
Rando is a contemporary homage to German Romanesque typefaces from the late nineteenth and early twentieth centuries, such as Anker Romanisch (Schelter & Giesecke) or Hamburger Römisch (Schriftguß A.G.). In this period many foundries published their own versions categorized "Romanesque," often with the same designs but with different names. The new Rando is designed in a text and display version with five weights.

CAM E LOT 7

TEXT

Regular +*Ita*
Medium +*Ita*
Semibold +*Ita*
Bold +*Ita*
Black +*Ita*

DISPLAY

Regular
Medium
Semibold
Bold
Black

FURNITURE
Żywiołowy
SQUEAKER
short-term
L'ÉNERGIE
juridique
ETNICZNY
diplômés
LA VALLÉE
exuberant

Entwickeln
ćwiczyć
Sociologie
Wysiłku
Standards
augmenté
traditional
Stężenie
philosoph
Autonomy

THE NEW PAGE of institutions is not a blank page. We might think about what's written on it by comparing the new institutional architecture to a uniquely modern machine rather *THAN TO A TRADITIONAL building-type like the pyramid specifically this new structure performs like an MP3 player.*

↓TYPEFACE
Renault Carname
↓DESIGN
Jean-Baptiste Levée°, Paris
↓RENAULT DESIGN
Sidonie Camplan
↓TEAM
Yoann Minet and Mathieu Réguer
↓FOUNDRY
Production Type
↓URL
productiontype.com
↓TWITTER
@ProductionType
↓MEMBERS OF TYPEFACE FAMILY/
SYSTEM
Condensed Regular, Condensed Bold,
Regular, Bold, Extended Regular,
Extended Bold, Condensed Italic,
Condensed Bold Italic, Italic, Bold
Italic, Extended Italic, Extended
Bold Italic, Condensed Italic Plus,
Condensed Bold Italic Plus, Italic Plus,
Bold Italic Plus, Extended Italic Plus,
and Extended Bold Italic Plus
↓CONCEPT
Renault Carname is a typeface
system for the interior and exterior
badges on Renault vehicles, designed
to remain visible even when the
car is in motion. Production Type
conceived and produced the type
with technical assistance from the car
design team at Renault. The flexible
family of various widths, weights, and
slopes covers the spectrum of visual
expressions in the Renault line, from
hulking, muscular trucks to swift,
nimble cabriolets. Renault Carname
manages to steer away from the
industry's typically "technical" look
while retaining a solid and dependable
mood.

Renault Carname

Regular	**Condensed Regular**
Italic	*Condensed Italic*
Italic Plus	*Condensed Italic Plus*
Bold	**Condensed Bold**
Bold Italic	**Condensed Bold Italic**
Bold Italic Plus	**Condensed Bd It Plus**

Extended Regular
Extended Italic
Extended Italic Plus
Extended Bold
Extended Bd Italic
Extended Bd It Plus

INTENTIONAL RADIATOR *DIAGNOSTIC EQUATION*

PLANCK TEMPERATURE *WHY IS THE SKY BLUE?*

PROGNOSTIC VARIABLE *TROPOSPHERIC OZONE*

LILJEQUIST PARHELION *METEOROLOGICAL DAY*

CANOPY INTERCEPTION *SPACE ALPINE TUNDRA*

EVAPORATIVE COOLING *LOCAL STORM REPORT*

ISOTHERMAL PROCESS *DEPOSITION (PHYSICS)*

SUN HELD-HOU MODEL *VIRTUAL TEMPERATURE*

TREND TYPE FORECAST *AFRICAN EASTERLY JET*

HIMAWARI (SATELLITE) *IRON AGE COLD EPOCH*

↓TYPEFACE
Stratos
↓DESIGN
Yoann Minet, Paris
↓ART DIRECTION
Emmanuel Labard
↓FOUNDRY
Production Type
↓URLS
productiontype.com and yoannminet.fr
↓TWITTER
@ProductionType
↓MEMBERS OF TYPEFACE FAMILY/
SYSTEM
Stratos ExtraLight, Stratos ExtraLight
Italic, Stratos Light, Stratos Light
Italic, Stratos SemiLight, Stratos
SemiLight Italic, Stratos Regular,
Stratos Italic, Stratos Medium, Stratos
Medium Italic, Stratos SemiBold,
Stratos SemiBold Italic, Stratos Bold,
Stratos Bold Italic, Stratos ExtraBold,
Stratos ExtraBold Italic, Stratos Black,
and Stratos Black Italic
↓CONCEPT
Stratos is a family that rethinks
concepts of weight and width,
spanning multiple hierarchies within
a single style. Stratos is a geometric
grotesque whose peculiar utility is
derived from unusual ideas about
proportion. It eschews conventional
notions of typographic relationships—
not just for novel effect but also
to empower the user to do more
interesting things with type.

Stratos (20 styles)

Thin
ABCDEFGHIJKLMNOPQRSTUVWXYZ
aabcdefgghijklmnopqrstuvwxyz
&!?§¶|@#€$¢£ƒ¥01234567890123456789

Thin Italic
ABCDEFGHIJKLMNOPQRSTUVWXYZ
aabcdefgghijklmnopqrstuvwxyz
&!?§¶|@#€$¢£ƒ¥01234567890123456789

Light
ABCDEFGHIJKLMNOPQRSTUVWXYZ
aabcdefgghijklmnopqrstuvwxyz
&!?§¶|@#€$¢£ƒ¥01234567890123456789

Light Italic
ABCDEFGHIJKLMNOPQRSTUVWXYZ
aabcdefgghijklmnopqrstuvwxyz
&!?§¶|@#€$¢£ƒ¥01234567890123456789

Regular
ABCDEFGHIJKLMNOPQRSTUVWXYZ
aabcdefgghijklmnopqrstuvwxyz
&!?§¶|@#€$¢£ƒ¥01234567890123456789

Italic
ABCDEFGHIJKLMNOPQRSTUVWXYZ
aabcdefgghijklmnopqrstuvwxyz
&!?§¶|@#€$¢£ƒ¥01234567890123456789

SemiBold
ABCDEFGHIJKLMNOPQRSTUVWXYZ
aabcdefgghijklmnopqrstuvwxyz
&!?§¶|@#€$¢£ƒ¥01234567890123456789

SemiBold Italic
ABCDEFGHIJKLMNOPQRSTUVWXYZ
aabcdefgghijklmnopqrstuvwxyz
&!?§¶|@#€$¢£ƒ¥01234567890123456789

Bold
ABCDEFGHIJKLMNOPQRSTUVWXYZ
aabcdefgghijklmnopqrstuvwxyz
&!?§¶|@#€$¢£ƒ¥01234567890123456789

Bold Italic
ABCDEFGHIJKLMNOPQRSTUVWXYZ
aabcdefgghijklmnopqrstuvwxyz
&!?§¶|@#€$¢£ƒ¥01234567890123456789

Black
ABCDEFGHIJKLMNOPQRSTUVWXYZ
aabcdefgghijklmnopqrstuvwxyz
&!?§¶|@#€$¢£ƒ¥01234567890123456789

Black Italic
ABCDEFGHIJKLMNOPQRSTUVWXYZ
aabcdefgghijklmnopqrstuvwxyz
&!?§¶|@#€$¢£ƒ¥01234567890123456789

↓TYPEFACE
EVUSCHKA
↓DESIGN
Petra Sučić Roje, Zagreb
↓URL
petraroje.eu
↓CONCEPT
A dramatic contrast between thick
and thin strokes, "ball" shapes at
stroke terminals, and straight hairline
serifs are main EVA characteristics. In
this font, the x-height is specifically
accentuated in relation to body height.
In spite of its extreme geometrical
shape, EVA exudes fairytale romance.
Belonging to decorative type fonts, it
is best suited for headlines, titles, and
small amounts of text in large sizes.

APPE

ND1X

BOARD OF DIRECTORS 2016–17

OFFICERS

President
Doug Clouse
The Graphics Office

Vice President
Paul Carlos
Pure+Applied

Secretary/Treasurer
Bobby Martin, Jr.
OCD | The Original Champions of Design

Directors-at-Large
Cara DiEdwardo
The Cooper Union

Abby Goldstein
Fordham University

Karl Heine
creativeplacement

Debbie Millman
Design Matters

Joe Newton
Anderson Newton Design

Dan Rhatigan
Adobe TypeKit

Douglas Riccardi
Memo

Bertram Schmidt-Friderichs
Verlag H. Schmidt GmbH Mainz

Christopher Sergio
Penguin Random House

Elizabeth Carey Smith
The Letter Office

Angela Voulangas
The Graphics Office

Chairman of the Board
Matteo Bologna
Mucca Design

Executive Director
Carol Wahler

BOARD OF DIRECTORS 2017–18

OFFICERS

President
Doug Clouse
The Graphics Office

Vice President
Paul Carlos
Pure+Applied

Secretary/Treasurer
Debbie Millman
Design Matters

Directors-at-Large
Ana Gomez Bernaus
Anenocena

Dawn Hancock
Firebelly Design

Karl Heine
creativeplacement

Bobby Martin, Jr.
OCD | The Original Champions of Design

Joe Newton
Anderson Newton Design

Dan Rhatigan
Adobe TypeKit

Douglas Riccardi
Memo

Christopher Sergio
Penguin Random House

Elizabeth Carey Smith
The Letter Office

Nina Stössinger
Frere-Jones Type

Angela Voulangas
The Graphics Office

Chairman of the Board
Matteo Bologna
Mucca Design

Executive Director
Carol Wahler

COMMITTEE FOR TDC63

CHAIRS
Joe Newton and Angela Voulangas

Call Poster Design (Electronic)
Leftloft

Coordinator
Carol Wahler

Assistants to Judges
Ana Andreeva, Matteo Bologna, Paul
Carlos, Graham Clifford, Doug Clouse,
Katrina Ellis, Abby Goldstein, Deborah
Gonet, Shivani Gorle, Karl Heine,
Paula Kelly, Carina Bolanos Lewen,
Khafeeon Love, Bobby Martin, Jr.,
Lauren Mendoza, Rusty Trump,
Anne Twomey, Diego Vainesman,
Richard Vassilatos, Allan R. Wahler,
Melinda Welch, Melanie Wiesenthal,
and Carey Wong

COMMITTEE FOR TDC 2017

CHAIR
Dan Rhatigan

Assistants to the Judges
Chris Andreola and Maxim Zhukov

NON-LATIN ADVISORY BOARD (NLAB)
NLAB is an informal group of experts
that provides guidance and advice to
the judges of the TDC Type Design
competitions in assessing typeface
designs developed for non-Latin
scripts (Arabic, Cyrillic, Greek, Indic,
and others).

TDC Non-Latin Advisory Board
included: Huda Smitshuijzen AbiFarès,
Misha Beletsky, Martin Heijra,
Kyoto Katsumoto, Dmitry Kirsanov,
Gerry Leonidas, Ken Lunde, Klimis
Mastoridis, Fiona Ross, Prof. and Dr.
Hyunguk Ryu, Dr. Mamoun Sakkal,
Danila Vorobiev, and Taro Yamamoto.

TYPE DIRECTORS CLUB PRESIDENTS

Frank Powers, 1946, 1947
Milton Zudeck, 1948
Alfred Dickman, 1949
Joseph Weiler, 1950
James Secrest, 1951, 1952, 1953
Gustave Saelens, 1954, 1955
Arthur Lee, 1956, 1957
Martin Connell, 1958
James Secrest, 1959, 1960
Frank Powers, 1961, 1962
Milton Zudeck, 1963, 1964
Gene Ettenberg, 1965, 1966
Edward Gottschall, 1967, 1968
Saadyah Maximon, 1969
Louis Lepis, 1970, 1971
Gerard O'Neill, 1972, 1973
Zoltan Kiss, 1974, 1975
Roy Zucca, 1976, 1977
William Streever, 1978, 1979
Bonnie Hazelton, 1980, 1981
Jack George Tauss, 1982, 1983
Klaus F. Schmidt, 1984, 1985
John Luke, 1986, 1987
Jack Odette, 1988, 1989
Ed Benguiat, 1990, 1991
Allan Haley, 1992, 1993
B. Martin Pedersen, 1994, 1995
Mara Kurtz, 1996, 1997
Mark Solsburg, 1998, 1999
Daniel Pelavin, 2000, 2001
James Montalbano, 2002, 2003
Gary Munch, 2004, 2005
Alex W. White, 2006, 2007
Charles Nix, 2008, 2009
Diego Vainesman, 2010, 2011
Graham Clifford, 2012, 2013
Matteo Bologna, 2014, 2015
Doug Clouse, 2016

TDC MEDAL RECIPIENTS

Hermann Zapf, 1967
R. Hunter Middleton, 1968
Frank Powers, 1971
Dr. Robert Leslie, 1972
Edward Rondthaler, 1975
Arnold Bank, 1979
Georg Trump, 1982
Paul Standard, 1983
Herb Lubalin, 1984 (posthumously)
Paul Rand, 1984
Aaron Burns, 1985
Bradbury Thompson, 1986
Adrian Frutiger, 1987
Freeman Craw, 1988
Ed Benguiat, 1989
Gene Federico, 1991
Lou Dorfsman, 1995
Matthew Carter, 1997
Rolling Stone magazine, 1997
Colin Brignall, 2000
Günter Gerhard Lange, 2000
Martin Solomon, 2003
Paula Scher, 2006
Mike Parker, 2011
Erik Spiekermann, 2011
Gerrit Noordzij, 2013
David Berlow, 2014
Louise Fili, 2015
Emigre, 2016

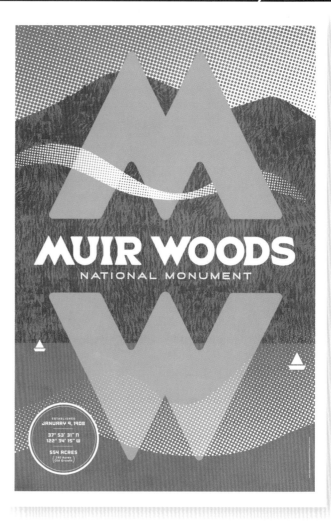

→JOE
NEWTON

Joe Newton's obsession with letters began at a young age, when he handlettered posters for his high school punk band, Aerobic Death (yes, really). Music continued to shape his style during Seattle's "grunge" era as he created album covers, comic books, posters, and videos for his band Gas Huffer (yes, really).

As grunge faded, Joe escaped the gravitational pull of music and became the design director for Seattle newspaper *The Stranger*, honing his type skills in a weekly trial by fire. This experience led to a position as deputy art director at *Rolling Stone*. But it was as head of type for Veer.com Joe found his type obsession taking its full form, as he soaked in the minutiae of all things type.

In 2012 Joe joined with Gail Anderson to launch AND (Anderson Newton Design), a creative agency dedicated to sophisticated yet playful design. Recent clients include Audible.com, the U.S. State Department, and the School of Visual Arts.

Joe's work has been honored by *American Illustration*, *Communication Arts*, *Print*, the Society of Publication Designers, and the Society of Illustrators.

In addition to his work at AND, Joe teaches "the kids" typography at the School of Visual Arts in NYC.

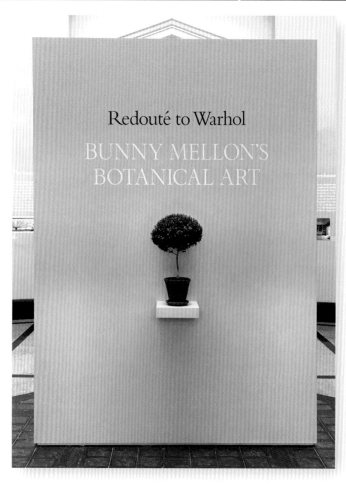

→ANGELA VOULANGAS

Angela Voulangas is a founding partner with Doug Clouse in The Graphics Office, a design firm in New York City focusing on exhibition and print work for museums, nonprofits, and galleries. She is the coauthor and designer, with Doug, of the award-winning *Handy Book of Artistic Printing* published by Princeton Architectural Press.

Her work has been recognized by the AIGA—including two book awards—as well as the Type Directors Club and the Art Directors Club. She served as a judge for TDC57.

Angela got her start at The New York Public Library, where she designed the graphics and collateral for five major exhibitions. (One of the banners made it into the *Seinfeld* "Library Detective" episode.)

Along the way she worked at Ralph Appelbaum Associates, wrote for *Print* and *Grafik* magazines, and even did some online time at Microsoft's sidewalk.com, an early digital city guide. Before founding The Graphics Office, she designed exhibits and books for the New York Historical Society, Harper Collins, the New York Transit Museum, and the Lower East Side Tenement Museum, among others. Angela strives to make history immediate, relatable, and surprising. She enjoys wordy things, esoterica, photography, and strictly nonfiction. She is a native New Yorker who got her education at Yale.

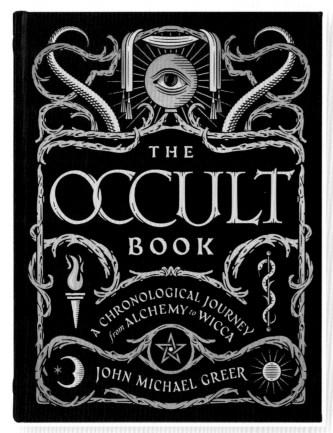

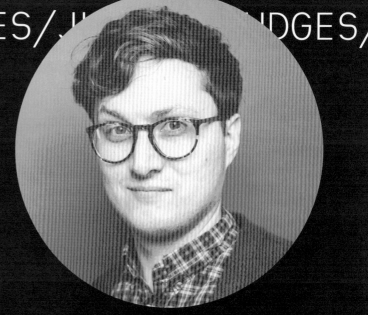

↓SPENCER CHARLES

A graduate of the University of Utah, Spencer Charles worked as a sign artist for Whole Foods before moving to New York City to work as senior designer at Louise Fili Ltd. from 2011–2014. In 2014 the Art Directors Club named him among its Young Guns 12. He currently teaches typography at the School of Visual Arts and is enrolled in the Type@Cooper extended program at the Cooper Union. He runs a small studio practice with his wife, Kelly Thorn, as Charles&Thorn in Greenpoint, Brooklyn. They create lettering, illustrations, and type-focused work for a variety of clients.

↓STEWART DEVLIN

Stewart Devlin is chief creative officer of NYC-based branding and marketing agency Red Peak. He has branded islands and created identities for companies in media and retail; he's packaged oils and hard liquor and tackled the typographic challenges of creating a global, proprietary font.

After graduating from the University of Central Lancashire in Preston, UK, Stewart started out in London before moving to New York, where he worked at Desgrippes Gobé, TAXI, and The Partners. He joined Red Peak in 2010.

Stewart's work has been recognized by the International Festival of Creativity at Cannes, The One Show, D&AD, CLIO, Type Directors Club, LIA Awards, Graphis, Art Directors Club, and Communication Arts, among others. Stewart was named one of Graphic Design USA's People to Watch in 2016.

stewartdevlin.com
@devlin7 [instagram]

Intel Clear is a font for all languages—unvexed by the squatly pocket sized and grandly jumbo sized screens of our world.

↓XERXES IRANI

Xerxes Irani is a third-generation creative professional. His career travels have included time spent as an international ad agency creative director, a professor at Alberta College of Art and Design for ten-plus years, and the founding partner of two successful design studios—both of which are still alive and well today. He was previously the creative director for Bill Gates' media licensing company, Corbis (and Veer), where he led a network of creative teams in Calgary, Seattle, China, and London that produced all marketing and advertising assets for the corporation's four global brands.

In his current role as principal designer on the Amazon homepage, Xerxes works with teams across the global organization, setting the content creative direction for Amazon's gateway for all devices.

This husband of one, father of two also finds time to pursue personal art projects. To date, he has had seven stamps printed and one coin minted by Canada Post, and he has specialized in brand-positioning projects with the estates of Muhammad Ali, Martin Luther King Jr., Albert Einstein, and Alfred Hitchcock, to name a few.

amazon.com
@xerxesirani [twitter]
@xerxes [instagram]

↘ALE PAUL

Ale Paul is one of the founders of the Sudtipos project and has contributed enormously in placing Argentina firmly on the map of graphic design.

Ale's career as an art director landed him in some of Argentina's most prestigious studios handling high-profile corporate brands. With the founding of Sudtipos, Ale shifted his efforts to typeface design, creating fonts and lettering for several agencies, media organizations, and magazines along with commercial faces.

In 2012 his font Piel Script was selected at Letter2. He has received four certificates of excellence from the Type Directors Club, eight from the CommArts type competition, and several awards at the Tipos Latinos biennial of typography.

He teaches a postgraduate typography program at the University of Buenos Aires, where he previously taught graphic design. He has also taught seminars and spoken at many conferences—such as the AGI Open Seoul, Type Master Weeks NY, TypoBerlin, TypeCon, Pecha Kucha, and Atypl conferences—as well as at the Type Directors Club in New York City, and at events and universities all around the world.

His work has been featured in publications around the globe, including *Eye*, *Étapes*, *Communication Arts*, *Print*, *Creative Review*, *Visual*, *Creative Arts*, *novum*, and many others.

He has been designated ATypl's country delegate and is a member of the Alliance Graphique Internationale (and the first one for Argentina).

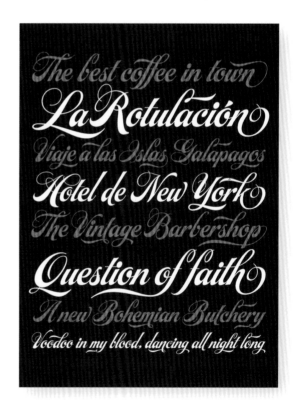

↓BEN SCHOTT

Ben Schott is the bestselling author and designer of the *Schott's Original Miscellany* and *Schott's Almanac* series. His most recent book is *Schottenfreude*, which contains 120 new German words to describe inexpressible moments of human existence: from "kicking through piles of fall leaves" to the "ineffable pleasure of a cool pillow." Together these books have sold more than 2.5 million copies and have been translated into 21 languages (including Braille).

Born in London in 1974, Ben was educated at University College School, Hampstead, and Gonville & Caius College, Cambridge, where he read social and political sciences. He graduated in 1996, taking a double first. After a fleeting career at the advertising agency J. Walter Thompson, Ben spent seven years as a professional photographer. He is now a contributing columnist to *The New York Times* and writes for a variety of publications, including *Bon Appétit*, *The Spectator*, and *Playboy*.

Ben undertakes design and strategic consultancy for a wide range of companies large and small. He divides his time between New York and London, and is married to travel journalist Pavia Rosati.

benschott.com
@benschott [instagram and twitter]

↓JANINE VANGOOL

Janine Vangool is the publisher, editor, and designer of *UPPERCASE*, a quarterly print magazine for the creative and curious. *UPPERCASE* publishes content inspired by design, typography, illustration, and craft. Her magazine and books celebrate the process of making, the commitment to craft, and the art of living creatively. Janine got her start working as a freelance graphic designer for arts and culture clients and has taught typography and publication design at the college level.

She has been a shop owner and bookseller, gallery curator, sold a line of greeting cards wholesale, made ten thousand books by hand (with lots of help!), and has sewn her own products for retail. She has a fondness for typewriters, a passion that has inspired a book about their graphic history. Her debut fabric collection launched in June 2016 with Windham Fabrics. She is often asked, "Do you ever sleep?"—to which she replies, "Yes! By the end of the day I'm exhausted!" She lives in Calgary, Canada, with her board-game-designing husband and curious son.

uppercasemagazine.com

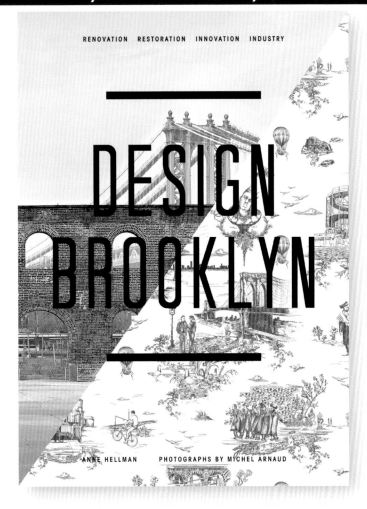

↓DEB WOOD

Deb Wood is a Brooklyn-based art director and book designer.

She has designed an impressive amount of notable books throughout her career, most recently with Abrams, Aperture, Martha Stewart Living Omnimedia, Penguin Random House, Princeton Architectural Press, Rizzoli, and Stewart, Tabori & Chang.

Her work has been recognized in various publications and competitions, including AIGA 365, 50 Books | 50 Covers, *Communication Arts*, and *The New York Times*. She was also featured as one of *Print* magazine's New Visual Artists of 2004.

Wood received a Bachelor of Fine Arts from Massachusetts College of Art and Design in Boston.

She is married to artist and musician David Konopka. They live in Brooklyn with their dog, Valentino.

hellodebwood.com
@deb_wood [instagram and twitter]

→DAN
RHATIGAN

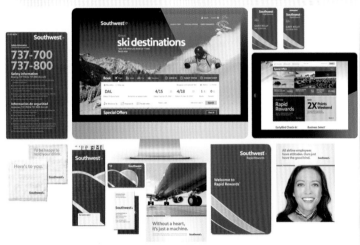

Dan Rhatigan works with Adobe Typekit in New York as the Senior Manager of Adobe Type. He has over 25 years of eclectic experience in various industries as a typesetter, graphic designer, typeface designer, and teacher, including several years in London and New York serving as Type Director for Monotype. He has a BFA in graphic design from Boston University, and MA in typeface design from the University of Reading in the UK, and a very tattered passport.

Fluggesellschaften

Minderheidsgroepen

Northumberland

Uafhængighedskrig

Posteriormente

Telekomunikaciju

Sünnipäevanädalalõpupeopärastlõunaväsimus

Muckanaghederdauhaulia

Quasquicentennially

Desarrollado

Lucca

↓BERTON HASEBE

Berton Hasebe is a type designer living in New York. He previously worked at Commercial Type, helping to develop typefaces for retail release, as well as custom typefaces for clients including *Bloomberg Businessweek*, *The New York Times*, Nike, and *Wallpaper**. Through Commercial Type, he has released the typefaces Druk, Platform, and Portrait. Since 2013 he has worked independently and teaches typography at Parsons School of Design and type design at Type@Cooper, at the Cooper Union.

Berton received his bachelor's degree in graphic design from Otis College of Art and Design in 2005, and he moved to the Netherlands in 2007 to attend the Type Media master's program at the Royal Academy of Art, The Hague (KABK). His typeface Alda, designed while attending TypeMedia, was released by Emigre.

Berton's work has been recognized by ATypl, Brno Biennial, the Type Directors Club, and Tokyo TDC. In 2012, he was featured as one of *Print*'s New Visual Artists.

↓BRENDÁN MURPHY

Brendán Murphy was born and raised in Dublin with three sisters, one brother, and a million cousins. His dad drove a cab and listened to Roy Orbison and The Strawbs. His mom was a mom—she preferred Charles Aznavour.

He had many jobs, including milk boy, paper boy, darkroom boy—and, after graduation, with 20 percent unemployment, dole boy. However, his main job growing up was to push his dad's car down a hill at five o'clock every morning to kick-start the engine.

Brendán came to the States on a track scholarship and bought a one-way ticket to Pittsburgh, Pennsylvania, only to learn the school was in Pittsburg, Kansas (who knew?). He got a master's degree in design from the University of Cincinnati, and, while there, he envisioned and designed a new wheelchair accessibility symbol. The symbol is now in use in many American cities and hangs on the wall at MoMA, albeit next to the bathroom.

This got him a prestigious job offer in New York ... which never materialized. And to add insult to injury, they misplaced his portfolio (Murphy's law).

Somewhere along the way, Brendán got married, joined Lippincott as a designer, had two kids, and wrote and illustrated a children's picture book. At Lippincott for longer than he can remember, he helps companies visually and verbally tell their stories.

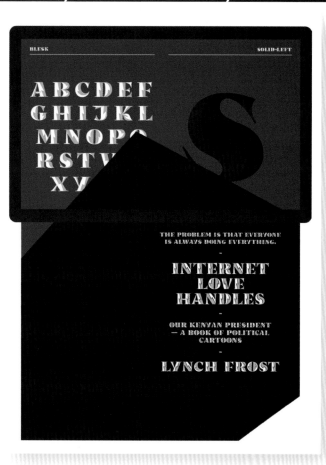

↓KSENYA SAMARSKAYA

Ksenya Samarskaya is the founding member of Samarskaya & Partners, drafting type to push the limits of technology, radiate legibly on small screens, and trigger nuanced algorithms of emotion and history. Clients and collaborators include Adobe, Apple, Best Made Co., Birnam Wood, Design MW, Font Bureau, Google, Frere-Jones, Hoefler & Co., Ideo, JaegerSloan, Light + Ladder, McCann, MCKL, Monotype, Snoop Dogg Marketing, and Trolbäck + Co.

↓ALICE SAVOIE

Alice Savoie is an independent typeface designer and researcher based in Lyon, France. She studied graphic and type design in Paris, and she holds an MA and a PhD from the University of Reading, United Kingdom. She collaborates with international design studios and type foundries (Monotype, Process Type Foundry, Tiro Typeworks, Our Type) and has specialized in the design of typefaces for editorial and identity purposes.

Between 2008 and 2010, Alice joined Monotype as an in-house type designer, working on custom projects for international clients and contributing to the design of new typefaces for the Monotype library. She collaborated with Tiro Typeworks on the development of the Brill type family, which received a Certificate of Excellence from the Type Directors Club in 2013. In 2014, she was awarded her PhD for research into the design of typefaces during the phototypesetting era.

Alice teaches type design and leads research projects at ANRT Nancy and ESAD Amiens.

→FREEMAN ("JERRY") CRAW 1917–2017

Freeman Craw, known to his friends and associates as Jerry, died in May 2017 at 100. He was a graphic designer and a type designer, best known for his two eponymous typefaces, Craw Clarendon and Craw Modern. Born in 1917, Craw attended Cooper Union, where he was a classmate of Herb Lubalin and Lou Dorfsman. Among his teachers was George Salter. After graduation, he worked for American Colortype Company and took evening classes in typography led by Eugene de Lopatecki. In 1943 Craw joined Tri-Arts Press where he worked as art director and then vice president until 1968. From then until he entered a retirement home over thirty years later, Craw operated as a freelance designer.

Craw designed a wide variety of printed material, including books, annual reports, magazines and house organs, paper promotions, announcements, stationery, and logos. Among his clients, both while he was at Tri-Arts Press and after, were the College Entrance Examination Board (and its successor, the College Board), Mohawk Paper, Communication Arts magazine, Bryn Mawr College, Martha Graham, the State University of New York Press, the Rockefeller University Press, and the brokerage firm Faulkner, Dawkins & Sullivan. Craw frequently used his own typefaces in his design work, often modifying the letters to add a swash to a letter or create a ligature. His work elegantly combined modernism and classicism with serif typefaces or calligraphy being deployed asymmetrically.

"Without modern art, modern typography does not exist," Craw wrote in 1958. His designs were heavily influenced by modern art, especially the work of the Impressionists, Fauves, and Cubists. He also studied ukiyo-e, Japanese woodcuts. Craw's modernism was not that of the Swiss school with its emphasis on grids and sans serif type. Instead, it was a more intuitive modernism marked by simplicity, use of white space, cropping, repetition, and a fascination with negative shapes and figure-ground relationships. This can especially be seen in his logos for Communication Arts and the Type Directors Club.

Throughout his long career, Craw won numerous awards for his work from the American Institute of Graphic Arts, the Art Directors Club, the Type Directors Club, the Match Book Industry, the Direct Mail Advertising Association, and Financial World Annual Reports. He was the recipient of the President's Citation Award from Cooper Union in 1967, the Frederic W. Goudy Award in 1981, and the Type Directors Club Medal in 1988. In 1955 Jan van der Ploeg, art director at American Type Founders, commissioned Craw to design Craw Clarendon, his first typeface and still his masterpiece. It was followed a few years later by Craw Modern and then in 1961 by Ad Lib. The latter was Craw's favorite design. He was especially proud of how he had designed several letters so that they could be turned upside down and used as other letters, thus providing variants at no extra cost (and, because it was a metal typeface, no extra weight or space). Its forms were inspired by Henri Matisse's paper cutouts.

Lou Dorfsman oversaw the signage and graphics for the new CBS headquarters (colloquially known as Black Rock) designed in 1965 by Eero Saarinen. He hired Craw, his Cooper Union classmate, to create custom typefaces CBS Sans and CBS Didot for the project. The former is closely related to Helvetica, Folio, and Standard (aka Akzidenz Grotesk) while the latter is an update of the display types of Firmin Didot and Molé le jeune.

Craw's last group of typefaces, and his least known, were created for the Headliners, a photo-process lettering company based in New York. All of them are strongly

AD LIB
(FOUNDRY)

18 pt. ABCDEFGHIJKLMNOPQRSTUVWXYZ
abcdefghijklmnopqrstuvwxyz $1234567890¢ &.,-;:?!'"

36 pt. ABCDEFGHIJKLMNOPQRSTUVWXYZ
abcdefghijklmnopqrstuvwxyz
$1234567890¢ &.,-;:?!'"

60 pt. ABCDEFGHIJKLMNOP
QRSTUVWXYZ   abcde
fghijklmnopqrstuvwxyz
$1234567890¢ &.,-;:?!'"

ADNEY TYPOGRAPHERS, INC.

CBS◉

CBS TELEVISION
ENTRANCE MEN
51 WEST 52 RING
COLUMBIA BELL
RECORDS RADIO

calligraphic: Canterbury is a textura, Classic is Craw's interpretation of Imperial Roman capitals, Chaucer is an uncial, and Chancery Cursive and Chancery Italic are Renaissance-inspired italics. The latter two are securely dated to 1966 and the others were probably designed the same year, but there is no solid documentation. The Headliners types were used extensively by Craw himself in his design work. They appeared regularly in his New Year's cards and in his work for Mohawk Papers.

List of Freeman Craw's Type Designs:

→   Craw Clarendon family (American Type Founders, 1955–1960)—Regular, Book, Condensed
→   Craw Modern family (American Type Founders, 1958–1964)—Regular, Bold, Italic
→   Ad Lib (American Type Founders, 1961)
→   Canterbury (The Headliners, mid-1960s)
→   Chaucer (The Headliners, mid-1960s)
→   Classic (The Headliners, mid-1960s)
→   Chancery Cursive (The Headliners, 1966)
→   Chancery Italic (The Headliners, 1966)
→   CBS Didot (CBS, 1965)
→   CBS Sans (CBS, 1965)

A personal note:

Jerry and I first met when I invited him to teach a calligraphy workshop for the Society of Scribes, Ltd. in the early 1980s. He was an outstanding calligrapher with a gorgeous chancery italic. But he was equally adept at Imperial Roman capitals, uncials, textura, and rotunda. (His uncial/rotunda logo for the TDC is still my favorite logo for the club.)

Jerry invited me to become a member of the TDC at a time when membership was by invitation only and a portfolio had to be presented. It was at my first TDC meeting that he introduced me to a Negroni, the powerful cocktail composed of equal parts Campari, gin, and vermouth. (That was back when the monthly TDC meetings were still luncheon affairs replete with alcohol in the manner of the Mad Men days of the 1960s.)

Jerry was a Francophile. He enjoyed traveling to France, viewing French art, drinking French wine. He usually asked me to meet him at a small French bistro in the old typesetting neighborhood near the United Nations. There he liked to start a meal with a mimosa, another drink that I discovered through him. He was quiet-spoken, almost courtly. He preferred to talk about wine and art more than type and design. We visited museums together, primarily the Metropolitan Museum of Art where he showed me the Japanese ukiyo-e collection and guided me through the European galleries. He avoided looking at every painting in a room, preferring to scan a gallery for the one painting that jumped out and then to devote his time to it. I still follow his precepts when visiting museums.

Whenever I visit a museum today or drink a Negroni, I remember Jerry.

Paul Shaw

kHyal™ 2010

Mike Abbink 2017
Michelle Abdelnour 2017lc
Naomi Abel 2017
Nick Adam 2016lc
David Adams 2016
Kevin Adams 2017
Donovan Adams 2016
Pouya Ahmadi 2016
Hannah Ahn 2014lc
Hyeona Ahn 2016lc
Bridget Akellian 2015lc
Sabri Akin 2016s
Seth Akkerman 2008
Salem Al-Qassimi 2016
Jawaher Alali 2016lc
Marta Cerda Alimbau 2015
Renee Alleyn 2014
Jackson Alves 2016
Lisa Amoroso 2015
Danielle Ancrile 2016lc
Heinz Anderhalden 2015
Gail Anderson 2011
Jack Anderson 1996
Lück Andreas 2006
Ana Andreeva 2016s
Christopher Andreola 2003
Cemile Armas 2015lc
Bob Aufuldish 2006
Yomar Augusto 2013

Luisa Baeta 2017
Dave Bailey 2015
Peter Bain 1986
Omar Baksh 2016
Sanjit Bakshi 2016
Andreu Balius 2016
Rachel Balma 2014s
Kevin Barclay 2016
Lindsay Barnett 2017
Jesus Barrientos 2013
Rebecca Bartola 2015s
Alessandra Basa 2017
Mark Batty 2003
Silvia Baz 2016
Allan Beaver 2012
Misha Beletsky 2007
Lauren Beltramo 2017
Felix Beltran 1988lll
Nim Ben-Reuven 2016
Sameu Bendriem 2017 lc
Ed Benguiat 1964lll
Anna Berkenbusch 1989
Sam Berlow 2009
Jennifer Bernabe 2015s
Ana Gomez Bernaus 2014
John D. Berry 1996
Peter Bertolami 1969lll

Michael Bierut 2010
Klaus Bietz 1993
Abe Bingham 2015
Henrik Birkvig 1996
Heribert Birnbach 2007
R. P. Bissland 2004
Marion Bizet 2016
Roger Black 1980lll
Jennifer Blanco 2017
Thierry Blancpain 2014
Elyanna Blaser 2015s
Marc Blaustein 2001
Susan Block 1989lll
Halvor Bodin 2012
Matteo Bologna 2003
Alexander Bomok 2015
Scott Boms 2012
Steve BonDurant 2016
Jason Booher 2016
Denise Bosler 2012
Chris Bowden 2010
Shaun Boyle 2016
Kelley Brady 2017
John Breakey 2006
Orin Brecht 2013
Greg Breeding 2016
Melinda Breen 2016
Jax Brill 2016s
Ed Brodsky 1980lll
Craig Brown 2004
Poul Allan Bruun 2014
Paul Buckley 2007
Ryan Bugden 2015s
Michael Bundscherer 2007s
Joanna Bury 2016

Christopher Cacho 2015
Susana Cadena 2016
Claudia Campbell 2004
Nancy Campbell 2017
Ronn Campisi 1988
Kevin Cantrell 2015
Wilson Capellan 2007
Nicole Caputo 2014
Marco Aurelio Cardenas 2014
Paul Carlos 2008
Gabriela Carnabuci 2016s
Erica Carras 2017
Scott Carslake 2001
Michael Carsten 2008
Matthew Carter 1988lll
Rob Carter 2012
James Castanzo 2008
Mariana Castellanos 2016
Ken Cato 1988
Francesco Cavalli 2012
Jackson Cavanaugh 2010
Eduard Cehovin 2003
Jamie Chang 2016s

Farid Chaouki 2014
Karen Charatan 2010
Christian Charles 2015lc
Frank Chavanon 2014
Len Cheeseman 1993lll
Abby Chen 2016
Alex Chen 2015s
Ying Chen 2016s
Yue Chen 2011
David Cheung Jr. 1998
Sherlene Chew 2014lc
Patricia Childers 2013
Todd Childers 2011
Alexandra Ching 2016
Francis Chouquet 2015
Robert Chu 2016
Shira Chung 2017s
Stanley Church 1997
Scott Citron 2007
John Clark 2014
Jamie Clarke 2015
Rob Clarke 2015
Graham Clifford 1998
Marc Clormann 2014
Jeff Close 2017
Doug Clouse 2009
Ethan Cohen 2016s
Christopher Colak 2014s
Ed Colker 1983lll
Brian Collins 2017
Nancy Sharon Collins 2006
John Connolly 2015
Cherise Conrick 2009
Jenn Contois 2015
Nick Cooke 2001
Kathleen Corgan 2015s
Owen Corrigan 2016
Madeleine Corson 1996
James Craig 2004
Lauren Crampsie 2016
Michael Crawford 2015s
Kathleen Creighton 2008
Travis Cribb 2016s
Andreas Croonenbroeck 2006
Dave Crossland 2016
Jay Crum 2016
Ray Cruz 1999
John Curry 2009
Rick Cusick 1989lll

Liang Dai 2016s
Luiza Dale 2016
Susan Darbyshire 1987lll
Anselm Dastner 2016
Simon Daubermann 2015
Carolina de Bartolo 2017
Josanne De Natale 1986
Roberto de Vicq de Cumptich 2005

Christopher DeCaro 2017
Meaghan Dee 2014
Raul De La Cruz 2017
Ken DeLago 2017
Kai Dellmann 2016s
Liz DeLuna 2005
Richard R. Dendy 2000
Mark Denton 2001
Ben Denzer 2015
James DeVries 2005
Mark DeWinne 2016
Cara Di Edwardo 2009
Tony Di Spigna 2010
Biagio Di Stefano 2017
Fernando Diaz 2016
Benjamin Dicks 2017
Daniel Dickson 2015
Chank Diesel 2005
Claude Dieterich A. 1984lll
Kirsten Dietz 2000
Joseph DiGioia 1999
Yiyuan Ding 2017lc
Skyler Dobin 2015
Stephen Dodds 2016
Tomo Doko 2015
Chelsea Donaldson 2016
Isil Doneray 2016s
Ross Donnan 2017
Danielle Donville 2016s
Megan Doty 2014lc
Vashenna Doughty 2017
Christopher Dubber 1985lll
Joseph P. Duffy III 2003
Denis Dulude 2004
Bianca Dumitrascu 2017s
James Dundon 2017s
Christopher Dunn 2010
Maguelone Dunoyer 2016lc
Ariel Duong 2016
Angie Durbin 2016
Patrick Durgin-Bruce 201
Megan Dweck 2017s
Simon Dwelly 1998

Lexi Earle 2014
Jeremy Elkin 2016
Jesse Ellington 2016s
Garry Emery 1993
Marc Engenhart 2006
Ilsa Enomoto 2016
Claudine Eriksson 2016
Juan Espinal 2016
Joseph Michael Essex 1978lll
Knut Ettling 2007
Florence Everett 1989lll
Michelle Evola 2017
Jesse Ewing 2011

Korissa Faiman 2009

Hamna Faisal 2016s
David Farey 1993III
Lily Feinberg 2014
Waner Feng 2017lc
Matt Ferranto 2004
Louise Fili 2004
Anne Fink 2013
Kristine Fitzgerald 1990
Linda Florio 2009
Andrew Footit 2016
Marissa Fornaro 2017
Louise Fortin 2007
Carol Freed 1987III
Christina Freyss 2017
Miranda Fuller 2015
Dirk Fütterer 2008

Evan Gaffney 2009
Louis Gagnon 2002
Maria Galante 2016
Emily Gallardo 2016
Viva Gallivan 2017s
Pam Galvani 2014s
John Gambell 2017
Felipe Garcia 2015
Christof Gassner 1990
David Gatti 1981III
Michael Christian Gaudet 2015
Carrie Gee 2015
David Genco 2016
Jake Giltsoff 2016
Pepe Gimeno 2001
David Giordan 2017
Laura Giraudo 2013
Mark Girgis 2016
Lou Glassheim 1947I
Howard Glener 1977III
Kimberly Glyder 2015
Mario Godbout 2002
Nurullah Gokdogan 2017lc
Abby Goldstein 2010
Deborah Gonet 2005
Megan Goodenough 2016
Jesper Goransson 2015
Baruch Gorkin 2015
Jonathan Gouthier 2009
Justin Graefer 2016
Diana Graham 1984
Amt Greenber 2017s
Shanna Greenberg 2016
Joan Greenfield 2006
Benjamin Greengrass 2016
Jon Grizzle 2012
Frank-Joachim Grossmann 2016
Michael Grover 2017
Katarzna Gruda 2009
Ben Ross Davis Gruendler 2016lc
Manuel Guerrero 2016
Artur Marek Gulbicki 2011

Nora Gummert-Hauser 2005
Raymond Guzman 2015
Peter Gyllan 1997

Andy Hadel 2010
Annette Haefelinger 2013
Elizabeth Haldeman 2002
Allan Haley 1978III
Debra Hall 1996
Tosh Hall 2017
John Haller 2017s
Jenny Halpern 2015
Carrie Hamilton 2015
Damian Hamilton 2015
Lisa Hamm 2015
Oen Hammonds 2016
Dawn Hancock 2003
Graham Hanson 2016
Jie Hao 2017lc
Egil Haraldsen 2000
Don Harder 2017
Vincent Hardy 2016
Kristen Hart 2016
Knut Hartmann 1985III
Luke Hayman 2006
Bonnie Hazelton 1975III
Amy Hecht 2001
Jonas Hecksher 2012
Eric Heiman 2002
Karl Heine 2010
Elizabeth Heinzen 2013
Anja Patricia Helm 2008
Cristobal Henestrosa 2010
Oliver Henn 2009
Kyla Henry 2017s
Bernadette Herrera 2016
Chris Herringer 2016
Aymeric Herry 2016
Klaus Hesse 1995
Cassie Hester 2016
Jeff Hester 2015
Joshua Hester 2015
Jason Heuer 2011
Fons M. Hickmann 1996
Lee Jacob Hilado 2015s
Bill Hilson 2007
Jennifer Hines 2017
Kit Hinrichs 2002
Jessica Hische 2010
Reid Hitt 2015
Amic Garfield Ho 2014
Serena Ho 2017lc
Fritz Hofrichter 1980III
Alyce Hoggan 1987
Jan Holmevik 2016
Karen Horton 2015
Kevin Horvath 1987
Colby House 2016
Paul Howell 2017

Debra Morton Hoyt 2016
Christian Hruschka 2005
Karen Huang 2012
John Hudson 2004
Aimee Hughes 2008
Keith C. Humphrey 2008
Ginelle Hustrulid 2014
Grant Hutchinson 2011
Kira Hwang 2016

Luca Ionescu 2016
Todd Irwin 2016
Yuko Ishizaki 2009
Alexander Isley 2012
Borna Izadpanah 2016

Donald Jackson 1978II
Alex Jacque 2014
Jessica Jaffe 2016
Torsten Jahnke 2002
Adriana Jamet 2016
Mark Jamra 1999
Moon Jang 2015
Etienne Jardel 2006
Alin Camara Jardim 2011
Song Jin 2017lc
Thomas Jockin 2016
Dean Johnson 2017
Patra Jongjitirat 2014lc
Alison Joseph 2014s
Giovanni Jubert 2004
Soomin Jung 2016lc

John Kallio 1996
Nour Kanafani 2015
Nakyeong Kang 2016s
Boril Karaivanov 2014
Pierre Katz 2016
Nana Kawakami 2017s
Ian Keliher 2015lc
David Kelley 2017
Margaret Kelly 2016
Paula Kelly 2010
Marcelo Kertesz 2016s
Joyce Ketterer 2016
Helen Keyes 2011
Ben Kiel 2014
Satohiro Kikutake 2002
Hayerim Kim 2015lc
Rick King 1993
Sean King 2007
Dmitriy Kirsanov 2013
Mdison Klarer 2016s
Amanda Klein 2011
Arne Alexander Klett 2005
Ros Knopov 2016
Judy Ko 2015
Akira Kobayashi 1999
Boris Kochan 2002

Markus Koll 2011
Scott-Martin Kosofsky 2015
Thomas Kowallik 2010
Dmitry Krasny 2009
Markus Kraus 1997
Stephanie Kreber 2001
Ingo Krepinsky 2013
Bernhard J. Kress 1963III
Gregor Krisztian 2005
Stefan Krömer 2013
Jan Kruse 2006
Henrik Kubel 2010
John Kudos 2010
Christian Kunnert 1997
Jessica Kuronen 2015lc
Julia Kushnirsky 2015
Caroline Kustu 2016s
Dominik Kyeck 2002

Gerry L'Orange 1991III
Belen La Rivera 2015s
Ginger LaBella 2013
Raymond F. Laccetti 1987III
Karolina Lach 2016
Nicole Lafave 2012
Caspar Lam 2017
Liliana Lambriev 2017
Karen LaMonica 2017
Meredith LaPerch 2017
Brian LaRossa 2011
Amanda Lawrence 2006
Kristen Leach 2016
Stephen Lechner 2016
Binna Lee 2015s
Edmund Lee 2016lc
Hyela Lee 2016s
Jessica Lee 2016
YunJung Lee 2014s
Pum Lefebure 2006
GG LeMere 2016
Simon Lemmerer 2016
David Lemon 1995III
Brian Lemus 2015
Dennis Lenarduzzi 2017
Gerry Leonidas 2007
John Lepak 2017
Mat Letellier 2010
Kristin Leu 2014
Olaf Leu 1966III
Jennifer Leung 2016
Jean-Baptiste Levée 2014
Aaron Levin 2015
Kent Lew 2016
Yuing Liao 2016s
Morgan Light 2016s
Jessica Lin 2017s
Jiaru Lin 2017
Maxine Lin 2013s
Armin Lindauer 2007

Sven Lindhorst-Emme 2015
Domenic Lippa 2004
Jason Little 2014
Wally Littman 1960lll
Xiaoyu Liu 2016s
Richard Ljoenes 2014
Sascha Lobe 2007
Ralf Lobeck 2007
Uwe Loesch 1996
Oliver Lohrengel 2004
Amy Lombardi 2013
Utku Lomlu 2016
Xin Long 2017
Dillon Looney 2016lc
Sabrina Lopez 2016
Frank Lottermann 2016
Hsin Yin Low 2014s
Christopher Lozos 2005
Wenjie Lu 2016
Luke Lucas 2012
Claire Lukacs 2014
Gregg Lukasiewicz 1990
Ken Lunde 2011
Annica Lydenberg 2016
Gary Lynch 2017

Bruno Maag 2013
Callum MacGregor 2009
Stephen MacKley 2015
Avril Makula 2010
Fouad Mallouk 2017
Daniel Mangosing 2016s
Eduardo Manso 2016
Joe Marianek 2016
Mary Marnell 2016
Bobby C. Martin Jr. 2011
Frank Martinez 2013
Jakob Maser 2006
Steve Matteson 2017
Scott Matz 2011
Ted Mauseth 2001
Andreas Maxbauer 1995
Elizabeth May 2017lc
Judith Mayer 2015
Jason McAloon 2016
Cheryl McBride 2009
Trevett McCandliss 2016
Mark McCormick 2010
Alistair McCready 2016s
Rod McDonald 1995
Lawrence McFarland 2017
Elizabeth McKinnell 2014
Maria McLauglin 2016
Kelly McMurray 2015
Marc A. Meadows 1996
Pablo Medina 2016
Uwe Melichar 2000
Jon Melton 2014
Adrien Menard 2016

Shenhui Meng 2014s
Trevor Messersmith 2017
Tessa Meyer 2016s
Abbott Miller 2010
John Milligan 1978ll
Debbie Millman 2012
Michael Miranda 1984
Manuel Molinari 2016s
Tara Molly-Aksar 2016
Sakol Mongkolkasetarin 1995
James Montalbano 1993
Mrk Montalbano 2017s
Maria Montes 2017
Ian Montgomery 2017s
Jessica Moon 2017
Aoife Mooney 2016
Richard Earl Moore 1982
Wendy Moran 2016s
Wael Morcos 2013
Joao Moreira da Silva Peres 2016
Richard Wade Morgan 2014
Minoru Morita 1975lll
Diana Mosher 2017
Jimmy Moss 2015
Brian Mulhlland 2016
Lars Müller 1997
Joachim Müller-Lancé 1995
Gary Munch 1997
Cleo Murnane 2016
Camille Murphy 2013
Kara Murphy 2006
Sean Murray 2016
Nicholas Musolino 2015
Jerry King Musser 1988lll
Mumtaz Mustafa 2015lc

Christof Nardin 2017
Jamie Neely 2013
Erik Nelson 2016
Titus Nemeth 2010
Mary Nesrala 2017s
Helmut Ness 1999
Christina Newhard 2016
Joe Newton 2009
Michelle Ng 2016
Vincent Ng 2004
Yoko Nire 2014lc
Charles Nix 2000
Stephen Nixon 2015
Dirk Nolte 2012
Gertrud Nolte 2001s
Heidi North 2013
Alexa Nosal 1987lll
Beth Novitsky 2013
Jan Olof Nygren 2014

Gemma O'Brien 2014
Teresita Olson 2017s
Jillian Ostek 2017

Robert Overholtzer 1994lll
Aimee Overly 2017
Lisa Overton 2017
Amanda Ozga 2016s

Michael Pacey 2001
Juan Carlos Pagan 2015
Kong Wee Pang 2016
Maureen Panos 3016
Amy Papaelias 2008
Niral Parekh 2015
Brian Parisi 2016s
Vivien Park 2017s
YuJune Park 2017
Amy Parker 2016
Jim Parkinson 1994
Michael Parson 2016
Blithe Parsons 2017s
Donald Partyka 2009
Mauro Pastore 2006
Neil Patel 2011
Gudrun Pawelke 1996
Alan Peckolick 2007
Yachun Peng 2016s
Andre Pennycooke 2008
Lilly Pereira 2016
Sonia Persad 2013
Max Phillips 2000
Stefano Picco 2010
Kate Pickworth 2017s
Clive Piercy 1996
Massimo Pitis 2012
M.Joane Pillard 2017
Leon Lukas Plum 205lc
Siri Poarangan 2015
J.H.M. Pohlen 2006
Maciej Polczynski 2016s
Niberca Polo 2016s
Albert-Jan Pool 2000
Yulia Popova 2017s
William Porch 2015
Jean François Porchez 2013
Carolyn Porter 2015
Linda Praley 2016
José Lus Preciado 2016
Nikita Prokhorov 2017
James Propp 1997
Caroline A. Provine 2015s
Viola Prueller 2017
Maggie Putnam 2015

Alan Qualtrough 2014s
Vitor Quelhas 2011lc
Nicholas Qyll 2003s

Ionut Radulescu 2015
Jochen Raedeker 2000
Jesse Ragan 2009
Erwin Raith 1967lll

Bjorn Ramberg 2016
Jason Ramirez 2016
Steven Rank 2011
Patti Ratchford 2012
Kyle Read 2016
James Reyman 2005
Dan Rhatigan 2013
Douglas Riccardi 2010
Morgan Riccardi 2016lc
Mike Rigby 2016
Tamye Riggs 2016
Michael Riley 2016
Phillip Ritzenberg 1997
Zackery Robbins 2016
Blake Robertson 2016
Thomas Rockwell 2014
Jeff Rogers 2012
Salvador Romero 1993lll
Kurt Roscoe 1993
Amy Rosenfeld 2016
Peter Rossetti 2015
Nancy Harris Rouemy 2007
Erkki Ruuhinen 1986lll
Nancy Ruzow 2016
Carol-Anne Ryce-Paul 2001
Michael Rylander 199

Stephanie Sadre-Orafai 2016
Aaron Sage 2014s
Jonathan Sainsbury 2016
Mamoun Sakkal 2004
Thomas Sakowski 2006
Richard Salcer 2014
Christy Salinas 2016
Ilja Sallacz 1999
Ina Saltz 1996
Rodrigo Sanchez 1996
Nathan Savage 2001
Joe Schafer 2017
Hanno Schabacker 2008
Paula Scher 2010
Robbin Schiff 2013
Hermann J. Schlieper 1987lll
Holger Schmidhuber 1999
Catherine Leigh Schmidt 2015lc
Hermann Schmidt 1983lll
Klaus Schmidt 1959lll
Bertram Schmidt-Friderichs 1989
Allison Schmitz 2015s
Thomas Schmitz 2009
Elmar Schnaare 2011
Guido Schneider 2003
Werner Schneider 1987
Uli Schoeberl 2016
Markus Schroeppel 2003
Eileen Hedy Schultz 1985
Eckehart Schumacher-Gebler 1985lll
Robert Schumann 2007

Peter Scott 2002
Neil Secretario 2016
Nicolette Seeback 2015lc
Ringo R. Seeber 2016
Alessandro Segalini 2015
Brian Seidel 2016s
Johnny Selman 2016
Charlene Sequeira 2016s
Christopher Sergio 2011
Thomas Serres 2004
Michelle Shain 2012
Ellem Shapiro 2017
Mohammad Sharaf 2014s
Paul Shaw 1987
Russell Shaw 2015
Benjamin Shaykin 2014
Nick Sherman 2009
Thomas Sherman 2016
David Shields 2007
Sonal Shintre 2017
Daniel Shires 2017s
Philip Shore Jr. 1992lll
David Short 2014
Bernardo Siaotong 2016s
Carla Siegel 2015
Nigel Sielegar 2016
Maria Sieradzki 2016lc
Carolyn Siha 2017
Maria Silva 2016lc
Scott Simmons 1994
Mark Simonson 2012
Dominique Singer 2012
David Skora 2016
Fred Smeijers 2916
Elizabeth Carey Smith 2010
Matthew Smith 2015
Ralph Smith 2016
Tina Smith 2016
Melissa So 2016
Ara Soghomonian 2017
Jan Solpera 1985lll
Brian Sooy 1998
William Sorrentino 2015
Tzeitel Sorrosa 2016
Christina Speed 2017
Erik Spiekermann 1988lll
Erik Spooner 2017
Will Staehle 2016
Adriane Stark 2017
Jamie Stark 2017
Steven Stathakis 2017
Rolf Staudt 1984lll
Gwendolyn Steele 2015
Olaf Stein 1996
James Stepanek 2017
Charles Stewart 1992
Roland Stieger 2009
Michael Stinson 2014
Clifford Stoltze 2003

Sumner Stone 2011
Tracy Stora 2015
Nina Stössinger 2015
DJ Stout 2010
Anastasia Strizhenova 2016
Ilene Strizver 1988lll
Mike Struna 2016
Hansjorg Stulle 1987lll
Molly Stump 2015
Micah Stupak 2015
Shantanu Suman 2017
Neil Summerour 2008
Qian Sun 2017
Stacey Sundar 2015
Derek Sussner 2005
Zempaku Suzuki 1992
Don Swanson 2007
Mark Swimmer 2017s
Paul Sych 2009
Lila Symons 2010

Yukichi Takada 1995
Yoshimaru Takahashi 1996lll
Megan Tamaccio 2017
Katsumi Tamura 2003
Trisha Wen Yuan Tan 2011
Matthew Tapia 2012
Abdullah Tasci 2014
Jack Tauss 1975lll
Pat Taylor 1985lll
Shaun Taylor 2015
Michaela Taylor-Becker 2017s
Anthony J. Teano 1962lll
Marcel Teine 2003
Simona Ternblom 2016
Martha Terry 2016
Eric Thoelke 2010
Peter Thottam 2016s
Jason Tiernan 2014
Eric Tilley 1995
Alexander Tochilovsky 2010
Laura Tolkow 1996
Andrea Trabucco-Campos 2016s
Hieu Tran 2015s
Tricia Treacy 2014
Jakob Trollbäck 2004
Klaus Trommer 2012
Niklaus Troxler 2000
Francesca Truman 2016lc
Elpitha Tsoutsounakis 2016
Ling Tsui 2011
Minao Tsukada 2000
Nina Tsur 2016s
Manfred Tuerk 2000
Natascha Tümpel 2002
François Turcotte 1999
Michael Tutino 2016
Anne Twomey 2005
Jef Tyler 2017

Andreas Uebele 2002
Ryota Unemura 2016
Diego Vainesman 1991
Oscar Valdez 2017
Patrick Seymour Vallée 1999
Jarik van Sluijs 2017
Arlo Vance 2014
Jeffrey Vanlerberghe 2005
Robert Vargas 2015
Richard Vassilatos 2017s
Rozina Vavetsi 2011
Inigo Vazquez 2016
Mirko Velimirovic 2016
Mathangi Venkatraman 2017lc
Hagen Verleger 2016s
Andrea Villanueva 2014s
Juan Villanueva 2013s
Adrian Vincent 2016s
Danila Vorobiev 2013
Angela Voulangas 2009

Emma Wade 2017
Frank Wagner 1994
Oliver Wagner 2001
Allan R. Wahler 1998
Jurek Wajdowicz 1980lll
Sergio Waksman 1996
Garth Walker 1992lll
Jennifer Wanderer 2016
Katsunori Watanabe 2001
James Wawrzewski 2016
Graham Weber 2016s
Harald Weber 1999
Kathryn Weinstein 2917
Terrance Weinzierl 2014
Melinda Welch 2017s
Laneen Wells 2017
Craig Welsh 2010
Sharon Werner 2017
Shawn Weston 2001
Alex W. White 1993
Anna Widdowson 2015s
Christopher Wiehl 2003
Ania Wielunska 2016s
Michael Wiemeyer 2013
Richard Wilde 1993
James Williams 1988lll
Luke Williams 2015
Steve Williams 2005
Grant Windridge 2000
Conny J. Winter 1985lll
KC Witherell 2014
Delve Withrington 1997
Youhee Won 2016s
Jason Wong 2015
Fred Woodward 1995
Annie Wu 2017

Man-Ping Wu 2016s

Oing Xu 2017
Wendy Xu 2011

Hui Chen Ou Yang 2016s
Susan Yang 2015
Henry Sene Yee 2006
Tanya Yeremeyeva 2016
Jieun Yoon 2016s
Kayci Younger 2017lc
Chen Yu 2015s
Ev Yu 2016s
Garson Yu 2005
Norika Yuasa 2015

Bibi Zafirah Hanfa Badil Zaman
2016
Xandra Zamora 2017
David Zauhar 2001
Roxana Zegan 2015
Zhao Zeng 2016lc
Chufeng Zhang 2016s
Haoqian Zhang 2014s
Wenting Zhang 2017
Siling Zhao 2016s
Ran Zheng 2017
Yijun Zhu 2016lc
Maxim Zhukov 1996lll
Roy Zucca 1969lll
Karolin Zuchowski 2017s

Corporate Members
Adobe TypeKit 2014
Bloomberg Businessweek 2017
École de Visuelle Communications
2011
ESPN The Magazine 2016
Font Bureau 2016
Grand Central Publishing 2005
OCD | The Original Champions
of Design 2016
Pentagram Design, New York
2014
RED Interactive Agency 2017
School of Visual Arts, New York
2007
St. Martin's Press 2017

l Charter member
ll Honorary member
lll Life members
s Student member (uppercase)
lc Lowercase student member

Membership as of May 16, 2017

Type Directors Club

NNNNNNNNNNNNNNN

TdC 12 BOOKLeT

For a typographic old-timer like myself (living in my ninetieth year), a glimpse into the professional past constitutes pure nostalgic delight. So it is with TDC12 and the reprint of the 1966 Type Directors Club show. Having switched during 1956 from being a metal (and wood!) type compositor and Linotype operator to being type director of advertising agencies, I started attending TDC meetings. And, after intensive vetting by their Membership Committee, I was admitted as a club member in 1959.

TDC12, perhaps because of an especially conscientious jury, contains only fifty-eight typographically outstanding 1965 works by some designers such as Lou Dorfsman, Milton Glaser, Herb Lubalin, and other "greats," well known during the second half of the twentieth century. My own typographic contribution as type director of the large ad agency Young & Rubicam is No. 35 in the catalog.

The TDC12 exhibition was opened on March 1, 1966—incidentally in the presence of Georg Trump, outstanding typeface designer and director of Germany's best-known printing academy. Professor Trump was in the United States for the opening of his work's show at Gallery 303 of the Composing Room, one of New York's advertising typography shops.

Georg Trump and Hermann Zapf (both good German friends of mine), Aaron Burns (who headed many TDC educational activities and with whom I founded the short-lived International Center of the Typographic Arts), Emil Klump of American Typefounders (yes, metal type was still being produced), and (even) myself were speakers during TDC luncheons in 1966 at the Roger Smith Hotel on Lexington Avenue. Lucian Bernhard, Paul Rand, Will Burtin, and other personalities of our field frequently attended.

Technologically speaking, 1966 was an interesting typographic year. Second-generation phototypesetting equipment such as Alphatype and Linofilm came into wide usage after the first generation with Intertype Fotosetter and Monophoto was being phased out. As a trained Linotype operator, I had set type on one of the first Intertype Fotosetters in Detroit during 1951. But in the late '60s, it did not take long for the beginnings of today's digital typesetting revolution to take hold.

The Sustaining Member list* in TDC12 shows names of well-known New York type shops, many of them located in "ad alley" (East Forty-Fifth Street): Advertising Agencies Service Co., Composing Room, Huxley House, Frederick W. Schmidt, Kurt H. Volk, and others besides manufacturers of metal type and typesetting equipment. All of them are gone today but not forgotten by us old-timers. So—enjoy TDC12!

Klaus F. Schmidt

*The 1966 TDC membership lists 134 names with some foreign countries.

The   Twelfth   annual

exhibit   of   the

Type   Directors   Club

of   New   York

SMALL SHOW/FEW ADS

This is the smallest show we've ever had.
We think it is our best.

Thank you for entering our exhibit.
We hope you will enter again next year.

Many entrants were disappointed this year.
We had over 2200 pieces submitted and only 58 were chosen.

Does this mean there was a lot of bad typography done
in the past year? No, not bad at all—
In fact we could easily have a second show of well crafted rejects.
But we feel taste and good craftsmanship are means,
not ends. If that's all good typography has to be we would soon
see similar looking and perhaps dull works (ineffective).

This year's winners are fresh, original and compelling.
They attract people to look, read, think and react.

Hopefully, the sternness of this year's judging will stimulate
designers to lift the level of typography beyond such
nice things as taste and craftsmanship to a level of *getting
the words across.*

With the number of entries as large as usual we were
disappointed in the small number of ads entered
this year. We make a special plea to correct this next year when,
I suspect we will have our biggest show yet.

Roger Ferriter, Chairman

Harvey Gabor is a graduate of The
Cooper Union Art School. He was
formerly the Associate Art Director
of *Redbook Magazine*, and is currently
the Art Director of the Coca-Cola
account with McCann-Erickson.
Mr. Gabor's work has been exhibited
many times in the Art Directors Show,
The Type Directors Club, AIGA,
Typomundus, *CA Magazine*, and the
Creativity on Paper shows.

same difference

Amil Gargano began his advertising
career with Campbell Ewald Co.
in Detroit, having attended Cranbrook
Academy of Art. In 1959, he moved
to Ewald's New York office, along
with Jim Durfee and Carl Ally. In 1961,
Mr. Gargano joined Benton & Bowles,
while Jim Durfee joined J. Walter
Thompson, and Carl Ally went with
Papert, Koenig, Lois. They regrouped
again as a threesome in 1962, this time
in partnership, and with their own
agency. Amil Gargano is the Creative
Director of Carl Ally, Inc.

$5.04 a day including meals.

William A. McCaffery was born in
Philadelphia, and has studied at
the Museum College in that city.
He has done considerable traveling
with jazz bands, both as a tenor
sax man and vocalist. He has also
written, and illustrated, children's
books. Mr. McCaffery has been Art
Director at Grey Advertising; with
Doherty, Clifford, Steers and
Schenfield; and with McCann-
Marschalk Co. He is now Creative
Director at de Garmo, Inc.

IRELAND

The best approach to washday problems

SCANDINAVIA?
WHAT'S THERE TO DO IN
SCANDINAVIA?

1
Designer: Herb Levitt
Type Director: Harold Black
Client/Agency: CBS Films
Typographer: Tri-Arts Press
          Typographic Service

The Twilight Zone

2
Designer: Lou Dorfsman/Peter Bradford
Type Director: Lou Dorfsman/Peter Bradford
Client/Agency: CBS, Inc.
Typographer: Tri-Arts Press

Worth Repeating

"The Columbia Broadcasting System turned in a superb journalistic beat last night, running away with the major honors in reporting President Johnson's election victory. In clarity of presentation the network led all the way...In a medium where time is of the essence the performance of C.B.S. was of landslide proportions. The difference...lay in the C.B.S. sampling process called Vote Profile Analysis ...the C.B.S. staff called the outcome in state after state before its rivals."

3
Designer: Dave Deutsch/Bill Alderisio
Type Director: Lepis/Zudeck
Client/Agency: Mead Papers
          McCann-Erickson, Inc.
Typographer: Advertising Agencies' Service Co.
          Petrocelli

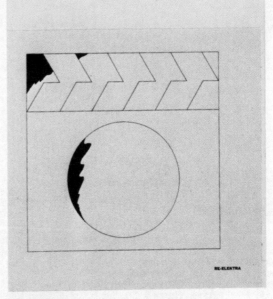

4
Designer: Milton Glaser/Vincent Ceci
Type Director: Milton Glaser/Vincent Ceci
Client/Agency: Elektra Films
Typographer: Metro Typographers

5
Designer: Edwin Gold
Type Director: Edwin Gold
Client/Agency: Hofstra University
          Barton-Gillet
Typographer: Service Composition

6
Designer: Herb Lubalin
Type Director: Herb Lubalin
Client/Agency: Farrar Straus & Giroux
Typographer: Hand Lettering: Tom Carnase
      Aaron Burns & Co., Inc.

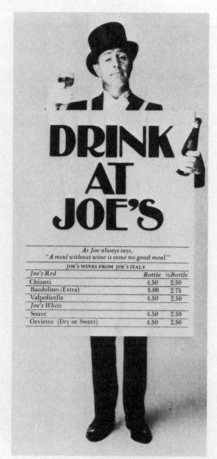

7
Designer: Ron Barrett
Type Director: Ron Barrett
Client/Agency: Horn & Hardart
      Carl Ally Inc.
Typographer: Tri-Arts Press
Letterforms: Bonder & Carnase

A Mural Sketch
Al Held

"A Mural Sketch" is like "pop" art, happenings, and other Dadaistic follies, a paradigm of the nonsequitur. Whoever heard of combining a single circle, square, and triangle, each characterized in a startlingly individual manner, in one painting? Yet Held, unlike the original Dada group and our contemporary neo-Dadaists, uses purely formal means to achieve nonsequitur. He is in no way trying to break down the barriers between art and life but rather to push traditional artistic expression as far as it can go without falling apart. This description of his work may make it sound tricky, but, on the contrary, his brand of avant-gardism is not the least bit self-conscious. Recently, Irving Sandler, a professor of art history at New York University and a free-lancing art critic, grouped Held with four other contemporary American artists in a show he called, "Concrete Expressionists." It so happens that these five artists all began as abstract expressionists and later transformed this idiom into fairly colored, dynamic, and highly individualized forms, thus making abstract expressionism "concrete." They usually retain from their previous style an ingrained, informal, or even painterly appearance. Held is, of all these artists, by far both the most far out and the most proficient, because he always manages to make his nonsequiturs look absolutely inevitable. Some of the other artists are often unable to make their precipitous combinations work. Furthermore, the fact that Held paints and repaints his canvas in order to get his leisures just right, lends his work an immediacy that most of the cooler, hard-edge painters miss however hard. Moreover, nothing is ever mathematically exact about Held's forms—his circles are usually squashed-looking, his triangles never equilateral, and his compositions never precisely symmetrical. And he is to be admired for resisting the temptation to introduce extra-aesthetic wittices into his art, which is about the easiest way to produce a weird, unsettling effect. All the same, his "Mural Sketch" will probably provoke a few scattered giggles, and for similar reasons that "pop" art is often humorous.

Al Held says he is trying "to give the gesture structure," gesture being an abstract expressionist term that refers to the presence of an emphatically personal signature in handling the brush, use of color, and composition. Irving Sandler recently made the following points about Held's manner of composing, "Held is not satisfied with a painting until the forms separate—until they 'leap' from what he calls the 'pictorial' (i.e. relational) to the 'non-pictorial' (i.e. self-contained and anti-relational). The tension between configurations (in his painting called Greco) kept reminding him of the 'electricity' between the figure of Adam and God in Michelangelo's Sistine Ceiling."

8
Designer: Tom Geismar/Dolores Battaglio
Type Director: Tom Geismar/Dolores Battaglio
Client/Agency: The American Federation of Arts
Chermayeff & Geismar Assoc.
Typographer: Clark & Way

9
Designer: Seymore Chwast
Type Director: Seymore Chwast
Client/Agency: Pioneer Moss
Typographer: Royal Typographers

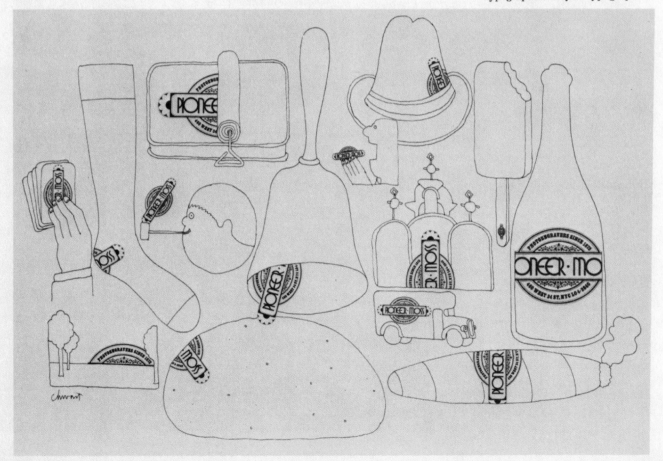

october 2 through october 29, 1965

edward
giobbi:
paintings

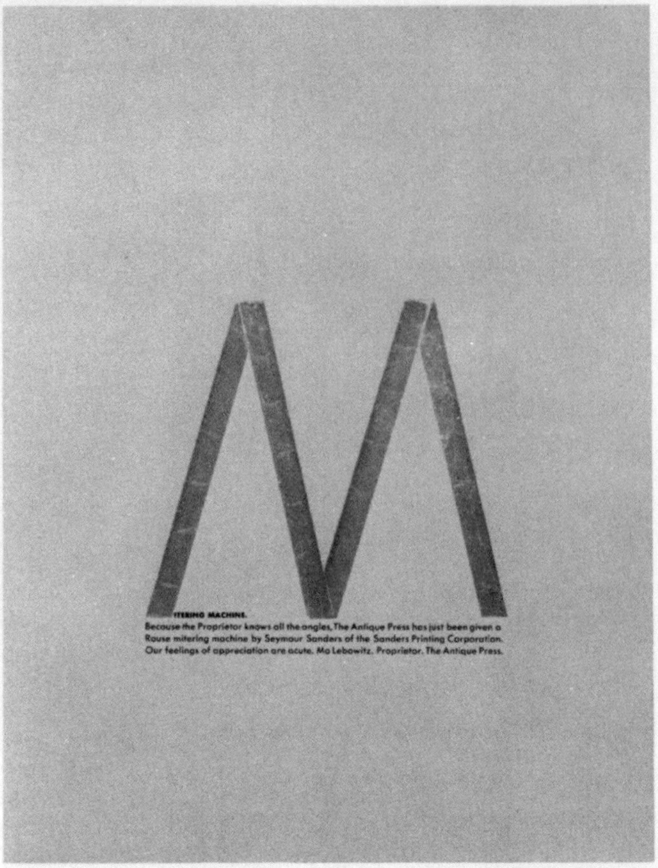

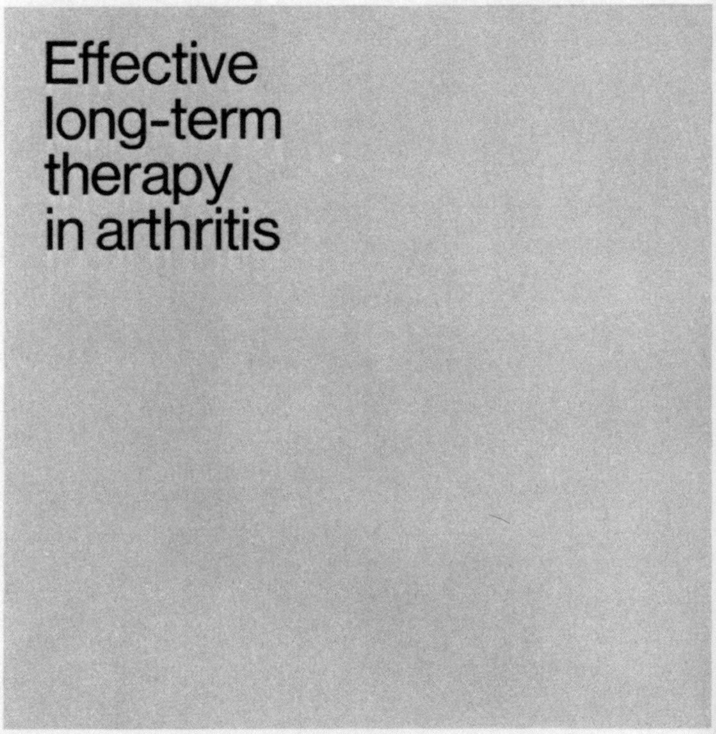

10
Designer: Eddie Byrd
Type Director: Eddie Byrd
Client/Agency: Mickelson Gallery of Art
Typographer: Progressive

11
Designer: Mo Lebowitz
Type Director: Mo Lebowitz
Client/Agency: The Antique Press
Typographer: The Antique Press

Effective
long-term
therapy
in arthritis

12
Designer: Theo Welti
Type Director: Theo Welti
Client/Agency: Geigy Chemical Corp.
Typographer: Empire Typographers

14
Designer: Robert Salpeter
Type Director: Robert Salpeter
Client/Agency: IBM World Trade Corp.
Typographer: Crosby

World Figure Skating Championships, Colorado Springs

13
Designer: Milton Glaser
Type Director: Milton Glaser
Client/Agency: Photo-Lettering, Inc.
Typographer: Photo-Lettering, Inc.

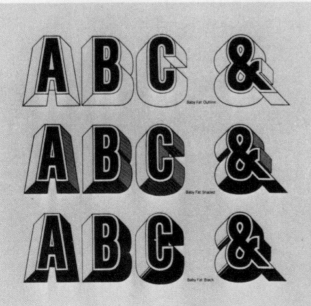

"Quarrels
would not
last long
if the
fault were
only on
one side."
La
Rochefoucauld

Baby Fat
Outline,
Baby Fat
Shaded
and
Baby Fat
Black
designed by
Milton Glaser

now are
available
at Photo-
Lettering, Inc.
216 East
45th Street,
New York
City
MU 2-2346

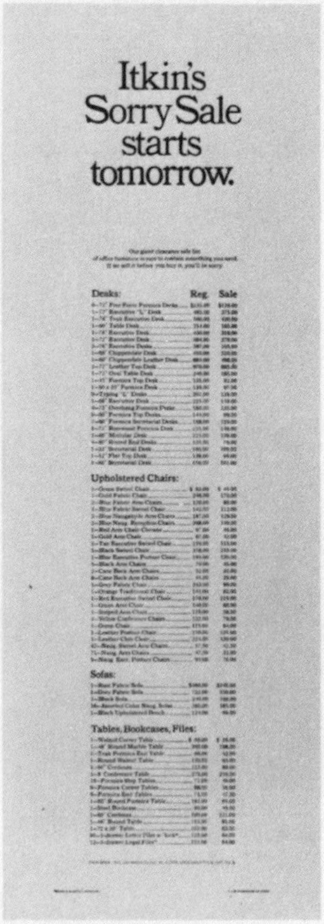

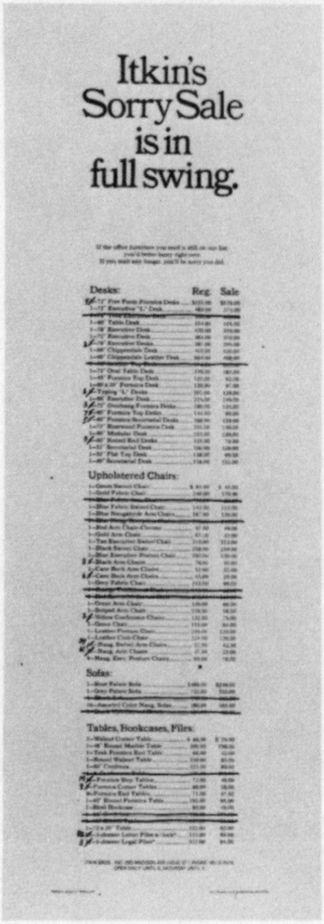

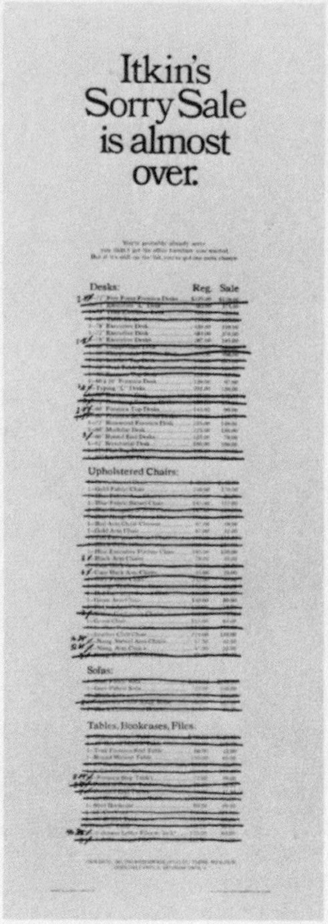

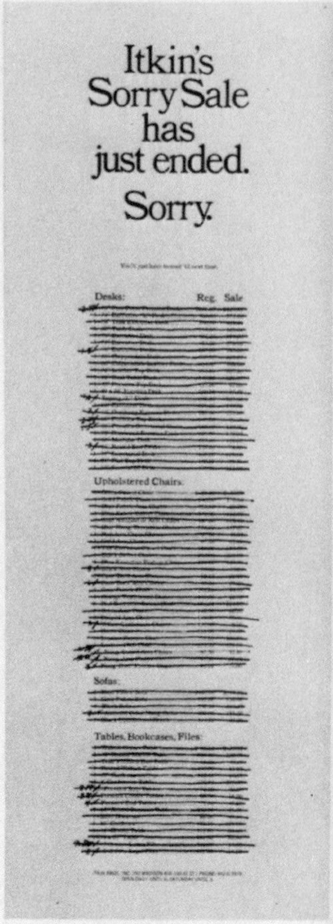

Itkin's
Sorry Sale
starts
tomorrow.

Itkin's
Sorry Sale
is in
full swing.

Itkin's
Sorry Sale
is almost
over.

Itkin's
Sorry Sale
has
just ended.
Sorry.

15
Designer: Burt Klein/Joe Lapinski
Type Director: Burt Klein
Client/Agency: Itkin Bros.
 Smith/Greenland Co. Inc.
Typographer: Royal Typographers

16
Designer: Ron Barrett
Type Director: Ron Barrett
Client/Agency: Horn & Hardart
 Carl Ally Inc.
Typographer: Tri-Arts Press
Letterforms: Bonder & Carnase

Posh Nosh.
Horn & Hardart Deluxe Tea Cakes.
$1.85

If you thought PREMIUM Saltines were crisp before, now hear this. New Slim Style PREMIUM Saltines are thinner, snappier, noisier, the crispest saltines you can buy. And kept fresher in the marvelous, moisture-proof stack pack.

PREMIUM SALTINE CRACKERS

17
Designer: Frank Nicolo
Type Director: Lou Lepis
Client/Agency: Nabisco
          McCann-Erickson, Inc.
Typographer: Photo Lettering, Inc.
Hand Lettering: Irving Bogen

18
Designer: Robert Wilvers
Type Director: Robert Wilvers
Client/Agency: Gillette
          Jack Tinker & Partners
Typographer: Aaron Burns & Co., Inc.

1903. The Gillette Razor Blade.

It took ages for civilization to hit on the idea you see below.
A flexible, disposable, affordable razor blade.
But soon (civilization being the pushy sort of thing it is), questions started popping up:
Why stop here?
Why not roll, say, 6 of these blades into a *band*?
Why not seal this band in a little cartridge, so you never have to touch its edge?
Why not put a lever on the razor, to unwind the band as you need it?
Why not indeed?

1965. The Gillette Razor Band.

The band idea is the basis of our new Techmatic Razor.
It replaces the whole blade-changing routine.
Gillette, however, does not judge a razor by how handy it is. We judge it by how well it shaves.
There is a light feel to this shave, a sheer comfort about it that cannot be compared to anything else in shaving.
There is also much less chance of a nick.
We believe the Razor Band is here to stay.
Though in another age or two, civilization may hit on a better idea.

Gillette Techmatic Razor, $2.95

19
Designer: Robert Pease
Type Director: Robert Pease
Client/Agency: Plumbing Contractors of
San Francisco
Typographer: Peter Kramer /Robert Pease

20
Designer: Ed Lukas /William Bossart /Dick Lopez
Type Director: Ed Lukas
Client/Agency: Kinney Service Corp.
Smith/Greenland Co. Inc.
Typographer: Royal Typographers

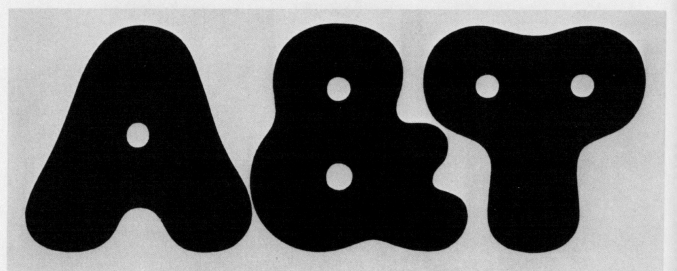

21
Designer: Arnaud Benvenuti Maggs
Type Director: Arnaud Benvenuti Maggs
Client: Antiques & Things
Letterer: Gerard Garneau

22
Designer: Werner Pfeiffer
Type Director: Werner Pfeiffer
Client/Agency: Department of Graphic Arts,
    Pratt Institute
Typographer: Huxley House

Pistilli Roman

AARON BURNS & COMPANY, DIVISION OF RAPID TYPOGRAPHERS, INC., 305 EAST 46TH STREET, NEW YORK, N.Y. 10017; TELEPHONE: HA 1-1470

23
Designer: Aaron Burns
Type Director: Aaron Burns
Client/Agency: Aaron Burns & Co., Inc.
Typographer: Aaron Burns & Co., Inc.

Side 1

Hamlet
the Fair
Adventure

8509 D-1

24
Designer: Gips & Danne
Type Director: Richard Danne
Client/Agency: Westinghouse Broadcasting
Company, Inc.
Typographer: Empire Typographers
Lettering: Martin Donald

Side 10

the Tempest
the Fair
Adventure

8509 D-10

TRUMP

TYPOGRAPHIC CRAFTSMEN, INC. / 311 WEST 43RD STREET / PLAZA 7-5252

25
Designer: Verdun P. Cook
Type Director: Verdun P. Cook
Client/Agency: Typographic Craftsmen, Inc.
Typographer: Typographic Craftsmen, Inc.

Scientist,

27
Designer: Tom Geismar/Jack Hough
Type Director: Tom Geismar
Client/Agency: Xerox Corporation
            Chermayeff & Geismar Assoc.
Typographer: Progressive

Taconic Foundation Report · December 1965

26
Designer: Peter Bradford
Type Director: Peter Bradford
Client/Agency: Taconic Foundation Report
Typographer: Aaron Burns & Co., Inc.

THE BANK OF NEW YORK

28
Designer: Lou Dorfsman/Peter Bradford
Type Director: Lou Dorfsman/Peter Bradford
Client/Agency: CBS, Inc.
Typographer: Tri-Arts Press

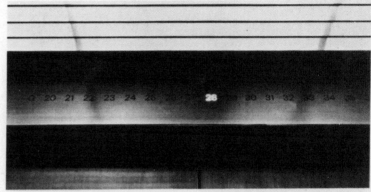

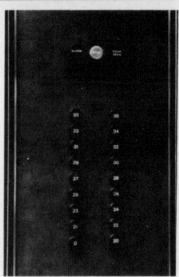

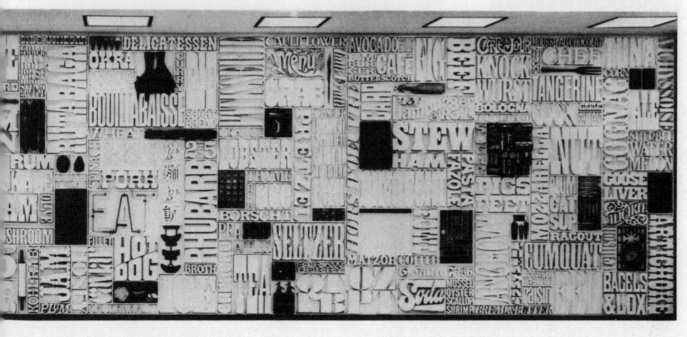

29
Designer: Bradbury Thompson
Type Director: Bradbury Thompson
Client/Agency: West Virginia Pulp and
Paper Company
Typographer: Wesco-Triangle

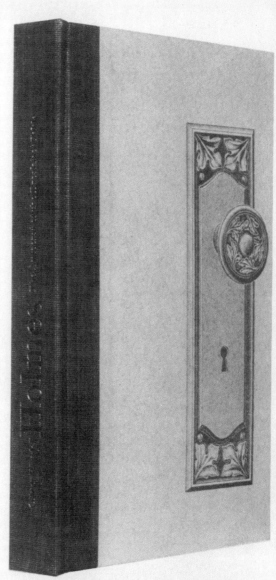

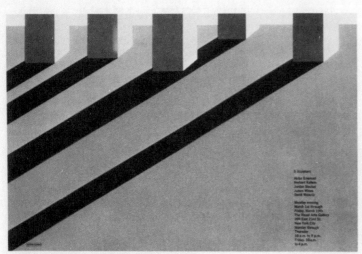

30
Designer: Milton Glaser
Type Director: Milton Glaser
Client/Agency: School of Visual Arts
Typographer: Metro

31
Designer: George Tscherny
Type Director: George Tscherny
Client: Financial Public Relations Association
Typographer: Tri-Arts Press, Inc.

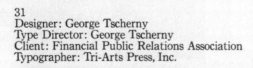

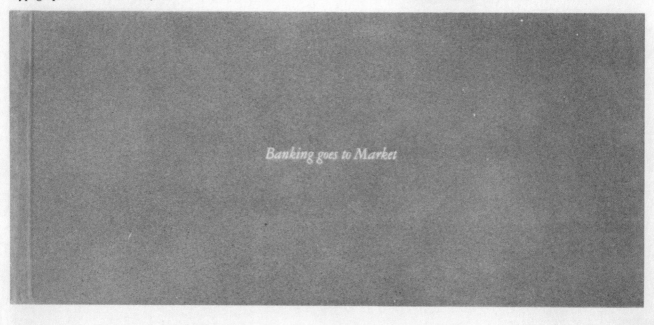

AVON/XXI/96¢

THE CAMP. FOLLOWERS' GUIDE!

EDITED BY NILES CHIGNON

96¢

MILTON GLASER

32
Designer: Milton Glaser/Vincent Ceci
Type Director: Milton Glaser/Vincent Ceci
Client/Agency: Avon Books
Typographer: Howard O. Bullard, Inc.

33
Designer: Bill Hyde–Lettering Design
            Bruce Butte–Illustration
Type Director: Bill Hyde
Client/Agency: David Davies
               Shell Chemical Company
Typographer: Hyde Lettering

Aaron Burns & Company
cordially invites you to attend
a preview of an exhibition featuring the work of

S. Odermatt
and Rosemarie Tissi
graphic designers of Zurich, Switzerland
Tuesday, January 18, 1966
Cocktails 5:00 pm to 7:00 pm
in the Visual Graphics Gallery
305 East 46th Street, New York,
Third Floor

The exhibition will be open to the public
from January 19, 1966 to February 18, 1966
10 am to 5 pm daily.

34
Designer: Rosmarie Tissi
Type Director: Rosmarie Tissi
Client/Agency: Aaron Burns & Co., Inc.
Typographer: Zurich, Switzerland

35
Designer: Mutsuo Yasumura
Type Director: Klaus F. Schmidt
Client/Agency: Young & Rubicam, Inc.
Typographer: Aaron Burns & Co.
          Kurt H. Volk, Inc.

36
Designer: Robert Salpeter
Type Director: Robert Salpeter
Client/Agency: IBM World Trade
               Headquarters Club
Typographer: Crosby

The World *ping* Trade Headquarters
Club *pong* is sponsoring *ping* a Table Tennis
Tournament starting *pong* Wednesday, *ping*
November 24. Participants *pong* will
be *ping* notified of dates for subsequent
rounds. *Pong* the tournament will take place *ping* in the
basement *pong* of *ping* 787 United Nations *pong* Plaza
at 5:30 p.m. on days of play. *Ping.*
If *pong* you are interested in trying your skills *ping* and
possibly *pong* capturing a trophy, *ping* please *pong* contact
Pauline Allen on extension 258
not later *ping* than Monday, November 22. *Pong.*

Fortunato Duranti   1787-1863

37
Designer: Jack W. Stauffacher
Type Director: Jack W. Stauffacher
Client/Agency: Dept. of Art and Architecture,
                 Stanford University
Typographer: Jack W. Stauffacher

38
Designer: Seymore Chwast/Allen Vogel
Type Director: Seymore Chwast/Allen Vogel
Client/Agency: Push Pin Studios
Typographer: Weltz Typographers

39
Designer: Joan Lombardi
Type Director: Joan Lombardi
Client/Agency: Joan Lombardi
Typographer: Photo Lettering, Inc./Quad, Inc.

40
Designer: John Clemmer
Type Director: Carl Brett
Client/Agency: Shirley M. Clemmer
Typographer: Howarth & Smith Monotype Ltd.

Jack Ward, photographer, 154 w 57, ny 10019, Lt 16251

Jack Ward, photographer, 154 w 57, ny 10019, Lt 16251

Jack Ward, photographer, 154 w 57, ny 10019, Lt 16251

Jack Ward, photographer, 154 west 57, new york 10019

copy

41
Designer: Allan Beaver
Type Director: Allan Beaver
Client: Jack Ward
Typographer: Aaron Burns & Co., Inc.

the village secretary · wilshire westwood office center · 1100 glendon avenue · suite 2101 · telephone 477-0070

42
Designer: Wayne Hallowell
Type Director: Wayne Hallowell
Client/Agency: The Village Secretary
Typographer: Advertisers Composition Company

43
Designer: Herb Lubalin
Type Director: Herb Lubalin
Client/Agency: Gerry Gersten
Typographer: Aaron Burns & Co., Inc.
Hand Lettering: John Pistilli

44
Designer: Herb Lubalin
Type Director: Herb Lubalin
Client/Agency: Steelograph Co.
Hand Lettering: Tom Carnase

HaHarvey Selig Ehrlich, 321 West 74th Street, New York, N.Y. 10023 **Cartoonist**

45
Designer: Robert Salpeter
Type Director: Robert Salpeter
Client/Agency: Harvey Selig Ehrlich
Typographer: Crosby

46
Designer: Bill Hyde
Type Director: Bill Hyde
Client/Agency: Bill Hyde/Designer
Typographer: Spartan Typographers

DÜSSELDORFER
GOLF-CLUB E.V.
4 DÜSSELDORF
KÖNIGSALLEE 70
PLATZANLAGE:
403 RATINGEN
RITTERGUT ROMMELJANS

47
Designer: F. G. Boes
Type Director: F. G. Boes
Client/Agency: Düsseldorfer Golf-Club
Typographer: F. G. Boes

FOR SALE

Horn & Hardart Pineapple Cheese Pie and Cocoanut Custard Pie. Excellent condition. Inquire within. 75¢ each.

48
Designer: Ron Barrett
Type Director: Ron Barrett
Client/Agency: Horn & Hardart, Carl Ally Inc.
Typographer: Tri-Arts Press

We give you fresh vegetables instead of canned music.

We don't wait for somebody to deliver our eggs. We use our own trucks. Fresh eggs taste better than fancy rugs.

We buy plump chickens instead of plush wallpaper. All our chickens are Grade A. Most places use Grade B.

Fresh rolls smell better than fake roses. They taste better, too. All Horn & Hardart baked goods are made fresh daily.

Our coffee goes down the drain every hour and a fresh batch is made. This costs us. But we save on chrome.

We're concerned with decorating your interior. Not ours.

Horn & Hardart. It's not fancy. But it's good.

49
Designer: Ron Barrett
Type Designer: Ron Barrett
Client/Agency: Horn & Hardart, Carl Ally Inc.
Typographer: Tri-Arts Press

VHS

Vortrag von
Hans-Peter Keller
Mittwoch, 17. März
20 Uhr
Elberfeld
Friedrich-Ebert-Str. 27
Volkshochschule
Wuppertal

Zur
Situation der
zeitgenössischen
Poesie

50
Designer: Albrecht Ade
Type Director: Jörg Hugendubel
Client/Agency: VHS Wuppertal
Typographer: Werkkunstschule Wuppertal

Torrington **Crossflo®**

51
Designer: Gene Sercander/Ivan Chermayeff
Type Director: Gene Sercander
Client/Agency: The Torrington Company
                Chermayeff & Geismar Assoc.
Typographer: Progressive

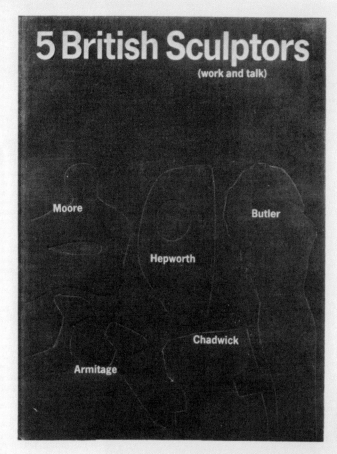

52
Designer: Arnold Skolnick
Type Director: Paul Seidenman
Client/Agency: Grossman Publishers
Typographer: Type Directions

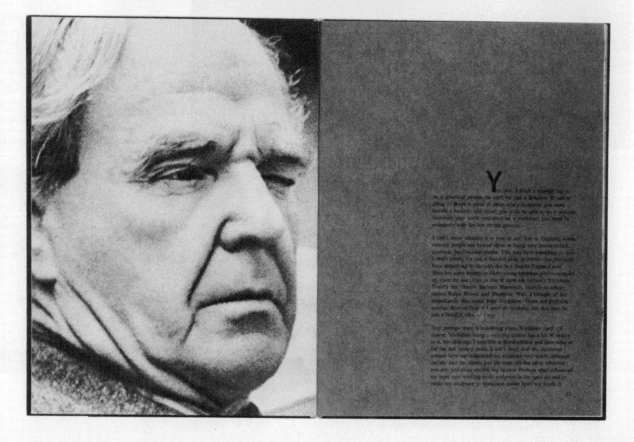

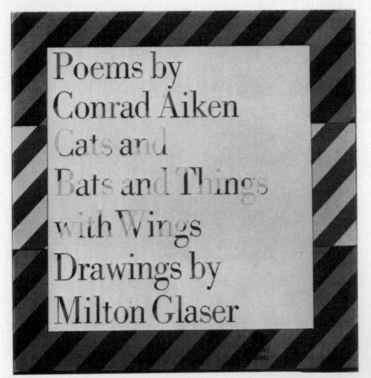

Poems by
Conrad Aiken
Cats and
Bats and Things
with Wings
Drawings by
Milton Glaser

53
Designer: Milton Glaser
Type Director: Milton Glaser
Client/Agency: Atheneum Publishers
Typographer: The Composing Room

The Owl.

To whit
to whoo
he stares
right through
whatever
he looks at
maybe
YOU
and so
whatever
else
you do
don't
        ever
            be
                a
                    mouse
                or
            if
        you
    are
    STAY
        IS
            YOUR
                HOUSE
old owl
can you be really
wise
and do those great big   or by jiminy
sunflower eyes   on a chimney
see THINGS   or whooshing by
that WE   on velvet wings?
can never see   Let's hie to bed
perched on the tiptop of your tree   and leave him be.

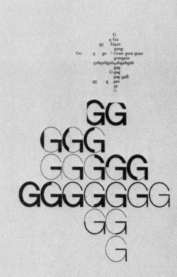

Guess who's wishing you a very Merry Christmas?

54
Designer: Gerhard Doerrié
Type Director: Gerhard Doerrié
Client/Agency: Herion Private Press
Typographer: Cooper & Beatty

55
Designer: Bernie Zlotnick
Type Director: Bernie Zlotnick
Client/Agency: Katz, Jacobs & Zlotnick, Inc.
Typographer: Haber

MARRIAGE

56
Designer: Herb Lubalin
Type Director: Herb Lubalin
Client: Visual Graphics Corp.
Typographer: Aaron Burns & Co., Inc.
Hand Lettering: Wayne J. Stettler

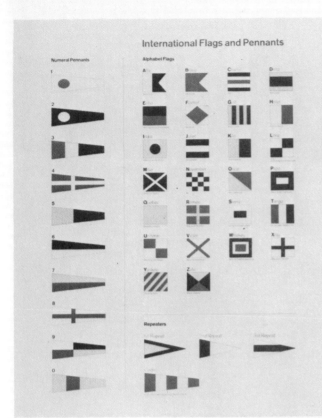

57
Designer: Ivan Chermayeff/Dolores Battaglio
Type Director: Ivan Chermayeff/Dolores Battaglio
Client/Agency: Champion Papers
     Needham, Harper & Steers
Typographer: Clark & Way
     Progressive Typographers

CHALET NORTHROP · 26e
SALON INTERNATIONAL
DE L'AERONAUTIQUE ET
DE L'ESPACE · · 10-21
JUNE 1965, PARIS, FRANCE

58
Designers: Jay Novak/Vern Simpson
Client/Agency: Northrop Corp.
Typographer: Vern Simpson

TYPE DIRECTORS CLUB MEMBERSHIP/1966

Robert J. Aldag
Kelvin J. Arden
Joseph S. Armellino
Leonard F. Bahr
Arnold Bank
Edward E. Benguiat
Paul A. Bennett
Ted Bergman
Pieter Brattinga
John H. Bright
Werner E. Brudi
Bernard Brussel-Smith
William Bundzak
Aaron Burns
Will Burtin
Travis Cliett
Mahlon A. Cline
Martin Connell
Verdun P. Cook
Nicholas A. Costantino
Freeman Craw
James A. Cross
Thomas L. Dartnell
Eugene de Lopatecki
William W. Demlin
O. Alfred Dickman
Louis Dorfsman

Cieman Drimer
Claude Enders
Eugene M. Ettenberg
Robert Farber
Sidney Feinberg
Roger G. Ferriter
Don Finck
Glenn Foss
Vincent Giannone
Lou Glassheim
Edward M. Gottschall
Austin Grandjean
James Halpin
Hollis W. Holland
Robert M. Jones
R. Randolph Karch
Frederick A. Kellar
Paul A. Keller
Lawrence Kessler
Wilbur King
Zoltan Kiss
Emil J. Klumpp
Edwin B. Kolsby
Ray Komai
Ray Konrad
Bernard Kress
Morris Lebowitz

Arthur B. Lee
Acy R. Lehman
Louis Lepis
Grace V. LeRoy
Olaf Leu
Irving Levine
Clifton Line
Wally Littman
Gillis L. Long
Melvin Loos
John H. Lord
Herb Lubalin
Edgar J. Malecki
Sol Malkoff
Saadyah Maximon
James H. McWilliams
Egon Merker
Frank Merriman
Lawrence J. Meyer
R. Hunter Middleton
Francis Monaco
Lloyd Brooks Morgan
Tobias Moss
Louis A. Musto
Alexander Nesbitt
Oscar Ogg
Robert J. O'Dell

Brian O'Neill
Gerard J. O'Neill
A. Larry Ottino
Dr. G. W. Ovink
Joseph A. Pastore
Eugene P. Pattberg
Michael N. Pellegrino
John A. Pfriender
Jan Van Der Ploeg
George A. Podorson
Frank E. Powers
Ernst Reichl
Andrew Roberts
Al Robinson
Richard Victor Rochette
Edward Rondthaler
Herbert M. Rosenthal
Frank Rossi
Gustave L. Saelens
Robert Salpeter
David Saltman
Lou Sardella
John N. Schaedler
Klaus F. Schmidt
James M. Secrest
William L. Sekuler
Arnold Shaw

Jan Sjodahl
Martin Solomon
James Somerville
Walter Stanton
Herbert Stoltz
Otto Storch
Herb Strasser
William A. Streever
Robert Sutter
David B. Tasler
William Taubin
Anthony J. Teano
Bradbury Thompson
M. Joseph Trautwein
Abraham A. Versh
Meyer Wagman
Beatrice Warde
Herschel Wartik
Stevens L. Watts
Kurt Weidemann
Joseph F. Weiler
Irving Werbin
Howard Wilcox
Hal Zamboni
Hermann Zapf
Milton K. Zudeck

SUSTAINING MEMBERS

Advertising Agencies' Service Co. Inc.
American Type Founders
Amsterdam-Continental Types & Graphic Equipment, Inc.
Composing Room Inc. (The)
Cooper & Beatty Ltd.
Craftsman Type Inc.
A. T. Edwards Typography, Inc.
Electrographic Corporation
Empire Typographers
Globe Printers Supply Corp.
Graphic Arts Typographers, Inc.
Highton Company (The)
Huxley House
Intertype Company
King Typographic Service Corp.
Lanston Monotype Company
Oscar Leventhal, Inc.
Linocraft Typographers
Ludlow Typograph Company
Mead Corporation
Mergenthaler Linotype Company
William Patrick Company, Inc.
Philmac Typographers
Rapid Typographers, Inc.
Frederick W. Schmidt, Inc.
Superior Typographers Inc.
Tudor Typographers
Typographic House, Inc. (The)
Typo-Philadelphia
Kurt H. Volk, Inc.
Westcott & Thomson, Inc.

OFFICERS OF THE TYPE DIRECTORS CLUB

Milton K. Zudeck: Chairman, Board of Governors
Eugene M. Ettenberg: President
Edgar J. Malecki: First Vice President
Morris Lebowitz: Second Vice President
Joseph A. Pastore: Secretary
Bernard J. Kress: Treasurer
Saadyah Maximon: Governor at Large
Jerry Singleton: Executive Secretary

COMMITTEE FOR TDC/12

Roger G. Ferriter: Chairman
Joseph A. Pastore: Co-Chairman
Saadyah Maximon: Associate
Herbert M. Rosenthal: Associate

CREDITS

Design: Paul A. Keller
Photographs: Bob Nacht
Copy Photographs: Photo Masters, Inc.
Typography: Tri-Arts Press, Inc.
Retouching: Miller/Guisto Inc.
Printing: Publication Press
Paper: Mead Paper Company

OBJECTIVES OF THE TYPE DIRECTORS CLUB:

To raise the standards of typography and related fields of the graphic arts.
To provide the means for inspiration, stimulation, and research in typography
and related graphic arts fields.
To aid in the completion and dissemination of knowledge concerning the use
of type and related materials.
To cooperate with other organizations having similar aims and purposes.

TYPOGRAPHY 38

First Edition
First published in 2017
by Verlag Hermann Schmidt
Gonsenheimer Str. 56
D-55126 Mainz
Phone +49 (0) 6131 / 50 60 0
Fax +49 (0) 6131 / 50 60 80
info@verlag-hermann-schmidt.de
www.typografie.de |
www.verlag-hermann-schmidt.de
facebook: Verlag Hermann Schmidt
twitter: @VerlagHSchmidt

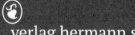

verlag hermann schmidt

ISBN 978-3-87439-898-5

Type Directors Club
Carol Wahler
347 West 36 Street
Suite 603
New York, NY 10018
Tel / 212.633.8943
E / director@tdc.org
W / tdc.org

Printed in China

ACKNOWLEDGMENTS

The Type Directiors Club gratefully
acknowledges the following for their
support and contributions to the
success of TDC63 and TDC2017:
Design: Leftloft
Production: Adam S. Wahler,
A to A Studio Solutions, Ltd.
Editing: Dave Baker,
Super Copy Editors

Judging Facilities:
Parsons School of Design

Exhibition Facilities:
The Cooper Union

Chairpersons' and Judges' Photos:
Catalina Kulczar-Marin

TDC63 Competition (call for entries):
Design: Leftloft
Online submission application and
development: adcSTUDIO

The principal typefaces used in the
composition of *Typography 38* are Heimat
Mono, designed and distributed by Atlas
Type Foundry, and Lab Grotesque, designed
and distributed by LettersfromSweden.
Heimat Mono was also used in the Call
for Entries campaign.

° Signifies TDC member in the credits.